JOURNAL FOR THE STUDY OF THE OLD TESTAMENT
SUPPLEMENT SERIES
228

Sheffield Academic Press

The Origins of the Ancient Israelite States

edited by
**Volkmar Fritz and
Philip R. Davies**

Journal for the Study of the Old Testament
Supplement Series 228

Copyright © 1996 Sheffield Academic Press

Published by
Sheffield Academic Press Ltd
Mansion House
19 Kingfield Road
Sheffield S11 9AS
England

Typeset by Sheffield Academic Press
and
Printed on acid-free paper in Great Britain
by Bookcraft Ltd
Midsomer Norton, Bath

British Library Cataloguing in Publication Data

A catalogue record for this book is available
from the British Library

ISBN 1-85075-629-5
ISBN 1-85075-798-4 pbk

CONTENTS

SOURCES

ABBREVIATIONS

AASOR	Annual of the American Schools of Oriental Research
AB	Anchor Bible
ABD	*Anchor Bible Dictionary*
ADAJ	Annual of the Department of Antiquities of Jordan
AfO	*Archiv für Orientforschung*
ANET	J.B. Pritchard (ed.), *Ancient Near Eastern Texts*
ARAB	Luckerbill, *Ancient Records of Assyria and Babylonia*
AS	Assyriological Studies
ATD	Das Alte Testament Deutsch
AUSS	*Andrews University Seminary Studies*
BA	*Biblical Archaeologist*
BASOR	*Bulletin of the American Schools of Oriental Research*
BETL	Bibliotheca ephemeridum theologicarum lovaniensium
BEvT	Beiträge zur evangelischen Theologie
BHS	*Biblia hebraica stuttgartensia*
BN	*Biblische Notizen*
BTAVO	Beiträge zum Tübinger Atlas des Vorderen Orients
BWANT	Beiträge zur Wissenschaft vom Alten und Neuen Testament
BZ	*Biblische Zeitschrift*
BZAW	Beihefte zur *ZAW*
CBQ	*Catholic Biblical Quarterly*
ConBOT	Coniectanea biblica, Old Testament
DBAT	*Dielheimer Blätter zum Alten Testament*
DTT	*Dansk teologisk tidsskrift*
EI	*Eretz Israel*
FRLANT	Forschungen zur Religion und Literatur des Alten und Neuen Testaments
HAT	Handbuch zum Alten Testament
HSM	Harvard Semitic Monographs
HTR	*Harvard Theological Review*
HUCA	*Hebrew Union College Annual*
IEJ	*Israel Exploration Journal*
IntEncSocSc	International Encyclopedia of the Social Sciences
JANES	*Journal of the Ancient Near Eastern Society of Columbia University*
JAOS	*Journal of the American Oriental Society*

JBL	*Journal of Biblical Literature*
JCS	*Journal of Cuneiform Studies*
JESHO	Journal of the Economic and Social History of the Orient
JNES	*Journal of Near Eastern Studies*
JSOT	*Journal for the Study of the Old Testament*
JSOTSup	*Journal for the Study of the Old Testament* Supplement Series
KAI	H. Donner and W. Röllig, *Kanaanäische und aramäische Inschriften*
KAT	Kommentar zum A.T.
OBO	Orbis biblicus et orientalis
OLA	Orientalia lovaniensia analecta
OLP	Orientalia lovaniensia periodica
OLZ	*Orientalistische Literaturzeitung*
Or	*Orientalia* (Rome)
PEQ	*Palestine Exploration Quarterly*
QD	Quaestiones disputatae
RA	*Revue d'assyriologie et d'archéologie orientale*
RB	*Revue biblique*
RLA	Reallexikon der Assyriologie
RSR	*Recherches de science religieuse*
SBB	Stuttgarter biblische Beiträge
SBLDS	SBL Dissertation Series
SBT	Studies in Biblical Theology
SHANE	Studies in the History and Culture of the Ancient Near East
SJOT	*Scandinavian Journal of the Old Testament*
SOTSMS	Society for Old Testament Study Monograph Series
ThS	*Theologische Studien*
ThWAT	G.J. Botterweck and H. Ringgren (eds.), *Theologisches Wörterbuch zum Alten Testament*
TZ	*Theologische Zeitschrift*
UF	*Ugarit-Forschungen*
VAB	Vorderasiatische Bibliothek
VT	*Vetus Testamentun*
VTSup	*Vetus Testamentum*, Supplements
WdO	*Welt des Orient*
WMANT	Wissenschaftliche Monographien zum Alten und Neuen Testament
ZAW	*Zeitschrift für die alttestamentliche Wissenschaft*
ZBK	Zürcher Bibel Kommentar
ZDPV	*Zeitschrift des deutschen Palästina-Vereins*

LIST OF CONTRIBUTORS

Philip Davies, Department of Biblical Studies, University of Sheffield

Volkmar Fritz, German Protestant Institute of Archaeology of the Holy Land, Jerusalem

Thomas L. Thompson, Institute of Biblical Exegesis, Copenhagen University

Baruch Halpern, Jewish Studies, Pennsylvania State University

Christa Schäfer-Lichtenberger, Kirchiche Hochschule, Bethel-Bielefeld, Germany

Niels Peter Lemche, Institute of Biblical Exegesis, Copenhagen University

David Hopkins, Wesley Theological Seminary, Washington DC

Diana Edelman, James Madison University, Harrisonburg, VA

Graeme Auld, Department of Hebrew and Old Testament, University of Edinburgh

Nadar Na'aman, Department of Jewish History, Tel Aviv University, Israel

Walter Dietrich, University of Bern, Switzerland

INTRODUCTION

Philip R. Davies

Minimum or Maximum?

Hardly any biblical scholar can be unaware that the issue of the 'United Monarchy' has come under scrutiny. The question of Israelite origins, of course, has dominated much of the twentieth century, but has focused in recent years on the emergence of new settlement patterns in the central highlands during Iron I (conventionally 1250–1050 BCE) and on whether, or to what extent, or at what point in the development of this society the term 'Israel' is appropriate. The debate is as much concerned with conceptual and methodological issues as with substantive conclusions. Although debate has been proceeding for several years, it has now erupted into a fairly heated confrontation, fuelled by the discovery of an inscription at Tel Dan which is alleged by some to refer to a king of the 'house of David', a claim which others dispute. (That inscription, and the controversy it has engendered, will form the topic of a forthcoming volume in the JSOT Supplement Series.)

Here the focus is on the formation of the Israelite and Judean state(s), which for some scholars provide the first legitimate occasion on which an 'Israel' can be spoken of historically. But what was this first 'Israelite state'? A united kingdom, composed of tribes of Israel and Judah, extending its influence through the whole of Palestine and beyond, but which subsequently split into 'northern' and 'southern' kingdoms? Or is this a fiction, the kingdoms of Israel and Judah having never been previously united? What was going on in the central highlands during the tenth and ninth centuries BCE? These are the issues addressed by the present volume.

Between proponents of different views of this period, the lines have been sharply drawn, in print at least. Rather than remaining a purely academic dispute over a couple of centuries in the distant past, something like a minor war has erupted. Those whose views explicitly or implicitly deny that the biblical account can form a basis for the early history of the ancient Israelite and Judean monarchies are dubbed 'minimalists' or 'deconstructionists' (one will find the former in Halpern's essay); while the charge of 'maximalist' or 'credulist' is beginning to be heard from the other side. Accusations of 'amateurism' and doubts about 'competence' are also being aired. The public, and biblical scholarship no less, is having a good time, though it is doubtful whether either audience is being well served. The colloquium from which these papers are taken was organized with the aim of bringing light rather than heat to the debate.

Why the Fuss?

For the issues are actually rather more complicated than the simplicities of popular debate suggest. Behind the entertaining joust of 'sceptic' and 'credulist', 'minimalizer' and 'maximalizer', lie fundamental issues which are not to be disposed of by slogans; indeed, they are not easy to analyse at all, for they comprise a number of interlocking components. (Not even all of the major protagonists always appear to recognize this.) First is the issue of what constitutes 'history': is there a 'real history' back there, which one can either 'minimalize' or 'maximalize'? Or is history rather a story that people tell, a story containing some data that are incontestable, yet organized into narrative, with the necessary gaps, causative and chronological links, cultural codes and an overall plot? The accusation of 'minimalizing' (or 'erasing') biblical history is a deceitful one, because no one is minimalizing the biblical *story* at all. Nor, of course, is anyone removing historical events from the stage of the past. What 'minimalizers' are doing is minimizing the extent to which the biblical account is taken as reliable history. Nothing else.

Putting aside, then, the rightness or wrongness of this position (on which no definitive verdict is possible at the moment, despite some confident claims) the interesting question is this: what has the *amount* of biblical history one believes in to do with historical scholarship? Why are 'maximalizing' and 'minimalizing' the terms on which the debate is being conducted (at least by one side)? After all, being either sceptical or credulous as a historian (which is what the issue amounts to) has to do with either one's style or one's method, and possibly one's personal inclination. But why should the alternatives so often be presented as *moral* options? In dealing with politicians or used car dealers or insurance salespersons scepticism would often be *advised*. In the case of friendships and marriages the opposite might be the case. Perhaps the problem is that for some people biblical history is not just about history but about Bible. Somehow, when the word 'Bible' is raised scepticism becomes bad and credulity ('belief') good. 'Sceptics' who employ labels like 'biblicist' and 'fundamentalist' merely accept that agenda and turn the issue on its head.

It does seem to me that the only *necessary* explanation for the violence of the current debate over the 'United Monarchy' is that religious value judgments are playing a role. Not only among laypeople (as the correspondence pages of *Biblical Archaeology Review* adequately confirm) but also among the many practitioners of biblical archaeology whose personal religion determines a prejudice in favour of as high an assessment of the historical reliability of the Bible as their conscience and their academic training will permit. I am personally less worried about this prejudice (for we are *all* guilty of prejudices) than about the way it both denies its own existence yet betrays itself so blatantly. I find individual scholars (with some notable exceptions) less to blame than the habits of academic research into ancient Palestinian history (which has rarely been studied other than within biblical scholarship).

But religious prejudice is not, cannot be, the only prejudicial factor exacerbating the discussion of two centuries of ancient Palestinian history. There are also political issues at stake. Biblical archaeology is a large industry, with many interests vested in it. Relatively disinterested pursuit of data about the past there certainly is; but even more evident are the financial, political and social stakes. For the state of Israel, archaeology has often gone, and goes increasingly, hand in hand with tourism. Unearthing the past has also played a dominant role in strengthening links between the modern state of Israel and the land it occupies; every Jewish artifact, inscription and ruin buttresses a claim to Jewish possession. This is understandable: many other countries do, or would do, exactly the same, for reclaiming the past is, and always has been, a dimension of national and ethnic identity. But it can lead to a tendency to exaggerate the Jewishness of the past and to 'maximize' the biblical history beyond what someone without this political stake might concede. It has to be affirmed, nevertheless, that the current generation of Israeli archaeologists displays a high level of scholarly objectivity and openness in its research. There is 'minimalism' in Tel Aviv as well as Copenhagen!

But there is a wider constituency: every year hundreds of scholars and students, mostly from the United States, go to Israel and pay for the privilege of working hard at uncovering its past. Why? The appeal of the Hebrew Bible/Old Testament (of which very much is rather dull to the layperson) lies pre-eminently in its link with history and archaeology. Putting aside the whole aspect of Christian pilgrimage, the mounds of Megiddo, Hazor, Lachish, Dan and Gezer testify to a real past, which in the minds of most of their visitors is the past given by the Bible. Any movement in scholarship which appears to cast doubt upon the ability of that biblical story to hold together the ancient relics and what most people nowadays imagine to be the 'real' past is a threat to what might be called the 'biblical archaeology industry', in which the state of Israel, countless academic institutions in the United States (especially) and several individual scholars have a high stake. It is paradoxical that from this last group come accusations of 'minimizing history', while their own industry of biblical archaeology has consistently overemphasized the 'Israelite' and 'Jewish' periods of Palestinian history at the expense of the pre-Israelite, Byzantine, Crusader and especially Islamic eras. Millennia of 'history' have been 'minimized' by biblical archaeologists. Their dismay, as the history in which they have invested so much comes under attack, is understandable, as are the terms in which that resistance is couched. Understandable yes—forgiveable? That is another matter.

Religious and political interests, then, explain the nature of the 'early Israelite state' debate more clearly than the substantive issue itself does. But not all disagreement is reducible to such prejudices. A number of historians defend as a reasonable method the assumption of the historicity of the biblical account as a premise, while subjecting it to stringent scrutiny so as to verify its probability. One reason often given for this is that the biblical narratives are the only full source we have, and so there is no choice but to use them. Archaeologists, too, unable to reconstruct adequately from their own data, find themselves obliged to use the Bible as a context for their interpretations of what they find. Pragmatic this may be, and a defensible method perhaps. But this approach does at least expose the extent to which the biblical story exercises its privilege over the reconstruction of parts of Palestine's past. Surely such a privilege deserves the most rigorous questioning that can be given?

There is a further complication to the debate about biblical historicity, which manifests itself at several points in this volume. In voting for or against some historical event or figure, the issue is not whether or not some kind of historical entity existed to whom the name 'David' (or 'Saul', or 'Solomon') can be attached, or to which the term 'empire' 'kingdom' or 'state' might be applied, but whether such a figure as the David of the Bible existed or such a kingdom as that of the united twelve tribes of Israel was founded. For the only David we know of, and the only twelve-tribe Israel we know of, are the biblical ones. Without the biblical story these characters would not belong to any history that we can recover. This means that attempts to show that a 'David' existed who was not a king, had no empire, did not kill Goliath, but did other things at the same period are guilty (in my view) of a ruse not uncommon among biblical scholars: to argue that the Bible presents a historical figure who was someone else! (This is rather like saying that Shakespeare's plays were not written by Shakespeare but by someone else called Shakespeare.) Hypothesizing a figure who is neither biblical nor attested in any other source is not really very satisfactory. Yet on the basis of such procedures both sides can claim victory: David (or Solomon) existed, and did not exist. Now what is to be made of that?

Contextualizing the Issues

If it is easy to see why disputes about 'biblical history' generate such heat, the flames only throw into deeper shadow what is really going on. For decades there have been arguments about biblical historicity: the historicity of the Flood and the tower of Babel (I pass over so-called 'creation science'), then the patriarchs, then the conquest under Joshua, then the 'amphitcyony' as reflected in the book of Judges. These battles were not without their heat either, and they still generate some warmth here and there. But the majority of professional historians of the period do not now regard the history of Israel as beginning before the creation of a society in Palestine in the Iron Age, and the process of interrogating the biblical story has come to focus on the United Monarchy. The context of this focus is not some 'revisionist' fad, but the logic of a process of questioning and clarifying the nature of the biblical story, and the role of archaeology in that task. However, one new element in the debate is the nature of the biblical narratives themselves: their ideological profile, the economic, social and political reasons for their production. For there is no point, or no purpose, in challenging an ancient story's historicity without asking why the story was produced and what ends it served. The thesis that these stories were not produced in order to preserve a memory but in order to establish a hegemony or to justify a present state of affairs adds a greater depth to the present phase of the historicity debate than previous episodes.

Another feature that distinguishes recent phases of the historicity debate from earlier ones is the frequency of the conference and the colloquium. In earlier decades Albrecht Alt and W.F. Albright attacked each other in print and from a distance (and less directly), as did John Bright and Martin Noth (a little more directly). Now scholars of different persuasions have to listen to each other, but can also cross-examine each other. Personal contact can lead to heightened aggression, but can also inject more humanity. Yet, rather like oral and literary traditions in an ancient society, personal conversation and published denunciation can exist side-by-side, and in a disconcertingly parallel rather than converging manner! Hence the curiosity of printed denunciations of 'incompetence' (and worse) in the popular forums by and against scholars who can converse in the friendliest of terms around a table or at the conference bar.

Most will agree that scholarship is not at its most effective when opponents polarize issues and demonize each other, but rather when it sets its sights on illuminating differences, explaining them, exposing the methods and data which underlie its disputes and aiming for whatever common ground can be won. What better context than a small collo-quium, where the participants are unable to avoid each other (and show little sign of wanting to), where the pleasanter aspects of human nature flourish, for the cultivation of true scholarship? Away from the circus arena, scholars focus on convergence as well as divergence, make concessions, aim for compromises where these can be glimpsed. They even socialize. It would be inaccurate to suggest that the colloquium from which these papers derive, held under the auspices of the German Protestant Institute of Archaeology in Jerusalem under its director Volkmar Fritz (archaeologist and biblical scholar), was in any sense 'cosy'. But, occasional outbursts apart, it was mostly good natured.

This volume does not, unfortunately, record some of the best moments of those three days, the conversations and discussions which interspersed the papers; nor have we a transcript of the impromptu seminar on the 'Tel Dan' inscription held in the hotel lobby. It was appropriate (or ironic, as you will) that a group of Israeli, European and American scholars were discussing (among other things) the historicity of United Monarchy centred in Jerusalem while the posters in that city were beginning to proclaim the celebration of 3000 years of the 'city of David'. What better illustration of my earlier remarks? But at any rate, in Jerusalem no archaeologist or biblical scholar feels engaged on an unimportant or socially useless occupation (as can happen elsewhere). There, as I think everywhere, all talk of history is talk about the present. And the future.

The Contents

It is customary for an editor to introduce or review the contributions in the volume. They have been grouped into three topics: method, society and sources. The methodological discussion about archaeology, literature and history is represented by Thomas Thompson and Baruch Halpern, who stand fairly far apart in their definitions and evaluations. Thompson starts off with an attack on William Dever. (The boot is usually on the other foot and one should not feel unduly sympathetic to the target, especially as he had been invited to the colloquium.) Dever has written much on the interface between biblical studies and archaeology, and has claimed some pre-eminence in this enterprise. But despite his vociferous claims to the contrary, he is here represented as really an old-fashioned biblical archaeologist. Rather than follow what he sees as the agenda of either Dever or Halpern, which is to make biblical and archaeological data fit as much as possible, Thompson argues for an understanding of biblical tradition as 'evoking' truth, not 'recounting' it, showing how reality can be drawn out of experience. Consequently, he finds the harmonizing agenda basically flawed. Although Thompson does not make this explicit, the two halves of his paper together address the question of whether modern archaeology and the biblical stories about the past are concerned with the same reality at all. And that is perhaps the most fundamental question in the whole debate about 'biblical history'.

For Halpern, on the other hand, there is no question that there is a single historical 'reality' which the biblical stories and the archaeological record represent. He offers as a definition of history 'the public form of memory' and his discussion ranges characteristically over the entire ancient Near East, scattering instances and assertions in profusion. The core of this lengthy paper is a claim that behind 2 Samuel 8 lies a genre called the 'display inscription' in which episodes are presented thematically rather than chronologically, and the methodological implication is that where the biblical text exaggerates it follows the cultural conventions of the day and when it does not, it is reliable. The source of the story of 2 Samuel 8 is a display inscription that David once set up. Indeed, this kind of (lost) inscription is claimed as the source from which much of the information about the United Monarchy in the biblical story probably came. It might fairly be said that Halpern does not merely harmonize using random texts. He can also conjure more 'history' out of less data (and with less method) than anyone. But Halpern's case is not for the historicity of the biblical 'Davidic-Solomonic' empire: this he clearly denies. He argues, instead, that early sources in 1 Samuel point to a more limited, though historically real, 'United Monarchy'.

The next three papers deal with the social organization of what is usually referred to as the early Israelite 'state'. Christa Schäfer-Lichtenberger begins with an analysis of what might be meant by the term 'state'. Discussing the notorious lack of royal inscriptions from Judah, she finds it less problematic than some scholars do, and concludes generally that archaeology cannot demonstrate the absence of the level of economic activity congruent to what we call a 'state' in the ninth–eighth centuries BCE. She also points out that notions of what the term 'state' implies vary between scholars (discussing Jellinek, Weber and Claessen in particular) and finally offers an analysis of Saul's reign as an 'inchoative state' and David's as a 'transitional early state'—basing her argument, as she says, on the biblical texts.

Schäfer-Lichtenberger's paper alluded to Weber's characterization of early states as 'patrimonial', the definition of which is close to Niels Peter Lemche's 'patronage society'. He considers that even on the biblical evidence there was no Judean state in the tenth century BCE, despite the portrait of David's huge empire. Here he disagrees with Schäfer-Lichtenberger, yet he agrees with her that a clear conception of 'state' is not evident in modern scholarship, and his paper aims to offer an appropriate model for the next stage of complexity after the tribal society (a definition he also challenges): the patronage society, in which ruler is patron ('godfather' in modern parlance) and subjects are clients. However, complexity is not unilinear, and cultures can collapse. This village culture in Iron I Palestine stands between two periods of patronage systems, in which rule was based less on individuals than patron lineages.

David Hopkins's contribution concentrates on the elusiveness of ancient economics, which lie hidden or in disguise behind material remains. He employs the graphic image of an opened tomb, from which the dead do not speak to us of themselves. How, then, can we reconstruct their economic life? Hopkins looks at the state as 'economic commander' ('demand economy' being the appropriate model), matching an eighth-century 'distinct Judean material culture' with an 'integrating economy' evidenced by the settlement landscape. Then he considers social stratification, an issue in which burials offer the primary evidence. On political economic decision-making he contrasts 'risk aversion' (by co-operative means at the village level) with specialization of production (e.g. wine and olive oil) concentrated around particular centres (such as Ekron for oil). Finally, he considers the implications of Judah's strategic position, politically and geographically and the economic implications of resistance to imperial rule and national identity.

There follow five papers dealing with source materials and centred on the chief biblical characters assigned to the period under review: Saul, David and Solomon. Saul is the object of Diana Edelman's investigation, which outlines methods for using biblical materials in aid of history (manuscript evidence, literary 'close reading', identification of original audience, dating). The 'literary Saul' was created, she believes, by the Deuteronomistic historian, using several literary techniques that can be identified. As older sources in this account she identifies scraps of folk-material (a *mašal* and two songs), two lists (administrative and genealogical), and a story underlying 1 Samuel 9–10. An Israelite story about Saul is said to have inspired the Deuteronomistic account. Of particular interest, however, are links between Saul and Gibeon, which the Deuteronomistic historian has tried to obscure. As invention she instances the account of Saul's death. As for the historical Saul, Edelman believes he was a petty king of Gibeon, of uncertain date.

Graeme Auld reviews recent analysis of the books of Samuel before turning back to Wellhausen's magisterial commentary of 1871 and the *Prolegomena* (1878). He points out that Wellhausen's low evaluation of Chronicles contrasts with his optimistic reading (historically speaking) of Judges, Samuel and Kings, which Wellhausen believed (with almost everyone else) Chronicles to have rewritten. The rest of Auld's paper then takes up his recent suggestion that both Kings and Chronicles rewrote an earlier (but still post-exilic) source. He presents instances of high literary artistry and evidence of later stages in the development of

Samuel–Kings and asks whether David and Solomon do not 'belong to the age of legendary beginnings rather than royal record'.

Nadav Na'aman belongs with those who feel able to rely on some biblical sources as bases for historical reconstruction, especially lists. But he also argues that the presence of (Egyptian) hieratic numerals and signs on Israelite and Judean ostraca in the eighth–seventh centuries BCE attest a high literacy level at an earlier period. This leads him to posit that reliable sources about David *could* have been written. He examines the biblical accounts of David's wars with Arameans, Philistines and Ammonites, and suggests the use of older sources in these accounts, inferring that the Deuteronomistic historian had access to an archival library, such as are attested in Egypt in the second half of the first millennium BCE and in seventh century BCE Assyria. On the matter of historicity he is cautious. Whether David's conquests took place he cannot say. But he believes that at least there is nothing impossible about them.

Volkmar Fritz's reappraisal of Solomon's kingdom concentrates on the archaeological evidence: the cities of Hazor, Kinneret (his own excavations), Megiddo and Gezer. He concludes that there is evidence of re-urbanization in the tenth century, which he associates with the establishment of monarchy. Solomon, though perhaps not the great ruler that the Bible depicts, was nevertheless a great builder. Here is a case where it is argued that archaeological data definitely come to the aid of the biblical narrative, though again not to the extent of endorsing the complete picture. Ascription to Solomon of complexes at these cities is not, of course, as certain as once held, but Fritz offers a considered defence of that interpretation. (The paper was especially interesting in view of the presence of Israel Finkelstein and David Ussishkin who have just begun a new dig at Megiddo which it is hoped will, among other things, clarify the dating of the 'Solomonic' buildings.)

Walter Dietrich concludes the volume with an excavation at 'Tell Tenak', the multi-layered mound of the Hebrew Bible, in which his trial trench is dug through the 'ban' or *ḥerem*. He starts, properly, at the surface level, with the post-state period, where he finds the notion of the ban as a devotion to annihilation receding into the background in the texts dated to that time. He turns then to a readily datable source, the inscription of Mesha, where the total population is exterminated, having been devoted to the deity. By comparison, the Deuteronomic laws can be seen as amelioration (Deut. 20.13 only prescribes the death of males), though the notion of extermination of Canaanites and the inclusion of property in the devotion is consistent with the practice described by Mesha. Dietrich sees two lines of tradition: a ruthless prophetic one and a pragmatic national-political one, converging in the Deuteronomic portrait of the *herem*. Moreover, accounts of such wars undertaken by Saul and David, being consistent with the national-political use, suggest the presence of ancient sources.

It is evident that little consensus is immediately conveyed by these papers. However, the discussions after the papers, and at other times, suggested a greater convergence and the astute reader may find it possible to reconstruct the gist of some conversations. A vote on the historicity of Solomon was in the end narrowly avoided; the participants (not all represented in this volume) had a clear estimate of the likely (majority) verdict on that occasion, but it seems to me proper that the readers of this book make up their own minds on whether, and why— or why not.

OPENING REMARKS

Volkmar Fritz

Let me formally open the colloquium 'The Formation of a State. Historical, Archaeological and Sociological Problems in the Period of the United Monarchy in Israel'. I want to say a few words at the beginning about our intention. During the last three decades critical scholarship has developed at a breathtaking speed. While during the twenties and thirties it was largely German scholars who stood with their critical attitude against the rest of the world, now we have the phenomenon that critical views are an integral part of biblical research everywhere. In addition to that development we witness the tremendous rate at which biblical archaeology is presenting new results concerning the history of this country. Altogether we have developed a new idea of biblical history. The main result of this is that biblical historiography has lost its dominant position and a new historiography based on all external sources available has been put in place. In this way an entirely new picture of the pre-monarchic period has replaced the story of the conquest given in the book of Joshua. The period of the monarchy has also undergone a critical re-evaluation. Not every sentence of the Deuteronomistic historian can now be considered a reliable tradition based on a historic fact. But criticism also means self-criticism. What are the standards of critical analysis, what are the methods for establishing a new historical picture? We are now confronted with a variety of opinions concerning the United Monarchy as well as the kingdoms of Israel and Judah. It was my intention to bring together at least some scholars with contradictory opinions for an open discussion. The main purpose of this colloquium is the presentation of critical views concerning the early period of the kingdom, an open discussion about the problems involved, and the attempt at a synthesis concerning the history of Israel during the tenth century.

This colloquium is held on behalf of the German Protestant Institute of Archaeology in Jerusalem. The German institute was founded in 1900 and opened in 1903 by its first director, Gustaf Dalman. After a long break, due to the two world wars, it was reopened by Martin Noth in 1964. In 1982 the institute moved to its present location within the Auguste Victoria Compound, which was once called the 'German peak' between the Hebrew University at Mt Scopus and the Mount of Olives. The Auguste Victoria Foundation was established at the turn of the century in connection with the visit of the last German emperor, Wilhelm II, to the Holy Land in 1898. The large building in neo-Romanesque style erected here was intended as a kind of recreation centre for clergymen of the Protestant churches. This purpose was never fulfilled, and instead it served as headquarters for the German-Turkish and, after 1917, for the British general command. Since 1948 the building has been used as a hospital for Palestinian refugees financed by the Lutheran World Federation and the United Nations. The church is still used for services and concerts by the Protestant church and frequently visited by German tourists. But let me assure you that this church does not go back to a very old tradition and that the place is not connected to any event in biblical history. The institute itself is housed in a small building which was erected for the gardener!

The purpose of the institute is research into the history and archaeology of the land of the Bible. Since German scholarship used to be very critical I think it can be a good place for critical analysis and open discussion. Let me stress again that in the name of the Institute you are cordially welcomed. And let me express again my wish for a successful colloquium with new ideas in an atmosphere of personal understanding.

METHOD

HISTORIOGRAPHY OF ANCIENT PALESTINE AND EARLY JEWISH HISTORIOGRAPHY: W.G. DEVER AND THE NOT SO NEW BIBLICAL ARCHAEOLOGY

Thomas L. Thompson

William Dever's discussions of biblical archaeology during the past years have led me to become increasingly convinced that, insofar as his discussion of the history of Palestine involves biblical studies or what he understands as the origins and development of Israel, it is not a new biblical archaeology and has not involved a new departure from our approach to the history of the southern Levant. It has rather been a reiteration of past approaches to the Bible and to history, however much it reflects a resilient assessment, adjustment and accommodation to the winds of change in both field archaeology and biblical studies. Dever's methods have remained rooted in an Albrightean harmony of ancient Near Eastern 'history' and illustrated Bible stories.

In his fundamental studies of Early Bronze IV, the patriarchal period's Amorites of Kenyon and Wright always played an explanatory historical role and provided Dever's historiographical perspective for understanding development and change in the archaeological record.[1] Although Haldar[2] and Liverani[3] had decisively severed the biblical archaeological linkage between the cuneiform texts relating to the *amurru* and the patriarchal narratives, it was not until the mid to late 1970s that Dever

---

1. W.G. Dever, 'The Pottery of Palestine in the Early Bronze IV–Middle Bronze I Period ca. 2150–1950 BC' (PhD dissertation, Harvard University, 1966); *idem*, 'The People of Palestine in the Middle Bronze Period', *HTR* 64 (1971), pp. 197-226; *idem*, 'The EB IV–MB I Horizon in Transjordan and Southern Palestine', *BASOR* 210 (1973), pp. 37-63; compare this with K. Kenyon, *Amorites and Canaanites* (Oxford: Oxford University Press,1966), *passim*, but especially pp. 15-18.

2. A. Haldar, *Who Were the Amorites?* (Leiden: Brill, 1971).

3. M. Liverani, 'The Amorites', in *Peoples of Old Testament Times* (ed. D.J. Wiseman; Oxford: Clarendon Press, 1973), pp. 100-33.

first began to separate himself from the historical implications of Kenyon's and Wright's hypothesis.[4]

In adjusting to these changes, Dever only recognized at first that Wright's earlier assessment of the continuity of pottery forms between the Early Bronze and the Intermediate period in Palestine needed to be reasserted.[5] It was not until after K. Prag independently and decisively had demonstrated that Glueck's longstanding insistence on the acceptance of a partially sedentary population during the Early Bronze IV period in the Transjordan had been after all correct[6] that Dever began to change his historical interpretations.[7]

Dever has long maintained his biblical framework for historical interpretations of archaeology. In his contribution, for example, to the Hayes–Miller *Israelite and Judaean History* of 1977,[8] Dever's 1966 dissertation's nomadic Amorite immigration theory for MB I was still sufficiently in place to have encouraged him to abandon this, by then, beleaguered period as a background for the tales of the patriarchs[9] (but not its historical description). Methodologically, Dever was still looking for synthesis and harmony, and so he invented a very strange—but not

4. See on this T.L. Thompson, *The Historicity of the Patriarchal Narratives: The Quest for the Historical Abraham* (BZAW, 133; Berlin: de Gruyter, 1974), pp. 52-164, and especially pp. 159-71—the typescript of which Dever saw in the spring of 1972.

5. G.E. Wright, 'The Chronology of Palestinian Pottery in Middle Bronze I', *BASOR* 71 (1938), pp. 27-34; Thompson, *Historicity*, pp. 160-62; W.G. Dever, 'The Beginning of the Middle Bronze Age in Syria-Palestine', in *Magnalia Dei* (ed. F.M. Cross; Garden City, NY: Doubleday, 1976), pp. 3-38; and *idem*, 'Palestine in the Second Millennium, BCE, The Archaeological Picture', in *Israelite and Judaean History* (ed. J.H. Hayes and J.M. Miller; Philadelphia: Westminster Press, 1977), pp. 70-120.

6. K. Prag, 'The Intermediate Early Bronze-Middle Bronze Age: An Interpretation of the Evidence from Transjordan, Syria and Lebanon', *Levant* 6 (1974), pp. 69-116; see also *idem*, 'Continuity and Migration in the South Levant in the Late Third Millennium: A Review of T.L. Thompson's and Some Other Views', *PEQ* 116 (1984), pp. 58-68; cf. Thompson, *Historicity*, p. 168; *idem*, 'The Settlement of Early Bronze IV–Middle Bronze I in Jordan', *ADAJ* (1974), pp. 57-71.

7. 'Beginning'.

8. Dever, 'The Patriarchal Period', in J.H. Hayes and J.M. Miller (eds.), *Israelite and Judaean History* (Philadelphia: Westminster Press, 1977), pp. 102-120.

9. Thompson, *Historicity*; J. Van Seters, *Abraham in History and Tradition* (New Haven, CT: Yale University Press, 1975).

archaeologically very cogent[10]—assertion of Rowtonian dimorphism as a 'sociological' and historical model for understanding the archaeological remains of the Middle Bronze II period. Then, in this article in the Hayes–Miller volume, he declared that to be his patriarchal period,[11] seriously expecting concurrence as he sincerely believed the biblical archaeological questions which he had proposed to have been historically appropriate. In his assertion of this peculiar MB II heuristic model for his own fieldwork on small one-period sites in the Judaean highlands, Dever tried to demonstrate the inseparable connection between archaeological fieldwork and what he understands as historical reconstruction. In the classical—and one must also say the now discredited—manner of biblical archaeology, archaeology and history were for him a single discipline. For him, there has been no other history of either Israel or Palestine than that of a critically revised, reconstructed one from the Bible. If, eventually, he has come to argue for a separation of archaeology from biblical scholarship—for a Syro-Palestinian rather than a biblical archaeology—such separation is merely an aspect of an academic territorial dispute: a fight over 'turf', but hardly one rendering a specifically critical perspective in scholarship.[12] In terms of the historiography of the southern Levant, Dever's Bronze Age—like Malamat's[13]—is ever cast in the context of the Bible's pre-history.

10. T.L. Thompson, 'The Background of the Patriarchs: A Reply to William Dever and Malcolm Clark', *JSOT* 9 (1978), pp. 2-43.

11. Dever, 'Palestine in the Second Millennium'.

12. W.G. Dever, 'Syro-Palestinian and Biblical Archaeology', in *The Hebrew Bible and its Interpreters* (ed. D.A. Knight and G.M. Tucker; Philadelphia: Scholars Press, 1985), pp. 31-74; *idem*, 'Archaeology in Israel Today: A Summation and Critique', in S. Gitin and W.G. Dever (eds.), *Recent Excavations in Israel: Studies in Iron Age Archaeology* (Baltimore: Johns Hopkins University Press, 1989), pp. 143-52; and especially, *idem*, 'Archaeology, Syro-Palestinian and Biblical', *ABD* I (New York: Doubleday, 1992), pp. 354-67. It is particularly notable that in this encyclopaedic survey of Dever's, dealing with the relationship between archaeology and the Bible—although written in a Bible dictionary—Dever's treatment is not only narrowly American in its focus and oriented to a particular group within American biblical archaeology, but the works of critical historians who had been most directly involved in the changes in biblical archaeology during the 1970s and 1980s—most significantly Ahlström, Knauf, Miller and Van Seters—do not appear even in Dever's bibliography, and one must wonder if such neglect is not a form of Harvard censorship of dissenting views.

13. A. Malamat, 'Die Frühgeschichte Israels: eine methodologische Studie', *TZ* 39 (1983), pp. 1-16.

It is important to point out that Dever has rarely tried to function as a historian. His ultimate rejection of the biblically derived picture of EB IV/MB I as a period reflective of migrant nomads came only as a result of the *bruta facta* of the sedentary structures he was finally to uncover in his excavations of transhumance pastoralist settlements at Beer Resisim.[14] It was this experience that was decisive in the development of Dever's interpretation—rather than any developments in the historiography of our field.[15] To his credit, he decisively turned away from the earlier positions of his dissertation and has abandoned biblical archaeology's Amorite and nomadic hypotheses not only for Transjordan and the Negev, but for the agricultural heartland of the southern Levant as well.[16]

Although Dever's field experience had led him in the early 1980s to give up the association of Genesis's Bible stories with EB IV, he had never recognized the methodological and historical issues that were involved. He, like Speiser—and for that matter Albright—had asked only *which* of the Bronze Age periods was the patriarchal period. He never seriously considered the question of whether any such period had existed. For Dever's history, only two factors pertained: that concerning materials derived from field excavation and that relating to the historical framework given to him by the Bible of Archbishop Ussher. His project has always been the relationship asserted by biblical and Christian fundamentalism to exist between the two. The same biblical archaeological perspective that Wright had pioneered and which had given

14. See W.G. Dever and R. Cohen, 'Preliminary Report of the Pilot Season of the Central Negev Highlands Project', *BASOR* 232 (1978), pp. 29-45; *idem*, 'Preliminary Report of the Second Season of the Central Negev Highlands Project', *BASOR* 236 (1979), pp. 41-60; *idem*, 'Preliminary Report of the Third and Final Season of the Central Negev Highlands Project', *BASOR* 243 (1981), pp. 57-77; W.G. Dever, 'Beer Resisim—A Late Third Millennium BCE Settlement', *Qadmoniot* 16 (1983), pp. 52–57; *idem*, 'Village Planning at Beer Resisim and Socio-Economic Structures in EB IV Palestine', *EI* 18 (1985), pp. 18-28.

15. Cf. Thompson, *Historicity*, pp. 167-68; *idem*, *The Settlement of Sinai and the Negev in the Bronze Age* (BTAVO, 8; Wiesbaden: Reichert, 1975).

16. W.G. Dever, 'New Vistas on the EB IV (MB I) Horizon in Syria-Palestine', *BASOR* 237 (1980), pp. 35-64; *idem*, 'From the End of the Early Bronze Age to the Beginning of the Middle Bronze Age', in *Biblical Archaeology Today* (ed. J. Aviram; Jerusalem: Israel Exploration Society, 1985), pp. 113-35; cf., however, already Thompson, 'The Background of the Patriarchs'; *idem*, *The Settlement of Palestine in the Bronze Age* (BTAVO, 24; Wiesbaden: Reichert, 1979).

Dever's dissertation a historiographic perspective has in the 1980s and 1990s dominated his efforts at historical reconstruction of archaeological data: from his vigorous defense of Solomon's legendary relationship to Gezer to his most recent efforts to try to find some biblical scenario—whether by way of Gottwald,[17] or of Fritz[18] or now more recently of Halpern[19]—with which he might shape a coherent consensus in contemporary scholarship regarding the history of Israel's origins.[20] Although Dever denies having approached the excavation of the Solomonic gate at Gezer, so to speak, Bible in hand,[21] it is my distinct memory that in the spring dig of 1967, all of us who were then at Gezer had gone, fully

17. So, W.G. Dever, *Recent Archaeological Discoveries and Biblical Research* (Seattle, WA: University of Washington Press, 1990); cf., however, the devastating critique of Gottwald's *Tribes of Yahweh* (1979) in N.P. Lemche, *Early Israel: Anthropological and Historical Studies on the Israelite Society before the Monarchy* (VTSup, 37; Leiden: Brill, 1985) *passim*; also T.L. Thompson, *The Origin Tradition of Ancient Israel* (JSOTSup, 55; Sheffield: JSOT Press, 1987), pp. 15-43, and, more recently, *idem*, *The Early History of the Israelite People: From the Written and Archaeological Sources* (SHANE, 4; Leiden: Brill, 2nd edn, 1994), pp. 50-76.

18. V. Fritz, 'The Israelite Conquest in the Light of Recent Excavations at Khirbet el-Meshash', *BASOR* 241 (1981), pp. 61-73; *idem*, 'Die Kulturhistorische Bedeutung der früheisenzeitliche Siedlung auf der Khirbet el-Meshash und das Problem der Landnahme', *ZDPV* 93 (1975), pp. 121-35; *idem*, 'The Conquest in the Light of Archaeology', in *Proceedings in the Eighth World Congress of Jewish Studies* (Jerusalem, 1982), pp. 15-22; *idem*, 'Conquest or Settlement? The Early Iron Age in Palestine', *BA* 50 (1987), pp. 84-90; *idem*, 'Die Landnahme der israelitischen Stämme in Kanaan', *ZDPV* 106 (1990), pp. 62-77.

19. So, most recently W.G. Dever, 'How to Tell a Canaanite from an Israelite', in *The Rise of Ancient Israel* (ed. H. Shanks; Washington, DC: Biblical Archaeological Society, 1993). In this same volume see B. Halpern's 'The Exodus from Egypt: Myth or Reality', .

20. For a clear statement of Dever's understanding of the history of Israel as an essentially corrected (however radical that may be) biblical history, see his 'Archaeology, Material Culture and the Early Monarchical Period in Israel', in D. Edelman (ed.), *The Fabric of History: Text, Artifact and Israel's Past* (JSOTSup, 127; Sheffield: JSOT Press, 1991), pp. 103-10; this also gives his perception of the Bible as essentially offering us a tradition of 'original events' 'lost in transmission', which, of course, historians of biblical scholarship, will recognize as the most fundamental premise of the 'old' biblical archaeology (see my *Early History*, pp. 10-13).

21. So, W.G. Dever, 'Of Myths and Methods', *BASOR* 277/278 (1990), pp. 121-30; in response to G.J. Wightman, 'The Myth of Solomon', *BASOR* 277/278 (1990), pp. 5-22, esp. pp. 15-17.

aware of Dever's quite explicit purpose of uncovering 'Solomon's' gate. Half of the gate had already been 'recognized' by Dever—following Yadin[22]—in Macalister's report on the Maccabean tower. No efforts to establish an independent interpretation or chronology were undertaken either in regard to stratigraphy or to the chronology of the pottery that was related to these gate structures. Although Dever certainly did not have the Bible in hand when he marked out the squares for excavation, he did have Yadin's article citing the relevant biblical passage. Far from the objective archaeological excavation that Dever claims in his *BASOR* article,[23] the sole purpose of this particular expedition was to confirm Yadin's thesis. There was no other reason for being there.[24] In Dever's then expressed opinion, the architectural similarities with the gates at Hazor and Megiddo were the sole and sufficient criteria for dating Gezer's 'Solomonic' stratum.

Dever's current efforts at creating a Bible History are clearly defined in his recent contribution to Shanks's *Rise of Ancient Israel*. Without acknowledging his indebtedness to the recent works of Ahlström, Lemche or Davies for bringing clarity to some of the historical problems involved,[25] Dever clearly attempts to clarify the nature of his allegiance

22. Y. Yadin, 'Solomon's City Wall and Gate at Gezer', *IEJ* 8 (1958), pp. 80-86; *idem*, 'New Light on Solomon's Megiddo', *BA* 23 (1960), pp. 62-68.

23. 'Of Myths and Methods', pp. 121-23. See on this, W.G. Dever, 'Archaeological Date on the Israelite settlement: A Review of Two Recent Works', *BASOR* 284 (1991), pp. 77-90. Indeed, in the square in which I worked, under the supervision of Anson Rainey, we uncovered immediately overlying the gate three large boulders ca. 85–110 cm in diameter, which did not make sense either in Macalister's descriptions or in Dever's reconstructions. These 'artifacts' were rolled down the slope of the mound by Rainey and Dever and never appeared in the field notes. When it came to questions of chronology and the gate itself, all pottery discrepancies were consciously discarded prior to recording.

24. Dever's effort at confirmation is to be stressed. Perhaps if we had found something that would have made Yadin's thesis entirely impossible, Dever may have re-examined the issue. Failing such overwhelming contradiction, however, all 'evidence' became malleable, and supported confirmation. The Gezer excavation's pragmatic and politically motivated observations, of course, depart substantially from Popperian preferences for the hypothetically falsifiable question that is the quintessentially scientific one.

25. G.W. Ahlström, *Who Were the Israelites?* (Winona Lake, IN: Eisenbrauns, 1986); N.P. Lemche, *The Canaanites and Their Land* (JSOTSup, 110; Sheffield: JSOT Press, 1991); P.R. Davies, *In Search of 'Ancient Israel'* (JSOTSup, 148; Sheffield: JSOT Press, 1992); see also, Thompson, *Early History*, pp. 310-15.

to biblical archaeology. He discusses his harmonization or 'synthesis' of the results of biblical and archaeological research in the context of what he believes to be the interrelationship and congruence of the literary concepts of 'Canaanite' and 'Israelite' with the—for Palestine—prehistoric and transitional period of Iron Age I.[26]

It is also in this article that Dever most clearly demonstrates his rejection of both historical methods and historical questions. For him, history—even in early periods of Palestine's past—is not itself a field of research, but is rather essentially the product of a harmony and joint project of two fields: archaeology and the Bible. For Dever, biblical archaeology is an 'interdisciplinary' project. However, he means by this that it is a project negotiated by—and between—two disciplines. Dever believes in experts; his, therefore, is history by committee.

Certainly Dever's understanding of the task at hand has modesty on its side. Dever's harmonizing perspective, wherein history lies between two disciplines, requires a view of research in our fields as possessing an objectivity—and this in both archaeological and biblical studies—such that our formulated conclusions and interpretations can be perceived as if they were *data*! This confuses the methods of both the social and human sciences (*Sozial-* and *Geisteswissenschaft*) with those of the natural sciences, and is excessively dismissive of the hard-won creative perspectives that form the very matrix of historical reconstruction.

Compared to archaeology—even compared to biblical studies, properly understood—history is a very soft science, especially that so very fragile branch of history that involves the pre-Hellenistic periods of the southern Levant. History involves very little that can be firmly asserted as knowledge or as 'known history', although there is a corresponding abundance of what we can confidently identify as unhistorical. It may well be ironic that it is this recognition of our ignorance of this period's history—indeed that the recognition of such ignorance is the hallmark of our field's cutting edge—that marks the most conclusive results of this generation's historical research! Dever's history by committee, for which no one discipline and therefore no one person can be responsible, is not history at all. At its best this might be Bright's

26. Dever's essentially harmonizing methods become particularly clear by comparing his *Recent Archaeological Discoveries* directly with either W.F. Albright's *The Archaeology of Palestine* of 1949 or G.E. Wright's *Biblical Archaeology* of 1962. For a critical perspective on the methods of this kind of biblical archaeology, see my *Historicity*, pp. 52-57.

'history of the possible' *redivivus*. Standing between archaeology and biblical studies and responsible to neither, it is wholly bereft of method. The example of the Dever and Halpern Smithsonian lectures is apt.

To be sure, Halpern and Dever here only 'visit ideas'.[27] Both largely summarize papers and talks that they have given over the past years. Although they claim to present an alternative to what they describe as current views about Israel's origins, they hardly advance beyond what had dominated the field back in 1962; namely, the three, formerly alternative, explanatory models of conquest, peaceful settlement and peasant revolt, which were given their canonical form by Manfred Weippert in 1967.[28] With some thirty years of hindsight, it is hardly surprising that they found none of these old theories viable.[29]

This audience well knows that not only archaeology, but history and biblical studies as well, have long abandoned such approaches.[30] Dever offers and identifies as his own position what he calls a fourth model and refers to it as a 'symbiosis model'. According to Dever, what had been

27. The *bon mot* here is provided by Kyle McCarter who, in H. Shanks (ed.), *The Rise of Ancient Israel* (Washington, DC: Biblical Archaeological Society, 1993), p. 128, describes his own historical reconstructions.

28. M. Weippert, *Die Landnahme der israelitischen Stämme in der neueren wissenschaftlichen Diskussion* (FRLANT, 92; Göttingen: Vandenhoeck & Ruprecht, 1967; ET = *The Settlement of the Israelite Tribes in Palestine* [SBT, 21; London, 1971]).

29. It might be pointed out here that the conquest model has been devastatingly reviewed by M. Noth, 'Der Beitrag der Archäologie zur Geschichte Israels', in *Congress Volume Oxford 1959* (VTSup, 7; Leiden: Brill, 1960), pp. 262-82; Weippert, *Landnahme*; and J.M. Miller, 'The Israelite Occupation of Canaan', in Hayes and Miller (eds.), *Israelite and Judaean History*, pp. 213-84. The settlement model was thoroughly undermined as early as 1968: H. Friis (originally unpublished gold medal essay at the University of Copenhagen), *Die Bedingungen für die Errichtung des davidischen Reiches in Israel und seiner Umwelt* (Heidelberg: Dielheimer Blätter, 1986); and N.P. Lemche, *Israel i Dommertiden* (Copenhagen: G.E.C. Gads, 1971); see also, Thompson, *Early History*, pp. 27-40. The model of peasant revolt, first comprehensively presented in N.K. Gottwald, *The Tribes of Yahweh* (Maryknoll: Orbis Books, 1979) was decisively overturned by Lemche, *Early Israel*; see on this, Thompson, *Early History*, pp. 41-76.

30. For reviews of the ongoing changes in scholarship, see especially Miller and Hayes (eds.), *Israelite and Judaean History*; R. de Vaux, *The Early History of Israel* (Philadelphia, Westminster Press, 1978); Lemche, *Early Israel*; Thompson, *Early History*; and G.W. Ahlström, *The History of Ancient Palestine from the Palaeolithic Period to Alexander's Conquest* (JSOTSup, 146; Sheffield: JSOT Press, 1993).

originally intended as a minor revision of Alt's thesis as presented by Volkmar Fritz now is presented as an alternative model:[31] that the original, immigrating Israelites had lived for some time in symbiosis with Canaanites. Also, in unwitting agreement with Alt, but no longer sharing Fritz's whole-hearted concurrence, Dever indicates a decided preference for the historicity of the book of Judges to that of Joshua. Such old-fashioned biblical archaeology, allowing the competitive selectivity of evidence, is based on the premise—attributed by Dever to Halpern, but also long ago asserted by Alt, and Albright, as well as by a half century of biblical scholarship prior to the 1970s—'that behind the literary tradition there must indeed be some sort of genuine historical memory'.[32] In filling out the historical character of his model, Dever then sees himself as adding to this biblical hypothesis as argued by Halpern what Dever views as the 'methods' of archaeological research in Palestine, which, of course, have played a central and critical role in discussions of Israel's origins since Alt first presented this thesis in 1925.[33]

In carrying this out, Dever partially follows the 1962 suggestion of George Mendenhall: that we should explore the possibility of Israel as a product of the indigenous population of Palestine. Dever also chooses to favor what he imagines to be a more sociologically oriented dichotomy of city commerce over against village-based agriculturalists, which Mendenhall asserted had been created by a religiously based revolution.

While Dever claims no longer to follow either Mendenhall's religious, or Gottwald's social, revolution hypothesis, his so-called 'proto-Israelites' of Iron Age I are, nevertheless, supposedly to be understood as agriculturalists indigenous to Palestine, and as—God knows how—

---

31. See A. Alt, *Die Landnahme der Israeliten in Palästina* (Leipzig, 1925; ET = 'The Settlement of the Israelite Tribes in Palestine', in *Essays in Old Testament History and Religion* [Oxford: Clarendon Press, 1966], pp. 133-69).

32. Dever, 'How to Tell a Canaanite', p. 31.

33. I am thinking here of the rich archaeological data relative to surface explorations and settlement patterns pioneered by such scholars as Alt, Albright and Glueck which has added so much to our understanding of the history of western Palestine with the more recent and systematic work of such scholars as Zori, Aharoni and Kochavi and most recently the extensive work of the Survey of Israel, including that of Finkelstein and Zertal. While it is true that very substantial synthetic interpretations such as that of Finkelstein have added new dimensions in the 1980s to this subfield of Palestinian archaeology, neither its importance nor much of the data is particularly new in our field. See, for example, Thompson, *Settlement of Palestine*.

having formed superior egalitarian village polities. Moreover, for unknown reasons, all this supposedly took place in the highlands in a social world that reflected the sharpest contrast to those equally hypothetically non-egalitarian Canaanite lowland town-dwellers.

Although Dever rejects Alt's pastoral nomads as having formed Israel's originating core as well as Alt's proposal of the later Israel's ultimate origin from beyond the Jordan, this is done without argument. The present audience will recognize certain uncredited similarities with the biblical side of Finkelstein's 1988 reconstruction. In Dever's update of Alt's paradigm, the historical methods pursued by Alt to synthesize biblical, historical and archaeological data remain largely unchanged from those so clearly described in Alt's 1925 seminal essay. Sooner or later we need to ask: What contribution has archaeology brought to Dever's (not Finkelstein's) adopted scenario during the seventy years which separate Dever from his source in Alt? Both Alt and Dever began with the observation of a significant transformation of Palestine from a world of Late Bronze 'city-states' to a world of assumed regional states in the Iron Age. Both Alt and Dever select Judges to be the most appropriate biblical story for archaeological illustration, and both Alt and Dever dismiss as irrelevant to the history of Israel's origins those biblical stories which fail the test of such illustrative promise.

Also echoing Borowski and Hopkins,[34] Dever's village agriculture in the Iron Age I highlands is found to reflect 'the kind of social and economic structure that comes right out of the pages of the book of Judges' (one might also mention Ruth). This seeming correspondence is understood as justifying Dever's model of Israel's origins as a 'biblical archaeology' of the 'right type'.[35]

What is problematic in Dever's methods—which have little to do with archaeology—was already problematic in Alt's; and they are problems endemic to a quite old-fashioned biblical archaeology. These are: a) the unfounded assumption that the biblical tradition of Judges is a recognizable reflection of historical memory; b) the belief that a history of Israel's origins can be written through a direct synthesis of the Bible and archaeology; c) the biblically and archaeologically indefensible assertion that the origins of Israel are to be discovered somehow through a

34. O. Borowski, *Agriculture in Iron Age Israel* (Winona Lake, IN: Eisenbrauns, 1987); D.C. Hopkins, *The Highlands of Canaan: Agricultural Life in the Early Iron Age* (The Social World of Biblical Antiquity, 3; Sheffield: Almond Press, 1985).

35. Dever, 'How to Tell a Canaanite', p. 48.

description of the Late Bronze/Iron Age transition; d) the naive assumption that Israel must have originated in a region of Palestine that centuries later came to be identified through place names as peculiarly belonging to the heartland of Israel in canonical biblical traditions, and—contrariwise—the assumption that Israel's origins could not have occurred in regions apart from this particular biblical view of the past, whether Judah, the Galilee, Issachar or Gilead; and e) the fundamentalistic faith in the existence of an Israelite monarchy during the tenth century as an unquestionable historical *datum*. What is 'new' in such biblical archaeology?

If Dever's effort to revive the united use of Bible and spade is judged as worn, timid and disappointing, the perspective of biblical scholarship and literature with which he seeks linkage is hardly less so. Halpern's effort to reassert the historicity of the Exodus story is also methodologically reactionary, reviving as it does some of the worst and already long-discredited aspects of the parallelomania of the old 'biblical archaeology'. Halpern argues for the historicity of the Exodus story not on the basis of a biblical interpretation of any texts we have, nor on the basis of a confluence of a critical exegetical understanding of biblical narrative with an independently derived understanding of ancient Near Eastern texts or history. Halpern rather presents a harmonizing amalgamation of a biblicistic interpretation of historical data from Egypt and the Levant with a historicistic reading of arbitrarily selected biblical stories, that have been equally as arbitrarily defined as early and judged as 'rooted' in historical events. One must forget for the sake of argument that these Halpernean 'events' are neither to be found in historical data from anywhere in the ancient Near East nor anywhere in biblical traditions that we actually have. They exist, rather, solely in Halpern's simulated reality.[36]

Dever's more recent contribution in the current issue of *Eretz Israel* to the issue of biblical archaeology does not substantially satisfy this need for sound method.[37] In this *ad hominem* attack on Ahlström and myself, Dever is quite engaged by concerns about credit for initiating the now

36. In the scholarly world these methodological issues have long been settled. See Thompson, *Historicity*; *idem*, 'The Joseph and Moses Narratives', in Hayes and Miller (eds.), *Israelite and Judaean History*, pp. 149-80, 210-12.

37. W.G. Dever, 'Archaeology and the Current Crisis in Israelite Historiography', *EI* 25 (1995). I am grateful to William Dever for an early pre-publication copy of the closing arguments of this paper.

dominant historiographical development in our field which understands Syro-Palestinian archaeology and the history of the southern Levant as independent disciplines. He is also much exercised in the checking of academic credentials. The disagreement between Dever and me—and between Dever and Ahlström—has little to do with either arrogating credit for work done—as Diebner might wish[38]—or with judgments about scholarly competence—as Dever would have it.[39] Those who have read my 1992 work are already aware that I have attributed pride of place in these present shifts of our historiography to the 1968 prize essay of the Danish scholar Heike Friis.[40] In his challenge against the credentials of Ahlström and myself, Dever avoids addressing any one of the many issues that we have raised, even that most important issue: that we have found his 'ancient Israel' to be a scholarly figment, rather than a goal of current research! The wish of Ahlström and myself—along with Liverani, Lemche, Helga Weippert, Knauf, de Pury, Niehmann, Niehr, Hübner, Nodet, Köckert, Diebner, Whitelam, Auld, Davies, Cryer, Carroll, Bolin and many others—is to see history as a discipline in its own right, with its own questions and its own methodology. Our topics have ever been historical, not archaeological, ones. However, such questions relate to a critical history and not to that of any specific view of the past projected by biblical tradition.

One of the major conclusions of the debates of the mid-seventies in our discipline as it relates to questions of historiographical method was the need to analyze separately and independently the data and evidence from the many sources we have related to southern Levantine history before bringing the results of our analysis into any form of synthesis. This was a hard-won gain that has been accepted by all but fundamentalists. Dever's and Halpern's search for harmonistic scenarios with which to wed their own hardly independently derived phantasms

38. See B.J. Diebner, *Dielheimer Blätter* 28 (1992, published 1994), *passim* and my response: 'Offing the Establishment: *DBAT* 28 and the Politics of Radicalism', *BN* 79 (1995), pp. 71-87.

39. So Dever argues against both Ahlström and me (in W.G. Dever, Review of A. Ben-Tor, *The Archaeology of Ancient Israel, JBL* 114 [1995], p. 122). Dever goes on not only to describe Philip Davies as a 'nihilist'—as G.E. Wright once did of Martin Noth—but also to refer rather obscurely to Davies's use of archaeology in his recent book, *In Search of 'Ancient Israel'* as 'a travesty'. Davies, of course, does not use archaeology in his book, but is among those whom Dever claims have been misled by Ahlström and myself.

40. *Die Bedingungen*; see my *Early History*, pp. 89-90.

abandons such gains in favor of historical syntheses which—much like the old assertion of patriarchal Hurrian family customs—can be supported neither by archaeological nor biblical studies. Independence in the analysis of our data allows us to ask questions appropriate to archaeological data, and *other* questions appropriate to biblical traditions.

Against any form of biblical archaeology, I am no longer convinced that biblical historiography is a legitimate point of departure for today's historiography of the southern Levant. I also doubt that the longstanding historiographical goals of biblical scholarship's historical criticism and tradition history any longer have much to say to a historian of the ancient Near East.

A critical affirmation or negation of classical historiographies, such as we often presume to find in the Bible and in similar traditions, has meaning and legitimacy only to the extent that we first assert that such historiographies in fact embody a view, however fictionalized, of a past that we also can perceive as 'real'. Such a judgment, however, engages us in a discussion—which we must begin—concerning the nature and referents of biblical historiography.[41]

The changes over the past generation in modern scholarship's understanding of the historiography of ancient Israel is not only limited to the way that we reconstruct our histories of Israel, as, for example, has been at the center of debate in our pursuit of a Syro-Palestinian over against a biblical archaeology, or to the search for a history constructed independently of biblical historiography. We have need for a history of Palestine and the east Mediterranean lands—as befits the largely prehistoric pre-Hellenistic world of the ancient southern Levant—rather than a history of Israel. That can, at best, be only part of this larger reality. Even aside from the not-insignificant question of whether such concepts as those of biblical 'Israel' and 'Canaan' are at all tolerable words in a modern historiography of this region, such issues and debates relate to what we are about in our duties as historians. However we might deal with such questions, a central premise of all who today engage in these debates, both implicit and explicit, is the seminal, historiographical

---

41. See, already, E.A. Knauf, 'From History to Interpretation', in D. Edelman (ed.), *The Fabric of History: Text, Artifact and Israel's Past* (JSOTSup, 127; Sheffield: JSOT Press, 1991), pp. 26-64; T.L. Thompson, 'Conflict Themes in the Jacob Narratives', *Semeia* 15 (1979), pp. 5-26; *idem*, 'Text, Context and Referent in Israelite Historiography', in Edelman (ed.), *Fabric of History*, pp. 65-92.

ideology or ideologies of the biblical traditions, which has or have created the historiographical questions we attempt to pose.

Contemporary historiography sets as its goal an understanding and an interpretation of the data that is reflective of the past which has survived. This data offers us in the limits and ambiguity of its mirror a fragmented, fractured past: one that is hardly identifiable or recon-structable as a past that was. This past, our history—hardly one that can be reconstituted in the form of a coherent historical narrative—never-theless does render us the means to evaluate critically ancient historio-graphies, and to evaluate their reflections on the quality of reality of any known past.

Modern historiography, which has defined our field, is inescapably tied to the Enlightenment's understanding of history in its signification of reality past. *Contemporary* scholarship's revisions may cast doubt on the influence of this perception of romanticism's assertion of historical reality's meaning, but to the extent that we continue to assert the relevance of history to our work, historicity, as the measure of the truth and reality of falsifiable historical statements, reasserts its deconstructive role on traditional historiography. The disturbing quality of historicism's lack of faith is awakened in the observation that answers to questions of historicity are only convincing when they render negative judgments. No wonder that biblicists and fundamentalists—whether religious or secular—needs must resort to charges of minimalism, skepticism, nihilism and the like. Historicity is not a question which faith can engage with hope of success.

In an effort to level the playing field, let us not continue any more with questions of historicity: a few fragments, a few lists, a story motif or character deriving from the Assyrian period might possibly give some comfort. Yet there is a question that has only rarely been engaged since the rise of the neo-orthodox reaction against Wellhausen. It is one which should have been engaged long ago and it is one that has the potential of re-establishing the continuity of biblical scholarship with its critical roots. This question simply relates modestly to the intention and function of biblical tradition in relationship to the understanding which it once both expressed and established. What is the early Jewish historiography that we call the Bible about?

In dealing with the dominantly narrative genres that are collected as tradition in the Bible, two chronistic referents commonly occur which stand in polarity to each other: that of tradition (such as the *Toledoth*) and that of the real (which is implicit to such tradition). They are both framed in the language of 'Israel's past'—which through reflective understanding (or 'philosophy') establishes confidence (that is, 'faith') in a new future, even eschatological reality. Biblical time, which, after all, is neither cyclical nor the linear historiography of our scholarly past generation's 'biblical theology', reflects a mirrored reality. Biblical history is ever *Heilsgeschichte*. However much its focus lies in the collections of tradition past, its interpretive matrix is transcendent of such mere accidental time, and seeks to gain a perspective of reality that transcends the transient experience of humanity's limited knowledge: an understanding in wisdom.

Also involved in this question is the contrast between natural theology (and here we should consider the entire spectrum of this ideology from the Egyptian theology of *maat* to the European and medieval philosophy of Albertus Magnus and Aquinas) and those central biblical perspectives which assert the theological way of unknowing and which are oriented towards the perception of reality as the arbitrary will of God. This we find dominating not only the Pentateuch and Samuel–Kings but Job, Qohelet and Jonah as well. Biblical *Heilsgeschichte* is not a theological understanding of history so much as it is an understanding of reality. But this biblical perspective of reality is radically foreign to the one that we have shared since the Enlightenment and which is fundamental to our understanding of history. The most disorienting difficulty with historicist readings of the Bible is that they attempt to transpose the perspective of reality that underlies biblical traditions in terms of a specifically modern understanding. It was such historicism that from the 1940s to the 1960s attempted to demythologize biblical theological perspective as if there were immediately accessible equivalencies of biblical theology in modern experience—as if the Bible had meaning apart from its miracles! Fundamental but contradictory assumptions lay on both sides of the Barth/Bultmann controversies over demythologizing. Biblical theology asserted the inadequacy of the world-view of the ancients and at the same time claimed that scripture could be transposed in such a way that these traditions might respond to modern historical concerns.

A central problem has been the use of language. Biblical *Heilsgeschichte* is not based in a perception of history as we might understand the word. The word 'history' does not even exist in Hebrew. In all its many stories of the tradition that has created Judaism's self-understanding, the Bible isn't talking about the past so much as it is talking about reality. History, events and their meaning, is a fundamental mode of *our* understanding of reality, and it lies at the crux of *our* historicistic distortions that swamp our biblical exegesis. Such a historically oriented perception of reality is far from the intellectual matrix of biblical tradition. Unlike events of history, events of tradition do not share in reality through their own individuality or significance. Rather, the referents of Bible lie quite far from both this world and its events. 'History', the past of human affairs, is, for the ancient traditionist, illusory—like the whole of this material and accidental world. Events in time are distortions. True reality is unknowable, transcendent of experience. Tradition is important in order to bring understanding: to evoke truth, not to recount it. In terms of the intellectual matrix of biblical traditions, events were not so much meaningful as *significant of a meaning* that resided apart from both this world and its events. 'History' was a distorting mirror. True reality was the will of God, and it does not matter how that was expressed. Such expressions and representations have not value in themselves; they are only important insofar as they bring understanding. Reality is not of this world; not even that of our gods. Yahweh and Jesus are not the divine in itself, but Emmanuel: god with us, significant specifically in what they signify.

Rather than history, the Old Testament ideology that was understood by Barth and others as *Heilsgeschichte* might better be expressed as reiterative and typological aetiology. I use the word 'aetiology' intentionally. It is not history, that narrative account of what brought about realities known, but rather aetiology, that story of the past that seeks to echo and evoke the truth of reality through metaphor. I use the words 'reiterative' and 'typological' intentionally as well. Unlike our perspective of historical event with its fundamental quality of singularity and historicity, true events of tradition are those markers of traditional motifs, themes and patterns that render the structural core of meaning which is reality. Typology is the systematic means by which the traditions' truths are organized and clarified, referencing not the specific individuality of events but rather a typicality evocative of ideal events. It is neither in people as individuals nor in the facticity of events wherein truth and reality reside.

Unlike our perception of post-enlightenment reality, the perception of the compilers of the biblical perception understand the events of this world as transient and refractive of a transcendentally real. The primary historiographical function of such a tradition is not to recount any past at all, but rather to draw out how reality can be found—even in the transience that is ever of this world, through the reiterative qualities intrinsic to experience. The philosopher appropriate to early Jewish historiography is Qohelet: there is nothing new under the sun. This is hardly a statement of cynicism so much as of the Hellenistic world's dominant paradigm that in our experience of this world, we see the reality of heaven, as it were, through a glass darkly.

The Bible speaks in a language which *we* understand as fictive. But unlike the language of our fictional genres, biblical language seeks to evoke not our fiction, but the truth and the reality that lie behind, but which are not revealed in, events or the illusions which constitute human experience.

The macrostructure of the Bible's historiography is developed in a binary historiographical succession: the continuous unbroken chain of ancestors and heroic leaders and the succession of periods or themes. 1 Chronicles and *Jubilees* are interestingly to be compared with the Pentateuch, where we have successively linked ancestor traditions, torah traditions and priestly aetiological traditions. In *Jubilees* we also have comparable ancestor traditions (including Moses) and priestly aetiologies, but 1 Chronicles is centered in David who plays Moses' and Joshua's and Ezra's roles. 1 Chronicles also recurrently breaks away from the chronological straitjacket not only of continuity of genealogy but of royal synchronisms as well: the succession of Samuel–Kings' forty servants of the eternal *Byt Dwd*.[42] In Chronicles David is eternal. David does it all: he establishes the temple's priesthood, brings the people through the wilderness and gives them their place in the land. It is David that gives hope to the returning exiles in Yahweh's temple.

In reiterative, typological historiography, a complex collage of ideological, thematic and emotive associations are made to coalesce. Biblical narrative is throughout reiterative not historical. Time is not linear and fluid, but a static framework organizing perspective and reference. The events of history lose their singularity and, in a kaleidoscope of consciousness wherein episode and character of one narrative echo and give remembrance to another, take on significance as vessels of understanding, containers of reference to a real world that lies apart from our human experience which is ever transient and intrinsically accidental.

42. N.P. Lemche and T.L. Thompson, 'Did Biran Kill David? The Bible in Light of Archaeology', *JSOT* 64 (1994), pp. 3-22; T.L. Thompson, ' "House of David": An Eponymic Referent to Yahweh as Godfather', *SJOT* 9 (1995), pp. 59-74.

If Israel and its king fear and serve Yahweh and listen to him, all will be well. However, if they do not listen, but turn against this word of Yahweh, Yahweh's hand will be against both them and their 'fathers' (1 Sam. 12.15 [MT]). Here, Israel's future destiny determines the fate of the tradition's past. That is what biblical historiography is about.

THE CONSTRUCTION OF THE DAVIDIC STATE:
AN EXERCISE IN HISTORIOGRAPHY

Baruch Halpern

I

Philosophers and even historians sometimes take up the question, what is history? Among students of the ancient Near East, Jan Huizinga's formulation has gained a certain currency: 'History is the intellectual form in which a civilization renders account to itself about its past'.[1] History is the organization and presentation of some aspect of the past.

This definition is serviceable because it is so broad. But in another sense, any representation meant publicly to preserve memory—any record—might be brought under the same umbrella. When (En)mebara(ge)si, king of Kish, inscribed his name and title on stone bowls, he may have meant to establish ownership, though given the number of people likely to see or able to read the text, it seems more likely that what he left was in fact a record of production. But when Pabilgagi, king of Umma, inscribed a statuette for Enlil, with his own name and title, it is more likely that he expected to project a record of both into the future.[2] Indeed, even paleolithic cave-paintings, whatever their motivation in superstition, were intended to provide a stable representation of animals seen in the past but presumed to exist in the present.

---

1. 'A Definition of the Concept of History', in R. Klibansky and H.J. Paton (eds.), *Philosophy and History: Essays Presented to Ernst Cassirer* (New York: Harper & Row, 1963), p. 9; picked up in Near Eastern Studies first by W.W. Hallo, 'Assyrian Historiography Revisited', *EI* 14 (1978), pp. 1-7; thereafter J. Van Seters, *In Search of History* (New Haven. CT: Yale University Press, 1983), p. 1 (Van Seters, however, contravenes Huizinga's intention, as in p. 1 n. 2).

2. For the texts, see J. Cooper, *Sumerian and Akkadian Royal Inscriptions*. I. *Presargonic Inscriptions* (AOS Translation Series, 1; New Haven, CT: American Oriental Society, 1986), 18 Ki.1; 91-92, Um. 1..

History cannot be described accurately—and the task is in fact to describe it, not to define it—without reference to a time beyond the past. History is always written, recording is always done, not for the present, except in its grossest form, but for the future. Only in that sense is the recording of events, even the researching of them, a purposive activity.[3]

In this respect, a text five millennia old or an entry in the History Book Club are the same. But they are also identical in their consumption. Bergson, in fact, argued that time is becoming, duration, rather than sequence: the past is encapsulated in the present.[4] As evidence, in the same way, a historical record is always part of the present in which it is contemplated.

Bergson also argued that our perception evolved in order to maximize our capacity to accumulate fuel, to reverse the principle of entropy in a macroscopic manifestation of subatomic indeterminacy.[5] We see doorways, for example, as empty, and walls as solid, instead of perceiving them accurately as looser and closer configurations of molecules. This stops us running into walls. Our senses evolved to organize the world in such a way as to facilitate our life in it. Even David Hume conceded, after completely demolishing our epistemology even about the present, that it made a difference whether he left his house by the door or the window.[6] Bergson explained how it was so.

In the same way, our minds have evolved to tell ourselves history, at

3.   This implies the inclusion of things like chronicles and annals in the category: contrast R.G. Collingwood, *The Idea of History* (Oxford: Clarendon Press, 1946), pp. 11-13. Collingwood claims that history is only the science of posing a question and ascertaining an answer of which the author was formerly ignorant. The contrast recapitulates the difference between Herodotean antiquarianism and Thucydidean insistence on contemporary history only: see A. Momigliano, 'The Place of Herodotus in the History of Historiography', *History* 43 (1958), pp. 1-13. The inclusive definition better reflects the true range of historical writing. Still, in regularly contrasting true 'history' with 'scissors-and-paste' history, Collingwood was mainly concerned to exclude not the chronicle so much as the florilegium, i.e., the uncritical parroting of 'authorities', into which category the medieval chronicle often fits.

4.   H. Bergson, *Creative Evolution* (New York: Henry Holt, 1911); the term 'encapsulated' is from R.G. Collingwood, *An Autobiography* (Oxford: Oxford University Press, 1948), p. 98 (see pp. 97-99). While the latter makes no reference to the former, the connection is sufficiently narrow to demand an inference of direct influence.

5.   *Creative Evolution*.

6.   D. Hume, *Dialogues concerning Natural Religion* (Library of Liberal Arts, 174; Indianapolis: Bobbs-Merrill, 1962).

the level of biological rather than atomic perception, because it is the most convenient and efficient method of organizing knowledge.

History is the way we organize, individually and in communities, our understanding of the world as it has been; and, using that knowledge, we project our experiences and the estimated efficacy of our responses to them into future situations. It is no coincidence that the earliest rationalizers of historical presentation in Greece drew the conclusion that their work could guide future policies:[7] memory, after all, is the school of hard knocks; and history is the reduction of memory about human intention. It is the public form of memory.

This description is broader than Huizinga's. It includes a huge variety of literary forms, even in the Bronze Age.[8] One could give a few examples: Egyptian tomb biographies, with parallels in Mesopotamian *narû*'s; poems celebrating the Battle of Qadesh or Merneptah's Libyan campaign, with parallels in epics concerning Tukulti-Ninurta and Tiglath-Pileser. Hittite materials, such as the Deeds of Suppiluliuma and the Annals of Murshili, with parallels in Mesopotamian and Egyptian royal inscriptions, undergo the same transition, from memoirs to demarcated annals, that occurs in Assyria under Tiglath-Pileser I. This is not to mention other documents often not considered historiographic such as treaty prologues, prologues to law codes, legal documents such as deeds, boundary markers, dedication inscriptions and the like, let alone chronographic devices such as king lists, eponym lists and year-name lists.

II

It has long been clear that biblical historiography, in the books of Kings at least, participated in some measure in this historical Republic of Letters. As early as 1934, J.A. Montgomery isolated 'annalistic'

7. See, e.g., Thucydides 1.22; Polybius; on the Hittite Old Kingdom annals, probably the closest analogy to 2 Samuel, see H.A. Hoffner, 'Histories and Historians of the Ancient Near East: The Hittites', *Or* 49 (1980), pp. 283-332.

8. Van Seters, *In Search of History*; D.B. Redford, *Pharaonic King-Lists, Annals and Daybooks* (Toronto: Benben, 1986); A.K. Grayson, 'Histories and Historians of the Ancient Near East: Assyria and Babylonia', *Or* 49 (1980), pp. 140-94; Hoffner, 'The Hittites'; H. Tadmor and M. Weinfeld (eds.), *History, Historiography and Interpretation* (Jerusalem: Magnes Press, 1983); F.M. Fales (ed.), *Assyrian Royal Inscriptions: New Horizons in Literary, Ideological, and Historical Analysis* (Orientis Antiquis Collectio, 17; Rome: Istituto per l'Oriente, 1981), to name just a few.

elements underlying Kings,[9] arguing that the phrase 'then' or 'at that time' reflected an origin in annals. However, subsequent analysis has shown that often these phrases represent a form of segue from one to another topic without any necessarily consecutive implications.[10] And in that respect, the phrases signal a relationship to the genre of display inscriptions, which are organized rather by topic or geography than by chronological sequence, a fact the full significance of which was

9.   J.A. Montgomery, 'Archival Data in the Book of Kings', *JBL* 53 (1934), pp. 46-52; for further, similar bibliography, see B. Halpern, *The First Historians: The Hebrew Bible and History* (San Francisco: Harper & Row, 1988), p. 237 n. 19.

10.   See H. Tadmor, 'History and Ideology in the Assyrian Royal Inscriptions', in Fales (ed.), *Assyrian Royal Inscriptions*, pp. 13-33; B. Halpern, 'A Historiographic Commentary on Ezra 1–6—Achronological Narrative and Dual Chronology in Israelite Historiography', in W.H. Propp, B. Halpern and D.N. Freedman (eds.), *The Hebrew Bible and its Interpreters* (Winona Lake, IN: Eisenbrauns, 1990), pp. 81-142; D. Glatt, *Chronological Displacement in Biblical and Related Literatures* (SBLDS, 139; Atlanta: Scholars Press, 1993). An exception may be the 'then' in 2 Kgs 12.18. If consecutive in function, it would imply a date for Hazael's depredations in Judah after 819 (Joash's 23rd year—12.7). This is a chronology that would allow Hazael time to recoup from his devastating defeats at the hand of Shalmaneser III in the 830s, then to dominate Israel before reaching the coast during the reign of Jehoahaz. This would accord with 2 Kgs 10.32-33, which attributes the loss of Transjordan to Hazael during Jehu's reign, and 2 Kgs 13.3, 7 which speaks of complete vassalship to Hazael under Jehoahaz. The point is that the terms in question sometimes do not, and at other times do signal consecution. It is precisely the ambiguity that makes them useful. Incidentally, if this 'then' is consecutive, our understanding of the stela from Tel Dan would be equally enhanced. As indicated in passing below, the stela is not attributable to Hazael, yet recounts his 'achievement' of 841, the deaths of Joram of Israel and Ahaziah of Judah. Both were victims, in fact, of Jehu, if the account of 2 Kgs 9 is to be credited. For a parallel, note the claim of Shalmaneser III to have killed, or alternatively that for fear of his approaching the locals killed, the king of the Balih region: E. Michel, 'Ein neuentdeckter Annalen-Text Salmanassars III', *WdO* 1/6 (1952), 464.2.20-21; 'Die Assur-Texte Salmanassars III. (858-824). 7. Fortsetzung', *WdO* 2/2 (1955), 149:54-55 (Black Obelisk): year 6: cities on Balih kill Giammu, lord of their cities. In the Kurkh Monolith, it is the 'nobles' who killed Giammu: D.D. Luckenbill, *Ancient Records of Assyria and Babylonia* (Chicago: University of Chicago, 1926), p. 610; on the Calah bull-colossi, it is the (people) of the region (Luckenbill, *Ancient Records*, p. 646). In the *Marmorplatte*, however, Shalmaneser claims to have killed him: E. Michel, 'Die Assur-Texte Salmanassars III. (858-824). 6. Fortsetzung', *WdO* 2/1 (1954), 32.13-14, or at least the (ambiguous?) logogram leaves that impression.

not appreciated until after the middle of this century.[11]

Among the materials in Kings that most closely relate to display inscriptions are those concerning Solomon. This has long been recognized: the organization of the chapters' contents is thematic, not chronological,[12] but the intention is to create the illusion of chronological sequence.[13] That is why the revolt of Hadad, in Edom, inspired by David's demise, is related at the end of Solomon's reign: news of David's death did not take 30 years to reach Egypt. Likewise, Rezin's revolt is linked to Solomon's senile apostasy, when in fact his career began at latest in the middle of David's reign, and must have concluded during the first half of Solomon's.[14] The Deuteronomistic historian understands that the revolt was early; he may claim that success came only late, or that the revolt was proleptic.

The motifs, too, of the Solomon account relate to historiography abroad. Kings portrays him as a natural philosopher (1 Kgs 5.13; 10.1ff.) and as an importer of exotic woods (10.11) and animals (10.22). This presentation, and the issue is one of literary presentation, comports very well with the portrait of the Assyrian king as a hunter of all sorts of animals and fish[15] and a breeder of exotic animals[16] and trees.[17] The ideal

11. Particularly in the pioneering work of H. Tadmor, 'The Campaigns of Sargon II of Assur: A Chronological-Historical Study', *JCS* 12 (1958), pp. 22-40, 77-100; 'The Inscriptions of Nabunaid: Historical Arrangement', in H.G. Güterbock and T. Jacobsen (eds.), *Studies in Honor of Benno Landsberger on his 75th Birthday* (AS, 17; Chicago: Oriental Institute, 1965), pp. 351-63. See further examples (including Tadmor's 'History and Ideology') in Fales (ed.), *Assyrian Royal Inscriptions*.

12. See J. Wellhausen, 'Die Composition des Hexateuchs', in F. Bleek, *Einleitung in das Alte Testament* (Berlin: Reimer, 4th edn, 1978), pp. 239-40; A. Šanda, *Die Bücher der Könige übersetzt und erklärt* (Exegetisches Handbuch zum Alten Testament, 9.1; Münster: Aschendorff, 1911), pp. 326-27; M. Noth, *Überlieferungsgeschichtliche Studien* (Halle: Niemeyer, 1943), pp. 66-67 n. 3.

13. See Halpern, *First Historians*, pp. 152-53; G.N. Knoppers, *Two Nations under God. The Deuteronomistic History of Solomon and the Dual Monarchies. I. The Reign of Solomon and the Rise of Jeroboam* (HSM, 52; Atlanta: Scholars Press, 1993), pp. 162-63. Incidentally, Ahijah's oracle is placed close to Solomon's 24th year: B. Halpern, 'Sectionalism and the Schism', *JBL* 93 (1974), pp. 519-32.

14. I address the chronology of David's reign in an excursus that will accompany the full publication of this study elsewhere.

15. A.K. Grayson, *Assyrian Rulers of the Early first Millennium BC I* (RIMAP, 2; Toronto: University of Toronto, 1991), hereafter cited as RIMAP 2: Tiglath-Pileser I 1.vi.55-84; 3.21-25; 4.67-71; 1001.12′-14′; Asshur-bel-kala 1(89):r. 8′-11′;

of the king as naturalist became a subject for written presentation in the inscriptions of Tiglath–Pileser I (1114-1076). It persisted as such into the ninth century. African simians were in special demand in Assyria as in 1 Kgs 10.22.[18]

Tiglath-Pileser made the transition from the display inscription to true annals. In this new form, the hunt and naturalism stand undated in the peroration. In a display inscription, in the course of a campaign, he also mentions killing a *naḥiru*, a sea-creature known to the locals as a sea-horse, and capable of producing 'ivory'.[19] Asshur-bel-kala lumped the *naḥiru* hunt with the report on the hunt and breeding in the annals' peroration.[20]

Asshur-Dan II (934–912) and Adad-Narari II (911–891) recall the hunt and husbandry at the end of the annals, without the *naḥiru*.[21] The latter reports getting his own monkeys from Bit-Adini during the course of a campaign:[22] Anatolian states were breeding them, as, apparently, were coastal sites. (Into this pattern, the claims concerning Solomon fit closely chronologically as well as thematically.) Tukulti-Ninurta II (890–884) reports hunting and collecting (imported!) breeding stock in the course of a campaign, but also maintains a segment on the hunt (but not breeding) at the annals' peroration.[23]

2.iii.29′-35′; possibly, 3(94).7′-9′; 7.iv.2-13,22-26; Asshur-Dan II: 1(135).68-72; Adad-Narari II 2(154).122-125; Tukulti-Ninurta II 5(173).45-46, (175).80-82, (178).134-35; Asshurnasirpal II 1(215f.).iii.48-49; 2(226).40-42; 30(291).84-91; 95(350); Shalmaneser III, E. Michel, 'Neuentdeckter', 454-474, 472.IV.40-474.IV.48; *idem*, 'Assur-Texte 6. Fortsetzung', 27-45.III.42-45; 40.IV.19-22.

16. RIMAP 2: Tiglath-Pileser I 1.vii.4-10; 4.27-28; perhaps 1001(72).7′-8′, 14′; probably Asshur-bel-kala 1.9-11; 7.iv.13-22,26-34; (as statuary, Tiglath-Pileser I 4.67-71; Assur-bel-kala 7.v.16-19); Adad-Narari II 2(154).125-127; Tukulti-Ninurta II 5(175).81-82; Asshurnasirpal II 1(215f.).iii.48-49; 2(226).30-38; 30(291-92).91-100. The zoo apparently begins with Asshur-bel-kala.

17. RIMAP 2: Tiglath-Pileser I 1.vii.17-27; probably 1001.9′-11′. Asshurnasirpal II, probably, RIMAP 2.A.0.101.30(290).36-52.

18. RIMAP 2.104.iv.29-30; 150.48; 226.30-31; 292.98-100.

19. RIMAP 2.37.21-25; 226.30.

20. RIMAP 2.103.iv.2-3 in the context of iv.1-33.

21. RIMAP 2.135.68-72; 154.122-127.

22. RIMAP 2.99.2(150).48. See also T. Dothan, 'The Arrival of the Sea Peoples: Cultural Diversity in Early Iron Age Canaan', in S. Gitin and W.G. Dever (eds.), *Recent Excavations in Israel: Studies in Iron Age Archaeology* (AASOR, 49; Winona Lake, IN: Eisenbrauns, 1989), p. 11 and fig. 1.9.

23. RIMAP 2.175.79-82; 178.134-35.

With Asshurnasirpal, the hunt and breeding apppear only in the course of his campaigns.[24] An early annals edition of Shalmaneser III places the hunt in the peroration, without the cultivation of herds or plants. Later editions integrate the hunt into a campaign and then drop it.[25] The breeding motif never occurs. Subsequent kings drop the motif from their annals; Assyrian and Persian palace reliefs attest that kings continued to build zoos and parks.[26] The motif continues, literarily, in building inscriptions:[27] thus, the 'garden' Ahab reportedly wanted was no mere 'vegetable garden' (1 Kgs 21.2), but a royal park filled with exotic imports. Still, this motif drops out of the literature of kings' self-presentation, the annals and displays.

From Tiglath-Pileser to Shalmaneser III, the hunt is a fixture of written royal propaganda. From Tiglath-Pileser to Asshurnasirpal II, the breeding of animals is such a fixture. But the last citation of herd-breeding in an annals' peroration stems from the early tenth century. The motif occurs in the ninth century, but is last central in the tenth.

Another fresh concern of late Middle Assyrian historiography is for aggregating the acquisition of horses and chariots,[28] which in later accounts are connected with individual campaigns. This concern is mirrored in the account of Solomon, who acquires and trades in horses in 1 Kgs 5.6; 10.25-26, 28-29. And Tiglath-Pileser's and his successors' concern with agriculture, prosperity and contentment[29] is another theme shared with 1 Kings 3–10. Related is the theme of the feast, both in

24. RIMAP 2.215f.iii.48-49; in a display, 226.30-38, with a summary, 226.40-42, before another campaign (227.43-51); 291f.84-101 is nearer being a peroration in another display.

25. Michel, 'Neuentdeckter', 472.IV.40-474.IV.48; 'Assur-Texte 6. Fortsetzung', 27-45.III.42-45; 40.IV.19-22.

26. See S. Dalley, 'Nineveh, Babylon and the Hanging Gardens: Cuneiform and Classical Sources Reconciled', *Iraq* 56 (1994), pp. 45-58.

27. E.g., RIMAP 2.55.71-75.

28. RIMAP 2.27.ii.28-35; 72.6'; Asshur-Dan II: A.0.98.1.60-67: repatriation, grain, horses; Adad-narari II A.0.99.2.121; Tukulti-Ninurta II 100.5.130f.; Michel, 'Neuentdeckter', 472.IV.40-474.IV.48; 'Assur-Texte 6. Fortsetzung', 44. left edge.

29. E.g., Tiglath-Pileser I, RIMAP 2.89.1.vi.85-vii.35; Asshur-Dan II, 98.1.64-67; Adad-Narari II, 99.2.120; Tukulti-Ninurta II, 100.5.132; Asshurnasirpal II, 101.30.78-83. Note Mesha's claim: he 'added (bovines) to the land' and sheep: *KAI* 181.29, 31.

Solomon's temple dedication and in Asshurnasirpal's dedication of Calah.[30]

These motifs do not disappear after the eleventh century. But in the royal inscriptions of the tenth and early ninth centuries, they cease to be showcased in the way that they were earlier. They cease, too, to occur as a complex. Considering, too, that the same motifs are largely absent from accounts of biblical kings later than Solomon, the parallels are worth dwelling on. It looks as though the royal ideal, particularly of the king as naturalist, reflected in 1 Kings 3–10 stems squarely from the late Middle and early Neo-Assyrian milieu.[31] Indeed, the Tyrian annals examined by Menander of Ephesus alleged that Hiram exchanged riddles with Solomon (*Ap.* 1.120); Dius gives this tradition (*Ap.* 1.114-115) a pro-Tyrian twist. Here is a claim that another monarch contemporary with Middle Assyrian culture was a natural philosopher. This is not to say that our texts are from the tenth century. However, underlying them are sources that faithfully preserve the concept of how one should project, literarily, the royal ideals of that time.

Of course, the same Assyrian implements to which we have adverted also deconstruct themselves, which is one way in which the genre of display inscriptions was originally unravelled. In his annals, Tiglath-Pileser claims to have pursued Ahlamu Arameans across the Euphrates 28 times, including twice in one year.[32] The claim deflates his other claim of taming the land from Suhu to Carchemish in a single day.[33] In fact, it deflates itself: an enemy against whom one successfully campaigns 28 times is suspiciously persistent. Indeed, Arameans made inroads into Assyria proper during Tiglath-Pileser's reign.[34]

---

30. RIMAP 2.101.30(292-93).102-154. See further A. Finet, 'Le Banquet de Kalaḫ offert par le roi d'Assyrie Ašurnasirpal II (883-859)', in R. Gyselen (ed.), *Banquets d'Orient* (Res Orientales, 4; Bures-sur-Yvette: Groupe pour l'Etude de la Civilisation du Moyen-Orient, 1992), pp. 31-44; see also D. Collon, 'Banquets in the Art of the Ancient Near East', in Gyselen (ed.), *Banquets*, pp. 23-30, with bibliography; and, for some literary representations, H.L.J. Vanstiphout, 'The Banquet Scene in the Mesopotamian Debate Poems', in Gyselen (ed.), *Banquets*, pp. 9-22; R.D. Barnett, 'Asshurbanipal's Feast', *EI* 18 (1985), pp. 1-6*.

31. Contrast Chronicles: so Gary Knoppers, in correspondence.

32. RIMAP 2, Tiglath-Pileser I 4.34-36; //3.29ff.

33. RIMAP 2 A.0-87.1.v.48-50; 2.28-29; 13(59).4′-6′.

34. So J.N. Postgate, Review of Khaled Nashef, *Die Orts- und Gewässernamen der mittelbabylonischen und mittelassyrischen Zeit*, *AfO* 32 (1985), pp. 95-101; the inroads may be earlier: Grayson, *Assyrian and Babylonian Chronicles* (Texts from

Another locution from this source invites comment. Of the recon-
quered Shubaru, Tiglath-Pileser writes, 'I imposed the heavy yoke of my
dominion...so that annually they send tribute and tax to my city Asshur
into my presence'.[35] The emphasis is on a resumption of lapsed
payment. But the formulation, unique in the king's writings, invites the
interpretation: they send tribute annually to Asshur, without my even
having to go and collect it!

Indeed, on close inspection, Tiglath-Pileser's inscriptions distinguish
several classes of conquered peoples: 1) those whose towns he loots and
burns; 2) those on whom he imposes his yoke; 3) those on whom he
imposes tribute (*biltu u madattu*), including some who submit voluntar-
ily; and, 4) those whose persons or territory he annexes. And yet, here is
a summary statement:

> Total: from my accession year to my fifth year, I conquered 42 lands... I
> subjected them to a single authority, took their hostages, imposed tribute
> and tax on them.

That is, in the campaign accounts the author details various treatments
he metes out, but he blurs the distinctions in the summary accounts.
Similarly, he claims to have conquered and ravished 'the land of
Katmuhu in its entirety' (l.i.91-92). Yet he concedes that within the
space of a year or two, he had to return, and conquer all the cities of the
region, annexing it (l.iii.7-31), although a later text (4.22-23) makes no
mention of this double appearance. And it would appear that a still later
campaign was necessary.[36]

For rhetorical purposes, a conquest of part of a territory is a conquest
of all of it. A looting raid is the same as the imposition of annual tribute.
But this does not mean that campaigns can be confected. Rather, the
technique is that of putting a maximal spin on the real events. And this
leads to a principle of interpretation, the Tiglath-Pileser principle: what is
the minimum the king might have done to lay claim to the achievements
he publishes? Looting a town? He shoplifted a toothbrush from the local
chemist. The same political hermeneutic applies reasonably well today.

The principle applies not to biblical historiography generally so much

Cuneiform Sources, 5; Locust valley, NY: J.J. Augustin, 1975), 189.2-7 or 10-11
precede a third campaign to Katmuhu (189.13).

    35. RIMAP 2.A.0.87 (Tiglath-Pileser I), l.ii.90-96.

    36. If the chronicle at Grayson, *Chronicles* 189 has a Katmuhu campaign after
the death of Marduk-nadin-ahhe.

as to its sources. To take just one example, 2 Kgs 16.8 relates that Hezekiah defeated the Philistines 'unto Gaza and its territories' (2 Kgs 18.8). What does this mean? Not a word is heard of Gaza in Sennacherib's reports. However, Hezekiah and his allies engineered a coup in Ashkelon, on Gaza's border, involving it in their revolt. So the verse records Hezekiah's successes, including the revolt in Ashkelon, up to but not including Gaza's territory. Instead of saying 'up to Ashkelon', the writer chose to maximize the area covered. By making the statement in a rubric to Hezekiah's regnal account, he also avoided stating that this territory was lost in 701.

So the principle of minimal interpretation seems to have abiding application.[37] And it is worth applying in particular not just to the account of Solomon's reign, but to that of David as well. For reasons too extensive to review here, in addition to the reasons given above, it seems to me that the majority of scholars have been right to derive 2 Samuel, at least, from the late tenth century.[38] If this is remotely right, then the lessons of Assyrian historiography are potentially valuable indeed.

III

Approaching 2 Samuel is a daunting task, however, because of its complexity. We have the civil war, the so-called 'ark narrative' and dynastic charter. Inside the 'succession narrative', one has not just the

37. Indeed, this is why the book of Joshua and Judges 1 distinguish 'conquest' from the supplanting of inhabitants in conquered territories: in their theory, the territory between Joshua's northernmost and southernmost battles (Josh. 10–11) was all conquered, though only in the highlands was Israel able to root out previous inhabitants. See my 'Settlement of Canaan', in *ABD*, V, pp. 1124-25. The Deuteronomistic historian was familiar with the canons of royal historiography.

38. A number of studies by T. Ishida buttress this conclusion, and these are forthcoming in collected form in the series, Studies in the History and Culture of the Ancient Near East (Leiden: Brill, 1997); see esp. 'Adonijah the Son of Haggith and his Successors', in R.E. Friedman and H.G.M. Williamson (eds.), *The Future of Biblical Studies—the Hebrew Scriptures* (Atlanta: Scholars Press, 1987), pp. 165-187; 'The Story of Abner's Murder: A Problem Posed by the Solomonic Apologist', *EI* 23 (1993), pp. 109-13; further, P.K. McCarter, *II Samuel* (AB, 7B; Garden City, NY: Doubleday, 1986); see also his 'The Apology of David', *JBL* 99 (1980), pp. 489-504; cf. J. VanderKam, 'Davidic Complicity in the Deaths of Abner and Eshbaal: A Historical and Redactional Study', *JBL* 99 (1980), pp. 521-39; finally, my 'Text and Artifact: Two Monologues?', forthcoming in a volume edited by L. Silberstein, NYU Press.

narrative itself, but the framework to the Uriah story of the Ammonite war in 2 Samuel 10 and 12, plus a series of lists and appendices in 2 Samuel 20–24. The 'succession narrative' dominates the book. However, all the supplemental materials contribute to the package. Among them, perhaps the most important is the compilation of 2 Samuel 8.

Among others, McCarter recognizes that the chapter is thematic, not chronological, in structure.[39] In this respect, it partakes of the character of the display inscription. But the details remain important. First, the chapter is placed thematically: David has become king of Judah, then king of Israel, then king in Jerusalem, and has brought the ark into his capital and received a dynastic oracle. In the narrative logic, the stage is set for a summary of David's positive achievements. What is to follow will be the succession narrative proper. 2 Samuel 8, thus, is the capstone of the narrative of David's royal career.

Secondly, the introduction to the chapter deliberately places it after the taking of Jerusalem, and for the most part this must be the case. But the chapter starts with a reference to the subduing of the Philistines, and the only narrative of such an encounter comes earlier, in 2 Samuel 5.[40] Possibly, traditions of conflict with the Philistines were otherwise confined to the appendices to 2 Samuel in order to imply that there were wars with them after the earliest part of David's reign.

Thirdly, 8.3 refers to a battle against Hadadezer of Aram Zobah, the conflict with whom is related in detail two chapters later in the run-up to the Bathsheba story. Fourthly, 8.12 refers to booty from Ammon that could not have been collected until after the events of chs. 10–12, when Ammon became David's tributary. In other words, this narrative is explicitly out of its time. 2 Samuel 8, in sum, is closely related to the conventions of display inscriptions. Indeed, the reports of conquest punctuated by statements that David was saved by Yahweh or made temple donations or was just[41] are reminiscent of Tiglath-Pileser's annals

39. *II Samuel*, p. 251.

40. 5.17-21, 22-25. On the placement of these texts between 2 Sam. 6.11 and 2 Sam. 6.12ff. in Chronicles, see B. Halpern, 'Chronicles' Thematic Structure— Indications of an Earlier Source', in R.E. Friedman (ed.), *The Creation of Sacred Literature. Composition and Redaction of the Biblical Text* (Near Eastern Studies, 22; Berkeley: University of California Press, 1981), pp. 36-37; *idem*, 'Historiographic Commentary on Ezra 1–6', p. 131; Glatt, *Chronological Displacement*, pp. 58-60.

41. 2 Sam. 8.6b, 10-11, 15.

with their intermittent strings of royal epithets and other formulaic celebrations of the king. There are additional parallels in Egyptian texts of the Late Bronze Age, which presumably furnished the inspiration for Tiglath-Pileser.

This being the case, 8.4 deserves renewed attention. This verse describes the celebrated hamstringing of Aramean chariot horses,[42] arguably but not certainly a literary reference to the prohibition on the multiplication of horses in the Law of the King (Deut 17.14-20, reflected in Josh 11.9). But it also constitutes the sole passage recounting the appropriation of foreign chariotry by any Israelite king. Again, this is a standard conceit of Middle Assyrian historiography, which enumerates totals of chariots and horses captured, although the same interest does register in the later Neo-Assyrian period.[43]

It is easy to overstate the weight of such parallels, particularly as the Assyrian monuments survived a considerable time. Still, it seems worthwhile to try reading ch. 8 as though it were a display inscription. This view coincides in effect, though not in the assumption, with previous treatments. My submission is that the effect reflects a reality that validates the assumptions of the study.

IV

1. *The Philistines*
The first verse of ch. 8 relates that David defeated the Philistines and subdued them, taking Meteg Ha-Ammah from the hand of the Philistines. The latter remains obscure.[44] Still, Alt, in 1936, argued that 8.1 was a *précis* of David's battles with the Philistines before the arrival of the ark in Jerusalem.[45] Alt's logic was that the text was a resumption of the narrative of ch. 5 after the insertion of chs. 6–7. But another perspective can also be offered.

---

42. The hamstringing is attributed either to an inability to integrate the chariot arm into the Israelite order of battle (Y. Yadin, *Art of Warfare in Biblical Lands* [New York: McGraw-Hill, 1963], II, p. 285) or to some cultic obligation (McCarter, *II Samuel*, p. 249). Lawrence Hutchinson, Professor of Veterinary Science at the Pennsylvania State University, suggests that a simple incision into a single front flexor tendon is the most likely operation.

43. E.g., A.G. Lie, *Inscriptions of Sargon II King of Assyria. I. The Annals* (Paris: Geuthner, 1929), 4.15-16.

44. See McCarter, *II Samuel*, p. 243 for some solutions.

45. A. Alt, 'Zu II Samuel 8,1', *ZAW* 54 (1936), pp. 149-52.

The story of David's confrontation with the Philistines in the area of Jerusalem ends with the following statement: 'He smote the Philistines from Geba (Chron., 'Gibeon') to the approaches to Gezer' (5.25). Here we have the defeat of some Philistines in the central hill passes. This is hardly Pentapolis territory. Further, the tendency to treat the Philistines as a monolithic group engenders the misleading implication that all the Philistines were bested. Yet had we the correspondence of the time, the resemblance would be to Amarna, with the king of Gezer complaining about David, the king of Ashdod complaining about Gezer, and so on. The image of Philistine unity in 2 Samuel and Kings is nothing more than a propagandistic myth.

Of the five cities of the so-called Pentapolis, the two inland centers were Eqron, at Tel Miqneh, and Gath, variably located just south of Eqron at Tel eş-Şafi or more recently, further south, at Tel Haror, on the Wadi Besor.[46] For the era of David and Solomon, our texts convey no reliable information about Eqron, which was in any event much reduced in size.[47] But even the territory of Gath was beyond David's reach: first, only one text refers to a battle at Gath, in an appendix to 2 Samuel (21.20-21), and it makes no territorial claims. At the end of the Goliath story, 1 Sam. 17.52 claims that Saul invaded Eqron's territory, but not Gath's. The claims of this legendary narrative are in any case suspect. Secondly, during the evacuation of Jerusalem in the Absalom revolt, David mentions that Ittay the Gittite is an exile from his own land—an indication that Gath was not subsumed in David's empire even as a vassal (2 Sam. 15.18-22).

Thirdly, 1 Kgs 2.39-40 relates that two slaves fled from Jerusalem to Gath, a sure indication that Gath was independent at the time. Their owner, Shimei, had to go to Gath in order to arrange for the extradition of his slaves. That he was able to retrieve them suggests treaty relations. But that he had to go personally suggests that extradition was not automatic, that Gath was not altogether subjected to the United Monarchy. It might be submitted that the slaves knew no better than to

46. See L.E. Stager, 'The Impact of the Sea Peoples in Canaan (1185-1050 BCE)', in T.E. Levy (ed.), *The Archaeology of Society in the Holy Land* (New York: Facts on File, 1993), pp. 342-43.

47. On Miqneh, see S. Gitin, 'Tel Miqne-Ekron: A Type-Site for the Inner Coastal Plain in the Iron Age II Period', in Gitin and Dever (eds.), *Recent Excavations in Israel*, pp. 25-26, 41; Dothan, 'Arrival of the Sea Peoples', p. 20 fig. 1.15.

flee to a town in a position of vassalage. But this claim presupposes a lack of sophistication that we have no basis to hypothesize, in support of a position for which there is no extrinsic evidence. Gath was outside David's ambit, and may have remained a parity partner.

What does our text allege, on the Tiglath-Pileser principle? That some Philistines established or even just travelling between Geba or Gibeon and Gezer were overwhelmed. As Gezer remained the border in the reign of David's son (1 Kgs 9.16), it is plain that this was the extent of David's expansion in that direction.

Despite traditions of combat, after all, in sites such as Gob and Nob (probably Geba or Gibeon), there is no evidence of combat with Philistia further than the fringes of the hill country. Likewise, the only tradition of hill country conflict between David and the Philistines involving a Philistine garrison (2 Sam. 23.13-17) refers to an event clearly anterior to the conquest of Jerusalem: David is 'in the hold' (cf. 1 Sam. 22.4-5), in a cave at Adullam; the garrison is in Bethlehem, on the road from Hebron to Jerusalem. The likelihood is that this conflict occurred while David was on the run from Saul or even still in his service:[48] Saul, after all, is given the credit for removing one such garrison (1 Sam. 10.5-7; 13.2-3),[49] and for recruiting David from Bethlehem. Probably, the Philistine presence at sites such as Tell en-Naṣbeh was contemporary with or anterior to Saul's, not David's monarchy. In fact, David, a Philistine collaborator, had no interest in rooting them out from the central hills: even the text speaks of him as a net importer of them (2 Sam. 15.18-22; 18.2).

The traditions in 2 Samuel 5 and 8 mention no Philistine garrisons. In sum, David's subjugation of the Philistines amounted to the removal of

48. So McCarter, *II Samuel*, p. 495. That the Philistines are encamped in the Rephaim Valley, and the overlap with 2 Sam. 5.7, 9 where David is also in 'the hold', namely of Jerusalem, when they come into conflict, suggests the possibility of a conflation in details. But as this text places David at Adullam, it is more likely that elements of this record, where the bravery is that of David's subordinates, and where no actual field victory is claimed, have been aggrandized in the connected narrative. That this was done in connection with the same story in the doublet in 1 Sam. 24, 26 I have argued previously (*First Historians*, pp. 62-65).

49. On the reduction of *gbʿ* (n?) in 1 Sam. 13.3 as the fulfilment of the command to Saul to 'do what comes to hand' at '*gbʿt hʾlhym*, where there is a garrison of the Philistines', see B. Halpern, *Constitution of the Monarchy in Israel* (HSM, 25; Chico, CA: Scholars Press, 1981), pp. 155-56.

Eqronite or Gittite or other filibusters from the Ayyalon Pass.[50] In contradistinction, thus, to the Moabites and Damascenes, the text does *not* allege that the Philistines—any Philistines whatever—accepted David's sovereignty or bore him tribute. The omission is not accidental.

This point has an edge to it. The text does not claim that David dominated Philistia. And it also does not claim that it was he who conquered the major Canaanite fortresses of the north, including such towns as Yoqneam, Megiddo and Beth Shan. At the last, the Philistines are said to have displayed trophies of their victory in the Jezreel. Since the historiography clearly indicates that Solomon was in control of the Jezreel fortresses, and of sites further north, who laid hold of them? The answer is: Ishbaal, or Saul and Ishbaal, must have completed the conquest of the Canaanites; and the authors of the sources underlying 2 Samuel neglected to mention this, because it was an achievement of the king of a previous dynasty. Ishbaal is the likelier conqueror. Above all, this would explain the absence of Philistine interference in the Israelite civil war. Otherwise, the lacuna is difficult to explain: Philistine forces were David's allies, and Israel's most menacing enemies. Here, however, they do not appear except as a nugatory impediment to David's move to Jerusalem. This is hardly believable.

To return, now, to the first difficulty with the text: the chapter opens, 'And it was afterward'. A sympathetic reader must assume that the smiting of the Philistines followed, and was therefore additional to, the exploits of David in 2 Samuel 5. One can of course rescue the text, and claim that a third battle with the Philistines took place (and that 2 Sam. 5.25 was proleptic). But the distance involved, and the unlikelihood of any major permanent investment by 'Philistines' in the Ayyalon Pass after Saul's expulsion of them, remind us that 'it was afterward' is a part of the editorial construction of the whole book: either it is a product of an editor believing that three or more battles occurred, or it refers to some, but not necessarily all, of the content of this chapter.

---

50. Oddly enough, between Baale Judah (or from Gibeon?) and Jerusalem, the ark stops at the house of Obed Edom the Gittite (2 Sam. 6.10-11); and Gittites, including Ittay, accompany David back to the capital (2 Sam. 15.18-22). The traditions of Ephraimite and Benjaminite conflict with Gittites in 1 Chron. 7.21, 8.13 might be adduced to support the idea of a Gittite thrust into the Ayyalon Pass. Thus the Ittay son of Ribai from Gibeah of the Benjaminites could be Ittay the Gittite!

2. *The Moabites*

The second claim of the chapter is that David defeated Moab, and killed two thirds of his captives, after which the remaining third paid tribute. The narrative does not provide guidance as to the history of warfare here; still, one may presume that some part of Moab was attacked. Can one conclude that the tribute was regularized? Based on the Tiglath-Pileser principle, the most likely scenario is of sporadic payment. That Moab resembled a productive, organized kingdom in this period, rather than what anthropologists call a chiefdom, if even that, seems unlikely on the basis of the archaeological remains. But again, in contradistinction to Edom and Damascus, the text does *not* allege that David installed a governor or garrison in Moab.

3. *David and Hadadezer*

8.3 relates that David defeated Hadadezer son of Rehob king of Zobah, when he (David/Hadadezer) went to erect his stela on the river. This verse is a *crux interpretum* for determining the extent of David's empire. Chronicles, $Q^e re$ and some versions have it that this was the Euphrates, to which David must have been *en route* when he encountered Hadadezer.[51] If it was some nearer river,[52] then the size of the empire diminishes. Which is it?

As Malamat has observed,[53] Hadadezer in ch. 10 intervenes in David's war with Ammon with an army consisting of Aram of the house of Rehob and Aram Zobah, along with allies, the king of Maacah and 'the man of Tob' (10.6); this last is a locution for a vassal. 8.3 presents Hadadezer as king of Zobah. Unlike Maacah and Tob, however, Beth-Rehob has no independent king. So Hadadezer's patronym seemed to reflect either direct filiation to a dynastic founder or the kingship over the 'house of Rehob'.

The northern states. This is of some import for the history of the tenth–

51. Note McCarter, *II Samuel*, p. 247; cf. H.W. Hertzberg, *I & II Samuel* (OTL; Philadelphia: Westminster, 1964), p. 291.

52. J. de Groot, *II Samuël* (Groningen: Wolters, 1935); A. van den Born, *Samuel* (Boeker van het Oude Testament IV.1; Roermond en Maaseik, 1956) for the Yarmuk (these citations from McCarter, *II Samuel*, p. 248); G.W. Ahlström, *A History of Ancient Palestine from the Palaeolithic Period to Alexander's Conquest* (JSOTSup, 146; Sheffield: JSOT Press, 1993), p. 484 and n. 4 for the orontes.

53. A. Malamat, 'Aspects of the Foreign Policies of David and Solomon', *JNES* 22 (1963), pp. 1-17 (2-3).

ninth centuries, and must be taken up in detail. In a forthcoming treatment, N. Na'aman argues that Hadadezer was the son of a dynastic
founder, Ruḫubu, of a state, Amqi, which he places, with Beth-Rehob,
between Dan and Zobah. He then holds that Baasha mār Ruḫubi KUR
Amanaya whom the Kurkh Monolith locates in the battle of Qarqar was
the dynastic scion of Beth-Rehob, associated with Mount Amana
(= Zobah). He suggests that the ninth-century Damascene usurper Hazael
stemmed from Amqi/Beth-Rehob. This relieves the tension arising from
the attribution of the Tel Dan stela to Hazael and the stela's reference to
a royal father, whose land Israel had invaded: Hazael was a king, but of
Rehob.

Though brilliant, this reconstruction is contraindicated. The first question is the location of Amqi. Na'aman sets out from the Hazael booty
inscriptions: *zy ntn hdd lmrʾn ḥzʾl mn ʿmq bšnt ʿdh mrʾn nhr*. Reading
hdd, correctly, as a personal name, Na'aman analyzes the text as: That
which Hadad gave :: to our lord, Hazael, from Amqi :: in the year that
our lord crossed the River. Hadad was a courtier of Hazael's; Hazael
was the one from Amqi.

But Late Bronze Age Amqi stretched to the northern Beqaʿ, on the
border between Egypt and Hatti (the region of Kumidi and Qadesh);
hence, whenever Hatti invades Egyptian territory, the first encounter is
in Amqi.[54] Whether this kingdom extended to Dan is moot. If Iron Age
Zobah was north of Rehob, it is a more likely candidate to be Amqi. If
Zobah and Rehob were coterminous in the southern Beqaʿ, then Amqi
was in the north, perhaps southern Hamath or P(/H)attina. The identity
of the latter with Unqi of ninth–eighth-century Assyrian royal texts
confirms its equivalence with Amarna Amqi, in the region of Qadesh.[55]

Secondly, around 800, Zakkur, king of Hamath, Luʿash and Hadrach,
confronted a coalition led by 'Bar-Hadad, son of Hazael, king of Aram'.
Were Hazael king of Amqi, Bar-Hadad would have succeeded in that
state as well as in Damascus, just as Zakkur reigned in Hadrach as well
as Hamath and Luash. In enumerating his opponents, however, Zakkur
mentions a king of Amqi in fourth place, not immediately after Bar-
Hadad, but after the king of Bit-Agusi and the king of Que, before the
kings of Gurgum, Sam'al and Melid. Again, the implication is that Amqi
is not Hazael's home kingdom, and, secondly, that it lies to the north,

54. See generally, O. Weber, 'Anmerkungen', in J.A. Knudzton (ed.), *Die El-
Amarna-Tafeln* (VAB, 2; Leipzig: J.C. Hinrichs Verlag, 1915), p. 1112.

55. See, e.g., RLA, s.v. Hattin.

where the vassals Bar-Hadad activated against Hamath in the literary context are otherwise situated.[56] A location on the border of Hamath is again preferable to one to the south.

Thirdly, the booty inscriptions may not say Hazael was from Amqi. It may be the gift that is from Amqi:

that which Hadad gave::	gift
to our lord, Hazael::	Hazael
from Amqi::	gift
in the year our lord crossed the river::	Hazael

A contentual consideration tips the scales: Hazael knew where he was from, and it would be impertinent to remind him of that fact rather than of his title, such as 'king of Aram'. This object came from a place under Hazael's sovereignty, through which he may have marched to reach 'the River', which here is probably the Orontes, on which Amqi verged. The gift was provenanced. And this means Amqi was not under Hazael's direct rule, was not his home city-state. It was Hadad's kingdom, just as it had a king different from that of Damascus in Zakkur's inscription. It was farther north than other kingdoms annexed by Damascus.

Beth-Rehob was Dan's neighbor (Judg. 18.28) in the southern Beqaᶜ. P sends spies 'to Rehob of Lebo Hamath' (Num. 13.21); but this may reflect archaizing, since Zobah was the name of the region in P's time. P's concern is that David should have extended Israel's territory 'to Lebo Hamath' (1 Kgs 8.65);[57] but his northernmost opponent was the king of Zobah and Beth-Rehob, so that the defeat of Zobah and Rehob must imply a grip on Lebo Hamath. The implication is that Rehob bordered Hamath—in other words, P's geography categorized everything from Dan, or the northern end of Israel, to Hamath as one territorial unit.

Beth-Rehob's actual geographic extent was never great, as the nearby town of Abel Beth-Maacah pertained to the dynasty of Maacah, which according to 2 Samuel 10 participated in the Ammonite war as Hadadezer's ally. However, Neo-Assyrian references to the province of

---

56. *KAI* 202.1-7. Amqi might even be north of the Beqa'.

57. Cf. 1 Chron. 13.5; 2 Chron. 7.8; the ideal borders as in Num. 34.8; Josh. 13.5; Judg. 3.3; Ezek. 47–48. Chronicles has Solomon conquer Hamath (2 Chron. 8.3-4), misreading Tadmor for 1 Kgs 9.18 Tamar. The locution, 'Hamath of Zobah' (2 Chron. 8.3) is explicable on the basis of a process of interpretation similar to that which produced P's 'Rehob of Lebo Hamath': David had overcome Zobah, so that Solomon could expand northeast, to Tadmor.

Subite/Subatu (Zobah) place this kingdom in the southern Beqaʿ: if Rehob and Zobah were separate territories, Zobah sat north of Rehob and south of Hamath in the tenth century, assuming the reliability of 2 Samuel.[58] In Sargonid times, Zobah lay farther north. Hence the identification of Tebah in 8.8 with Tubihi, in the northern Beqa'.[59]

Zobah, thus, bordered Hamath in the tenth century. So its defeat established Israelite bragging rights to Lebo Hamath.[60] Samuel never takes up this bragging right. DtrH does (1 Kgs 8.65; Judg. 3.3; Josh. 13.5; 2 Kgs 14.25, 28). And Chronicles, conditioned by 2 Samuel 8, expands the brag to include the Euphrates (2 Chron. 8.3-4, 'river' in 1 Kgs 5.1, 4): the expansion takes in Gen. 15.18; Deut. 1.7; 11.24; Josh. 1.4; 1 Chron. 5.9; 18.3. This predictable exaggeration over time cautions us against overestimating the extent of the kingdom of Zobah.

Following Malamat, Na'aman identifies Hadadezer son of Rehob king of Zobah (2 Sam. 8.3, 12) as Hadadezer, scion of the house of Rehob, and king of Zobah. But the locution RN son of GN is not otherwise current in biblical historical works. Nor does any other biblical text identify a king as the son of a dynastic founder and use for his title the kingship of a kingdom not connected to that founder. As a strategy of legitimation, this would be bizarre: why name someone as 'son of' a dynastic founder from a kingdom more restricted than his own, unless he was in fact the 'dynastic founder's' biological offspring? Assuming Hadadezer's pedigree means anything, it probably names his actual father.

Na'aman appeals to a parallel: the Kurkh Monolith's *Baasha mār Ruḫubi KUR Amanaya*. This cannot, he submits, be Ammon, which in later Assyrian inscriptions is always 'the house of Ammon'. Rather, it must be the northern Anti-Lebanon, Mount Amana. Baasha son of Ruhubu is the dynast of Beth-Rehob, whose kingdom is Mount Amana/ Zobah. (Both Ammon and Ammana are usually written with doubled

58. E. Forrer, *Die Provinzeinteilung des assyrischen Reiches* (Leipzig: Hinrichs, 1920), pp. 62, 69; McCarter, *II Samuel*, pp. 248-49.

59. The identification is near certain: S. Ahituv, *Canaanite Toponyms in Ancient Egyptian Documents* (Jerusalem: Magnes Press, 1984), p. 191. d[wlbḫ appears with Qadesh in pap. An. I 19:1 and under Thutmosis III, as well as in EA 179. Beerothai's identification with modern Bereitan, and the latter as Cun—McCarter, *II Samuel*, p. 250—is less secure (cf. Ezek. 47.16).

60. On Lebo Hamath's identity, outside of P, with Neo-Assyrian Lab'u, see H. Tadmor, *The Inscriptions of Tiglath-Pileser III King of Assyria* (Jerusalem: Israel Academy of Sciences and Humanities, 1994), pp. 148:25 and 149 n. 25.

-mm-, against a single -m- in this reference.)

A dynasty founder is used as the patronym of many kings in Assyrian royal inscriptions, from Asshurnasirpal II and Shalmaneser III, for example.[61] We even have a text in which RN the son of GN is signalled with a geographic determinative.[62] In the Zakkur stela, Atarsamek is son of Gush (i.e., king of Bet Agusi), perhaps under Assyrian influence.

There are problems, however. First, in the absence of other evidence, 'RN son of N' may not denote dynastic affiliation. Thus, the king of Gath in Solomon's day, 'Achish son of Maacah', was not a scion of the house of Maacah.[63] And Adini son of Dakkuri may have himself had heirs, who were sons of Adini, without being kings of Bit-Adini! Secondly, Rehob is a common toponym and occurs in the onomasticon of Cisjordan (Rehoboam, Rehaviahu). But a third point is most daunting.

If Baasha son of Ruhubi of KUR Amanaya was king of Beth-Rehob, Shalmaneser's scribes violated a convention that Assyrian records otherwise consistently maintain. To signal that RN son of GN was a king from the dynasty GN, one used the dynastic name and *omitted* the name of the country. Nowhere else, in all the cases where Assyrians employ the formula, 'RN son of X king of GN', does X have a value other than the name of a king's father. To assign it such a value therefore plunges the reader into ambiguity. For example, right next to the mention of Amme-Ba'li son of Zamani (king of Bit Zamani), Asshurnasirpal II mentions Labturu son of Tupusu of the land of Nirdun.[64] No one would dream of suggesting, even in that context, that Tupusu was a dynastic name; had it been, either it or Nirdun would have been omitted. Similarly, in 1 Kgs 2.39, there appears 'Achish son of Ma'akah king of Gath': the point is that Achish was the biological son Ma'akah, king of Gath; he was not a scion of the dynasty, Ma'akah, attested in the petty state north of Israel.

Na'aman thus reads 'Hadadezer son of Rehob king of Zobah' and 'Baasha mar Ruhubi KUR Amanaya' in parallel. For the latter, he proposes 'Baasha king of Beth-Rehob and Mt. Amana', citing Zakkur's

61. RIMAP 2.202.ii 12; 2.203.ii 22; Michel, 'Neuentdeckter', 466: II 52; 466; 458; 460; 462; *idem*, 'Assur-Texte 6. Fortsetzung' 38.4.11; *idem*, 'Assur-Texte 7. Fortsetzung', 137-157: Black Obelisks: 14OB; 152.95; 156.125.

62. E. Michel, 'Die Assur-Texte Salmanassars III', *WdO* 2/3 (1956), 221-233, *226.154: at Kinalua, precisely in P/Hattina.

63. 1 Kgs 2.39; Achish son of Ma'ok in 1 Sam. 27.2

64. RIMAP 2.202.ii 12-13

title as 'king of Hamath and Luʿash'. (This solution identifies the other-wise unattested kingdom of 'Mt Amana' with Zoba, and Mt Amana/Zoba must then be Amqi.) But Zakkur, again, is not 'son of GN'. Yet what is the likelihood that each of two literary traditions would produce a singleton formulary, and each about a dynast from Beth-Rehob, a kingdom otherwise unattested?

The more banal reading is in each case preferable: Baasha was the son of king Ruhubu of the land of the Ammonites—a typical form of expression in the ninth-century annals, in which, as in many examples cited above, the element Bit- was frequently dropped. Hadadezer was the son of king Rahab of Zobah. Rahab may well have been the dynastic founder, but if so, he was the founder of the dynasty of Zoba, and the house of Rehob and Zobah were in fact identical. More likely, Rahab was Hadadezer's father and was not connected to Ammon or Rehob at all.

This would explain why Beth-Rehob is mentioned only in 2 Sam. 10.6, which aggregates its troops with those of Zobah, in contrast to Tov and Maacah. In ch. 8, only Zobah appears. Rehob is singled out because of Hadadezer's patronym. But, to proceed to the most elegant part of Na'aman's edifice, it seems to preclude Hazael's identification with Rehob's dynasty.

Hazael's ninth-century predecessor, Hadad-idri, bore the same name as 2 Samuel's Hadadezer, suggesting possible dynastic continuity between the overlord of the tenth century and the ruler of the ninth. Secondly, Hadad-idri disposed of a coalition throughout Syria, in partnership with a strong Israel to his south. That a petty kingdom of Zobah survived in the southern Beqaʿ without annexation by Damascus or the Omrides seems improbable. Thirdly, and most important, Shalmaneser and Kings both report that Hazael was a usurper, in Shalmaneser's case, 'son of nobody'.[65] Were Hazael the ruler of Beth-Rehob, adversion to the point might be expected, certainly from Shalmaneser.[66] Na'aman points to a putative parallel: Rezin II, in the eighth century, was not born in Damascus, but in [X]-Hadara, just as

65. In the case of 2 Kgs 8.7-15, it is reasonably clear, *pace* Na'aman, that Hazael did murder his liege lord.

66. Add: 1) Hazael's 'river' may be the Orontes; 2) 'beyond the River' (2 Sam. 8:3) isn't the west of the Euphrates; 3) no later source would assume Damascus was garrisoned; 4) Damascus under Hazael is a capital of a major state, unlike its role under Hadadezer of Zobah, all contrary to Na'aman's submission.

Na'aman's Hazael originates from Rehob; still, the Assyrian annals signal Rezin's relationship to his birthplace unambiguously, not by styling Rezin II 'son of [X]-hadara, king of Damascus'.[67] Hazael was a usurper, without a patronym—something he would have had every reason to invoke, thus claiming to be the conqueror, rather than usurper, of Damascus. It is unlikely, too, that he was the author of the Tel Dan stela. No more is it likely that David's opponent Hadadezer was a filibuster from Rehob who claimed the kingship of Zobah, or that Baasha son of Ruhubi of KUR Amanaya represented Rehob in Zobah.

Hadadezer. To return to the main thread of the discussion, there has been broad agreement latterly that David's Aramean opponent, Hadadezer, was the unnamed 'king of the land of Arumu' who, in the time of Asshur-rabi II seized Pitru and Mutkinu, the latter east of the Euphrates.[68] This hypothesis depends on the nature of Hadadezer's coalition in ch. 10. After Hadadezer's first field force—Beth-Rehob, Zobah, Maacah and Tob—is put to rout, a new one is formed. 2 Sam. 10.16: 'Hadadezer sent and called out the Arameans who are beyond the river'. Again, most scholars follow Malamat in identifying 'the river' as the Euphrates, though some have championed an identification with the Jordan or Yarmuk.[69] This has been the interpretation since antiquity; Chronicles, Psalm 60 and Josephus all adopted it.[70]

This dominant view has two flaws. First, the river here is surely the same river as that where David or Hadadezer erected a stela, but the odds that David reached the Euphrates are low. Secondly, north of Zobah sat the kingdom of Hamath, David's ally (2 Sam. 8.9-10).[71] Hamath was at least neutral toward and probably hostile to Zobah. So Arameans pouring south from the Euphrates would have been interdicted there. Of Hamath's active assistance to David, or passivity

67. Tadmor, *Tiglath-Pileser III*, 80 (Ann. 23):13'-14': *[...]-ha-a-da-ra É AD-šu ša ᵐRa-hi-a-ni KUR Ša- ANŠE-šu-a+a [a]-~šar~ i'-al-du.* The 'house of his father... the place where he was born' may have borne a dynastic name, (Hadad?)-ʿadara (Hadadezer), but the relationship is not telegraphically signalled.

68. A. Malamat, 'The Kingdom of David and Solomon in its Contact with Aram Naharaim', *BA* 21 (1958), pp. 96-102, widely followed. For the reference from Shalmaneser III see Luckenbill, *Ancient Records*, 1.603.

69. See McCarter, *II Samuel*, pp. 272-73.

70. 1 Chron. 19.6; Ps. 60.2; Josephus, *Ant.* 7.121 read Aram Naharaim for Aram Bet Rehob in 10.6.

71. For Solomon's attack on Hamath (2 Chron. 8.3-4), see above.

toward Zobah, we have no indication. In geopolitical terms, in fine, it is more likely that it was Toi or a more northerly neighbor who took land from Asshur-Rabi II than that it was Hadadezer.

Further, after enumerating Hadadezer's losses, ch. 8 lists neither Tov nor Maacah nor anyone else as his allies, citing only the case of Damascus. 8.6: Aram Damascus came to assist Hadadezer the king of Zobah, and David smote of Aram 22,000 men. The passage continues, 'David placed garrisons in Aram Damascus, and Aram became David's tribute-bearing servants'.

Two points, again, deserve attention. The text relates that Aram Damascus was occupied. But it makes no such claim concerning any territory in the Beqaᶜ. In other words, there is not a single report here of military action west of the Anti-Lebanon. It was the ally or vassal, Damascus, that suffered occupation, and Zobah, Beth-Rehob, Maacah and Tov, the first three, at least, in the Beqaᶜ, went unmolested.

In addition to prescinding, however, from any claims regarding Aramean territory north of the Bashan, 2 Sam. 8.6 engages in some delicate sleight of hand: David occupied Aram *Damascus*, but Aram, unqualified, became his tribute-bearers. Does this mean all Aram? Not if we include Hamath in the designation. Indeed, the term is deliberately vague, and the principle of propagandistic economy suggests that the tribute of Aram Damascus does literary duty for the other Aramean states. It is not coincidental that in the enumeration of David's extractions and dedications in 8.11-12, after all, the contributions of Hadadezer alone are referred to as 'booty'. There is no implication of the payment of tribute, just as there is no such implication when Tiglath-Pileser collects spoil, but does not mention imposts.

Having intimated, however, that Hadadezer's double defeat was a triumph over all Aram, the text continues to press. David retrieved military regalia from Hadadezer's vassals (10.7) and considerable bronze from two of Hadadezer's cities, Tebah, and Berotai or Kun. The impression is that David campaigned in the northern Beqaᶜ. But the kings of these towns might have been part of the field force relieving Amman, and the bronze lost in the despoiling of their camp. In other words, the text promotes two unwarranted assumptions: that Zobah was a unified nation-state, rather than a territory containing various kinglets, whose existence is attested in 10.19 (1 Sam. 14.47); and, that David campaigned there. Yet after the encounters with Aram, David's army still had unfinished business at the Ammonite capital, which it prosecuted in a succeeding year. The text, as distinct from the subtext, affords no evidence for a northern campaign.[72] But it is, again, the method of royal inscriptions to aggrandize by implication, to lead the reader without prevaricating.

Having created an impression, the text hastens to reinforce it. In 8.9-10, Toi king of Hamath dispatches his son, Joram, with precious gifts, to congratulate David on his victory. Here, the basis is laid for a claim (as in 1 Chron. 18.3) that David's sphere of influence extended beyond Zobah, and on to the Euphrates. In this respect, perhaps too much has been made in the past of Joram's Yahwistic name: it has been supposed that he changed his name from Hadoram, to show fealty to a suzerain Israel. More likely, Yahweh was a name indigenous to the Hamath region, as Stefanie Dalley has argued.[73] In any case, Hamath probably entered relations with David as a peer, rather than submitting formally. By treating the gifts from Hamath, which were undoubtedly reciprocated, just like the exactions from Aram (read: an area south of Damascus), Moab, Ammon, 'the Philistines', Amaleq and 'the spoil of Hadadezer', the author of 8.11-12, however, reinforces the impression of Israelite sovereignty in Syria. All this was tribute, is the implication. And yet a close reading of the text indicates the contrary.

4. *The Edomite Campaign*

The narrator next relates in 8.13 that David 'made a name when he returned from defeating Aram', closing the segment of the text that deals with this episode.[74] The reference, as is widely acknowledged, is to a monument, likely the monument mentioned at the outset of the war with Hadadezer, in 8.3. Even if not, references to stelae frame the Aramean war. The frame is then augmented with a report on the subduing of the Edomites, the garrisoning of their territory and their bearing tribute as vassals. The parallel is to the decimation of Moabites in 8.2, before the Aramean war.

What is important about the Edomite campaign is that all three

---

72. Contrast J.M. Miller and J.H. Hayes, *A History of Ancient Israel* (Philadelphia: Westminster Press, 1986), p. 185.

73. Hadoram in 1 Chron. 18.10; see Malamat, 'Foreign Policies', pp. 6-7, with the argument for Israel's sovereignty, followed by McCarter, *II Samuel*, p. 250. Further S. Dalley, 'Yahweh in Hamath in the 8th Century BC: Cuneiform Material and Historical Deductions', *VT* 40 (1990), pp. 21-32.

74. On the text of 8.13 see McCarter, *II Samuel*, pp. 245-46.

elements of David's ideal policy are combined: inflicting heavy casualties during a victory on the field, as in the case of Zobah and Damascus; the reduction of the Edomites to vassalage, as in the case of the Moabites; and the garrisoning of the country, as in the case of Aram Damascus. Edom is placed at the climax of the account to leave the reader with the impression that all the previous conquests were as thoroughgoing and permanent as that of the impoverished south. The direct parallel is to the summary statements in the annals of Tiglath-Pileser I, which level all distinctions among the nations he harassed.

Particularly telling is one locution, in 8.14: 'He placed garrisons in Edom, in all of Edom he placed garrisons, and all of Edom were servants to David'. Why the repetition?[75] It is to stress that the entire country was under David's rule. What is the contrast: to Aram Damascus, where garrisons are also located, again, with the implication, but without the explicit remark, that the entire territory of Damascus was subdued.

From this observation, one of two conclusions flows. If David took the town of Damascus itself, the garrison he installed was probably headed by Rezon the son of Eliada, Hadadezer's breakaway vassal. It is, after all, unlikely that Rezon, a fugitive, took a royal city from a strong empire. This scenario fits 1 Kgs 11.23-24 (MT): when David defeated Hadadezer, Rezon took Damascus where his men proclaimed him king.

The second possibility is that David did not achieve a hold over the town of Damascus. Again, 2 Sam. 8.5 implies that in the second encounter—the one with kings from across the river—Damascus was newly enlisted in Hadadezer's cause. The suggestion is that it was independent. In that case, the defeat of Hadadezer and his Damascene ally may have precipitated Rezon's filibuster, and perhaps a temporary accommodation with Israel. His revanchism in Solomon's day may have represented only an attempt to recover territories ceded to David by Rezon or his predecessor. This too fits the evidence from Kings.[76]

5. *The Ammonites*

One other oddity of 2 Samuel 8 is its failure to mention the fall of Rabbat Ammon (12.26-29) or any conflict there. It is true that it speaks of exactions from the Ammonites (8.12). But one might have expected some passing mention of the reduction of the capital and the taking of

---

75. Against McCarter, *II Samuel*, p. 246, read MT here.
76. So, basically, Malamat, 'Foreign Policies', p. 5.

its special booty (12.30). Indeed, 12.31 lodges the claim that David impressed 'all the towns of the children of Ammon'. But, fortified watchtowers aside, this may be a summary statement, on the Tiglath-Pileser principle.[77]

For the omission of the Ammonite campaign, several explanations suggest themselves: a first, that the campaign against Ammon would be treated in detail in 2 Samuel 10–12, does not commend itself, since the author of that account felt no compunction about repeating the history of the Aramean conflict, with details differing from 2 Samuel 8. A second explanation is better: Ammon regained partial independence in the course of the Absalom revolt, a few years later.[78] In favor of this inference is the fact that neither Maacah nor Tov appears in 2 Samuel 8. It may be that neither became a vassal, despite the claim (10.19) that Hadadezer's vassals submitted: perhaps formal sovereignty was achieved—but there is no mention of tribute. More likely, however, the implication is that their active intervention in Transjordan ceased:

> David slew of Aram 700 chariot teams and forty thousand horsemen, and he smote Shobach, commander of its army and he died there. And all the kings, the vassals of Hadadezer, saw that they were defeated before Israel, so they made peace with Israel and served them, and Aram feared to succour the Ammonites any further (10.18-19).

The whole point of the passage is that the Arameans no longer obstructed David's advance against Ammon. Thus, the continuation reads, 'At the turn of the year, when kings go forth to war, David sent Joab and his servants with him, and all Israel, and they attacked the Ammonites and laid siege to Rabbah' (11.1).

The extent of Aramean servitude is in the context concession of Israelite domination in Transjordan. Read minimally, the text may claim nothing more than that some Damascenes entered into vassalship, while the other Arameans withdrew.

Conversely, the phrase about Aramean submission in 10.19 may reflect later developments. The sequence in 10.18–11.1 indicates that David was deflected from campaigning in the north by his need to reduce Rabbah: perhaps neither Maacah nor Tov became a vassal at this

77. The 'fortified watchtowers' date to the seventh century at earliest. See H.O. Thompson, 'The Ammonite Remains at Khirbet al-Hajjar', *BASOR* 227 (1977), pp. 27-34.

78. McCarter (*II Samuel*, p. 274) and Miller and Hayes (*History*, p. 175) date the Absalom revolt before the Aramean conflict.

time. Thus, a third possible reason for the omission of Ammon from ch. 8 is that the source of ch. 8 was written in the interval between the conflict with Aram and the taking of Rabbah.

After all, Maacah was later at least partly integrated with the kingdom: by Asa's time, Ben-Hadad's idea of an attack on Israel was to strike at 'Iyyon, Dan and Abel Beth-Maacah (1 Kgs 15.18-20)—Abel, city of the dynasty Maacah; nor is it likely that Abel was integrated into Israel under Solomon or Jeroboam. Already at the end of the Absalom revolt it is to Abel that Sheba ben-Bichri flees. Then, under siege, Abel extradited him (2 Sam. 20.14-22). Whether or not the absence of a town king from this story is authentic, the flight and sheltering of Sheba suggests Abel was extraterritorial and at least partly independent, as does Joab's siege.[79] The extradition, and especially the 'wise woman's' protestations that Abel was an Israelite 'matriclan',[80] indicate submission. But this came late in David's reign, and not on the heels of the conflict in Transjordan. And that, or its annexation, may explain the absence of any notice about it in 2 Samuel 8, despite the report in ch. 10 that Maacah participated in Hadadezer's coalition.

Thus, there is at least a good chance that the source of 2 Samuel 8 was written early in David's reign, perhaps even before the fall of Rabbah.[81] And in that case, one source suggests itself as most likely. That is the display inscription that 2 Samuel 8 refers to at least once, and possibly twice, and that David erected. The river in question is probably the Jordan, for there is no evidence that he ever approached the Euphrates, nor that Hadadezer raised troops any further afield than Damascus (across the Jordan). Depending on the location of Helam, site of the second confrontation with Hadadezer, or rather, with his general, Shobach, it is not clear that David penetrated very far into Damascene territory. Indeed, the ongoing independence of Geshur, whose royal house furnished Absalom's mother and his own refuge in exile, rather

---

79. For the archaeology, see W.G. Dever, 'Abel-Beth-Maʿacah: Northern Gateway of Ancient Israel', in L.T. Geraty and L.G. Herr (eds.), *The Archaeology of Jordan and Other Studies Presented to Siegfried H. Horn* (Berrien Springs, MI: Andrews University Press, 1986), pp. 207-22, esp. p. 220.

80. On 'a mother and a city in Israel' see R. Tomback, *A Comparative Semitic Lexicon of the Phoenician and Punic Languages* (SBLDS, 32; Missoula, MT: Scholars Press, 1978), pp. 22-23; A. Malamat, 'UMMATUM in Old Babylonian Texts and Its Ugaritic and Biblical Counterparts', *UF* 11 (1979), pp. 527-36.

81. The Edomite campaign (2 Sam. 8.13-14) is in this case narrated out of sequence. For the reasons, see above.

suggests that the small kingdoms of the north were not wholly or, with the exception of Abel, even partly overcome until Damascus expanded under Rezin and his successors in the late tenth or even ninth century.[82] Had David campaigned in Geshur, Tov, Beth-Rehob or Zobah, we would surely have heard about it in print.

There is a more cynical explanation for the condition of 2 Samuel 8, and it is difficult to exclude: namely, that the text as it stands decontextualizes the Aramean war; and this reinforces the impression that '(the) river' of 8.3 is indeed the Euphrates. After all, having turned from the war against Moab in 8.2, the text next states that David 'smote Hadadezer...king of Zobah'. The connection to the war against Ammon is altogether absent, and the succeeding action takes the reader to Damascus (8.6) and Hamath (8.9). By including Ammon only in a generalized list of those 'conquered' (8.12), the author of the text further insulates the 'Aramean campaign' from the Ammonite war.

But what is the implication of this technique? Again, no mention is made of later conquests—the capital of Ammon, Abel Beth-Maacah. Further, it is the succession narrative itself (in the frame around the Bathsheba story) that enables us to recontextualize ch. 8 and to understand that David fought Hadadezer in Transjordan, not in the north. In other words, the implication of the technique employed in ch. 8 is that it was anterior to and was imported into the history of David's reign. Even if the chapter's source postdated the fall of Rabbat Ammon, it would still bear the look and employ the propagandistic technology of the royal display inscription.

In sum, the authors of 2 Samuel, or of its sources, deliberately employed writing techniques closely akin to those of Near Eastern display inscriptions. They suggested, implied, insinuated that David's achievements were a great deal more extensive than in reality they were. But they did not openly prevaricate, on this subject at least. Their method was a good deal more subtle than outright forgery, and very much at home in the historiographic traditions of the chanceries of the ancient Near East.[83] The Republic of Letters embraced, and did not stop at, ancient Israel.

---

82. Occupations at Ein Gev and Tel Hadar indicate a continuous Aramaic presence, or at least a distinctive regional culture.

83. Hence the lack of textual or archaeological evidence of Davidic construction: had David constructed an empire reaching into Syria and to the Litani (as Ahlström, *History of Ancient Palestine*, p. 486 and Map 14), a more aggressive program of fortification and display would have been in evidence.

V

Against this perspective, a number of objections might be lodged. First, no West Semitic display inscriptions are attested before the ninth century.[84] This, however, is not a major impediment, as the recovery of inscriptions depends on the accidents of secondary state formation and archaeological recovery, both of which are differential in different contexts. Most royal sites in Israel, after all, have modern occupations, and Jerusalem, the Davidic capital, was torn up repeatedly by ancient engineers. The recovery of stelae in the countryside, conversely, is relatively unlikely, as excavation tends to be on mounds. Thus, only something massive and in a protected location is likely to be found.

Further, the annals of Asshurnasirpal II and Shalmaneser III already indicate Assyrian contact with the southern trade in the early ninth century. This indicates that trade was already recovering in this period, and the report that Solomon exploited southern trade connections accrues credibility as a result. The Suhu texts, including one that speaks of the hold-up of a Sabean caravan at Hindanu, indicate just how much verisimilitude the Solomon reports enjoy.[85] It is not at all implausible that a trading state gained ground in the tenth century, particularly as Assyrian annals mention such states south of the Euphrates. Where there are royal states, there can be royal inscriptions, and the existence of a monument of Absalom—that could be seen in the King's Valley (2 Sam. 18.18)— confirms the likelihood of tenth-century monument-building in Israel.

Again, some scholars maintain that Jerusalem's population was insufficient for it to function as a state center until its expansion in the late eighth century.[86] This is misleading. The earliest territorial state in

84. So, in conversation, Nadav Na'aman.

85. See A. Cavigneaux and B.K. Ismail, 'Die Statthalter von Suḫu und Mari im 8. Jh. v. Chr', *Baghdader Mitteilungen* 21 (1990), pp. 321-456, pp. 327-29, 339 and n. 61.

86. See, e.g., T.L. Thompson, *The Early History of the Israelite People. From the Written and Archaeological Sources* (SHANE, 4; Leiden: Brill, 1992); P.R. Davies, *In Search of 'Ancient Israel'* (JSOTSup, 148; Sheffield: JSOT Press, 1992); J.W. Flanagan, *David's Social Drama: A Hologram of Israel's Early Iron Age* (The Social World of Biblical Antiquity, 7; JSOTSup, 73; Sheffield: JSOT Press, 1988); D.W. Jamieson-Drake, *Scribes and Schools in Monarchic Judah: A Socio-Archeological Approach* (The Social World of Biblical Antiquity, 9; JSOTSup, 109; Sheffield: JSOT Press, 1991).

Canaan/Israel pursued a deliberate policy of distancing domestic population from state centers. Thus, Megiddo VA-IVB and Hazor X-IX are both elements of a central state structure: their gates exhibit a homologous character, similar to those of Gezer, and, perhaps slightly later, Lachish and Ashdod; probably, the fortifications also are similar, consisting in the initial phase of casemates.[87] At Megiddo, Hazor and Gezer, the relevant gates are associated with the first Iron Age layers in which burnished red-slipped pottery appears, again suggesting contemporaneity. And the end of each layer can be associated with Shishaq's Asian campaign, ca. 921.

What is particularly striking, however, about Megiddo VA-IVB (and IVA) and Hazor X-IX is that both lack domestic architecture. Nor, in the case of Megiddo, was there a significant hinterland population, at least in the western Jezreel. Here, then, is evidence of a central state. Something can even be said about the policies of that state: a disembedded capital, including a provincial capital, is something to which an elite resorts in order to be shut of the influence of prior elites and structures.

David's taking of Jerusalem with his private army leads us to expect this sort of disembedment. Among Solomon's district capitals (1 Kgs 4.7-19), too, are a number of settlements that before the inception of the monarchy were surely extra-territorial: Beth-Shemesh, which was Philistine; Dor, previously a Sea-People site;[88] Arubboth, its earlier status unclear; the Bashan, likely unconquered before David; probably, Gilead; and, Taanach, Megiddo and Beth Shan. Solomon's other governors may have been as inspecifically based as Amarna commissioners seem to have been, having the power to rove rather than being assigned to sit. But, as Alt observed, the urban centers are frequently those unconnected with Israelite populations.[89] Insofar as recent accessions of

---

87. For this vexed issue, see Y. Yadin, *Hazor* (Schweich Lectures; London: British Academy, 1972), pp. 150-64; Y. Yadin, Y. Shiloh and A. Eitan, 'Megiddo', *IEJ* 22 (1972), pp. 161-64; D. Ussishkin, 'Was the "Solomonic" City Gate at Megiddo Built by King Solomon?', *BASOR* 239 (1980), pp. 1-18; Y. Shiloh, 'Solomon's Gate at Megiddo as Recorded by its Excavator, R. Lamon, Chicago', *Levant* 12 (1980), pp. 69-76, both with bibliography; more recently, D. Ussishkin, 'Megiddo', *ABD*, IV, pp. 666-79.

88. E. Stern, *Dor, Ruler of the Seas* (Jerusalem: Israel Exploration Society, 1994), pp. 101-11, speculates that Dor was taken from the Tjeker by Phoenicians. More likely, Saul or Ishbaal took it, and a peaceful transition to Davidide rule ensued.

89. See A. Alt, 'Israels Gaue unter Salomo', *Kleine Schriften zur Geschichte des*

the Israelite kingdom are concerned, then, Solomon seems to have to recapitulated David's policy. Administrative centers were so far as possible divorced from existing populations. The policy is consistent with Solomon's general attempt to remove fiscal power from the lineages.[90]

These administrative centers confirm the presence of a central Israelite state before the Omrides. So, too, does the fact that by the mid-ninth century, Israel already had a massive chariotry arm with a distinctive tactical tradition, as evidenced by Ahab's contingent at the battle of Qarqar.[91] The massive public structures of Megiddo IVA are related to this arm, whether as stables or storehouses.[92] The presence of a central state in the tenth century is confirmed, just as the mention of 'the house of David' in the Tel Dan stela should lead us to expect.

VI

Overall, then, our text makes remarkably conservative explicit claims. The grandiose claims are all in its implications. And yet the implications are so palpable that, taken up into later biblical literature, they have resonated in the form of an extensive empire through the millennia.

The implication is that the text is early, before its author felt he had the license to aggrandize the accomplishments: the contrast is to parts of the Solomon account, in which claims to parts of Syria are asserted, and even more so to Chronicles. 2 Samuel was only lightly edited in the Deuteronomistic era, which accounts for the differences in the claims.

This point comports with other details. Thus, Rehoboam's birth a year before Solomon's accession, to an Ammonite mother, follows from Ammonite support for David during Absalom's revolt: the marriage to an eligible, if unlikely, successor, was a reward to Shobi ben-Nahash. Similarly, Rehoboam's marriage to Absalom's daughter indicates a policy of reconciliation with Adonijah's supporters early in Solomon's

Volkes Israels (Munich: Beck, 1953), II, pp. 76-89. Cf. P.S. Ash, 'Solomon's? District? List', *JSOT* 67 (1995), pp. 67-86.

90. See Halpern, 'Sectionalism and the Schism'.

91. See ARAB 611; esp. S. Dalley, 'Foreign Chariotry in the Armies of Tiglath-Pileser III and Sargon III', *Iraq* 47 (1985), pp. 31-48.

92. For stables, see J.S. Holladay, 'The Stables of Ancient Israel. Functional Determinants of Stable Construction and the Interpretation of Pillared Building Remains of the Palestinian Iron Age', in Geraty and Herr (eds.), *Archaeology of Jordan*, pp. 103-65.

reign.[93] It is also a marriage to the father's brother's daughter, the ideal in Israelite theory.[94] None of this is the invention of a later period—the connections are simply too rich, too unorthodox, including as they do connections to the Absalom revolt, and the anathema of the Persian period, intermarriage (without censure!).

An interesting sidelight on the same question comes from 1 Sam. 27.6: Ziklag belongs to the kings of Judah 'to this very day'. Given settlement patterns in the Negev, no such statement could be made after the early ninth century, and probably not after Shishaq's campaign. It would certainly be possible to claim a western Negev settlement in the seventh century, but the plain was dominated by Assyria. If Haror, for example, turns out to be ancient Gath, then Sharia, as a candidate for Ziklag, could not conceivably have been attached to Judah: Haror was a major Assyrian fortress. Even less likely is a Persian date for the claim. This text, whatever its history, makes an assertion consistent only with a tenth-century date. There are later elements in Samuel, but again, there are early elements.

Overall, the implication of this study is that large parts of our information on the United Monarchy stem from roughly contemporary sources. Some of the information may even derive from monuments. Indeed, this is the reason that, when read carefully and literally, the claims—and the silences—of the texts are so conservative. There was certainly, on the evidence of texts and of such archaeology as we have, no extensive Davido-Solomonic empire in Syria. In fact, were we to find a monument of Toi of Hamath or his successors, it might even claim hegemony 'unto Israel' in the south, as his own ascendancy over Zobah is at least as likely to have been asserted as David's. Still, the relatively modest claims of the first generation of Davidic propaganda suggest strongly that the United Monarchy was real, and in fact that it achieved significant territorial gains in Transjordan, and modest gains to the north. It was only in subsequent generations that the original, careful, claims were expanded, a sure sign that the Davidic 'myth' did not spring up full-blown in some late era, as some have maintained. This reading of Samuel, then, may imply a drastic reduction in traditional views of the early empire; it has the merit of confirming that the central state indeed existed.

93. See further my 'Text and Artifact: Two Monologues', forthcoming.

94. See my 'Sybil, or the Two Nations. Archaism, Kinship and Alienation in Judah in the Era of Reform', in J. Cooper (ed.), *Near Eastern Studies in the Twenty-first Century* (Albright Centennial Volume; Winona Lake, IN: Eisenbrauns, 1996).

SOCIETY

SOCIOLOGICAL AND BIBLICAL VIEWS OF THE EARLY STATE

Christa Schäfer-Lichtenberger

The 'Histories of Israel' written during the past thirty years generally view and portray tenth-century Israel-Judah as a state.[1] This position has been challenged recently. Some authors contend that archaeological and ancient Near Eastern sources are to be used exclusively for reconstructing the Israelite society of the tenth century. Archaeological data and the silence of ancient Near Eastern sources are pronounced the ultimate evidence of a position, which denies state-status to tenth-century Israel-Judah,[2] or which considers the first kings and their political organization of the people as ideologically motivated projections—dating from the post-exilic period—of idealized figures in early times.[3]

I would like to make a few consequential inquiries into this situation before continuing with my deliberations on the emergence of the state in Israel-Judah.

---

1. Cf. among others H. Cazelles, *Histoire Politique d'Israel des origines à Alexandre le Grand* (Paris, 1982), pp. 117ff.; H. Donner, *Geschichte des Volkes Israel und seiner Nachbarn in Grundzügen* (ATD Ergänzungsreihe, 4.1; Göttingen: Vandenhoeck & Ruprecht, 1984), pp. 169-232; J.A. Soggin, *Einführung in die Geschichte Israels und Judas. Von den Ursprüngen bis zum Aufstand Bar Kochbas* (Darmstadt: Wissenschaftliche Buchgesellschaft, 1991), pp. 30-75; G.W. Ahlström, *The History of Ancient Palestine from the Palaeolithic Period to Alexander's Conquest* (ed. D.V. Edelman; JSOTSup, 146; Sheffield: JSOT Press, 1993), pp. 421-542. The terminology among the individual authors varies between empire/kingdom/monarchy/national state/territorial state and policy.

2. Cf. H.M. Niemann, *Herrschaft, Königtum und Staat. Skizzen zur soziokulturellen Entwicklung im monarchischen Israel* (Tübingen: Mohr, 1993).

3. Cf. G. Garbini, *Storia e ideologia nell'Israele antico* (Breschia, 1986); P.R. Davies, *In Search of 'Ancient Israel'* (JSOTSup, 148; Sheffield: JSOT Press, 1992); T.L. Thompson, *The Early History of the Israelite People. From the Written and Archaeological Sources* (SHANE, 4; Leiden: Brill, 1992).

Excursus: Implicit Suppositions of Positivistic Historicism

The ancient Near Eastern silence is eloquent but not meaningful (or expressive). ('Das altorientalische Schweigen ist zwar beredt aber nicht eindeutig aussagekräftig.') Apart from the Bible, the lack of written documents on Israel during Iron Age I in ancient Near Eastern sources could have at least four causes, each independent from the others. 1) There was no political entity of any consequence by the name Israel at this period. 2) The historical hegemonic powers of Syria/Palestine, Egypt or Assyria failed politically in their attempt to extend their claim to power in that region and, consequently, no written accounts about it exist. 3) No records remain because they were probably written on papyrus.[4] Contracts, documented in writing at this time probably occurred with Egypt rather than Mesopotamia. 4) The records have not been found yet. In my opinion, arguments 2-4 offer a sufficient explanation of the ancient Near Eastern silence.

Architecture and epigraphy provide the data considered historical fact that supposedly argue against a political organization of Israel at this time. The absence or the lack of monumental buildings, of building inscriptions, or of other evidence in written form is noted.

Stones and walls do not speak for themselves and even their descriptions are not unambiguous. Data derived from archaeological artifacts exist only in linguistic form. Being elements of a linguistic structure, however, they are subject to an interpretation as well. The description of archaeological findings is already interpretation and it is subject, like any other literary form of expression, to the singular choice of the narrative procedure, to the concept of explanation, as well as to the value-

---

4. Cf. the exposition of A. Millard, 'An Assessment of the Evidence for Writing in Ancient Israel', in J. Amitai (ed.), *Biblical Archeology Today. Proceedings of the International Congress on Biblical Archeology* (Jerusalem, 1984), pp. 301-12, in particular 304-306. The possibility of papyrus having been the preferred writing material in Israel until the eighth century BCE is also suggested by D.W. Jamieson-Drake (*Scribes and Schools in Monarchic Judah* [The Social World of Biblical Antiquity, 9; JSOTSup, 109; Sheffield: JSOT Press, 1991], pp. 124-25). Millard points out that the use of hieratic numeric symbols in Israel and Judah is an indication of the hieratic script having been a predecessor of the alphabetic script in this region (personal communication).

orientation of the descriptive archaeologist.[5] And—depending on the perspective of the describer or the observer—there are various interpretational levels which can be differentiated, ranging from the singular data to the immediate context, or from the immediate and the extended environment to a geographical region or even beyond.[6] The anwer to the question whether there were centrally organized fortifications in Israel-Judah during this time period is not only dependent on material findings, but is determined largely by the conception of the term 'state', by the understanding of society, as well as by the evaluation of biblical texts used as historical sources.[7] Yet there appears a negative conception of 'state' paired with an idealistic idea of society, and both notions correspond with the fundamental skepticism toward the accounts of the books of Samuel and Kings.[8]

Monumental inscriptions from this period have not been found until now.[9] This only needs an explanation when putting Israel-Judah on the same level as Egypt and Assyria, and when regarding the existence and maintenance of monumental inscriptions as an indispensable criterion of a state. The application of this criterion to small and medium powers, in

5.   Following Hayden White, *Tropics of Discourse: Essays in Cultural Criticism* (Baltimore, 1982).

6.   Even the apparently simple comparison of a handle from Tell es-Sheba with another handle from Tel Megiddo implies a complex interpretational chain. The differences in regard to dating the multi-chambered gates of Lachish, Gezer, Hazor and Megiddo, which have appeared among various excavators, may not be entirely linked to the material substratum; they may also have been caused by the applied theoretical conceptualization. Cf. also the exposition of J.M. Miller, 'Is it Possible to Write a History of Israel without Relying on the Hebrew Bible?', in D. Edelman (ed.), *The Fabric of History: Text, Artifact and Israel's Past* (JSOTSup, 127; Sheffield: JSOT Press, 1991), pp. 93-102.

7.   Consensus on the archeologically provable existence of monumental buildings in the tenth century may still be as distant as an agreement on connecting the relative stratigraphy—supplied by excavation—to an absolute chronology; cf. the debate in *BASOR* 277/278 (1990).

8.   Cf. Niemann, *Herrschaft*. It is not surprising that, according to this view, fortifications, which indicate centralized planning, cannot be dated back to the early period of kings; failing this, if they cannot be dated to another time period, they are accounted as an evolutionary moment in the aspiration for security of local associations which were not in need of a centralized organization (*Herrschaft*, pp. 97-98, 110-11).

9.   The Ophel fragment is dated to the seventh century by J. Naveh, 'A Fragment of an Ancient Hebrew Inscription from the Ophel', *IEJ* 32 (1982), pp. 195-98.

my opinion, lacks a sociological basis. Monumental inscriptions are always indicative of specific sociological conditions. They point out a state's considerable need for legitimation. The societies of large ancient Near Eastern states and those of small states may well differ structurally. That is why Hebrew monumental inscriptions of this period are not necessarily to be expected. It is noticeable that ancient societies of pre-Roman times, which used alphabetical scripts, have left behind few or no building inscriptions from the early periods of the formation of their state. Measured by this criterion the states of Athens or Sparta of the seventh century BCE or the Carolingian empire of the eighth century CE would have their statehood denied.

If there were monumental inscriptions in early Israel, they would be conceivable only in Jerusalem. The limited possibilities for excavating the sites in question are commonly known. Assuming there were inscriptions on buildings addressed to the public, it should be expected that, in accordance with ancient Near Eastern building inscriptions, the names of deities would be mentioned. Research to date on Israelite religious history of the pre-Josianic time allows the assumption that other deities were mentioned next to Yahweh.[10] It is unlikely that such inscriptions would survive the religious reforms of later times, to say nothing of the massive military destruction following the fall of Samaria as well as Jerusalem.

The epigraphic findings of the time period between the tenth and the eighth centuries are rare. The respective epigraphic findings from Athens and Sparta from before the sixth century BCE are also meager.[11] The evaluation of these findings is dependent on the preconceived conception of the term 'state'. Taking the viewpoint of a thoroughly organized state which registers every potentially exploitable unit up to the individual, the meager yield of ostraca becomes clear: there were no sociopolitical organizations which could have necessitated written notes on clay shards. But let us put aside the model of a bureaucratic-totalitarian state for a moment in order to enquire—aside of any such expectations—into the possible causes of these findings. In this region, papyrus was probably

---

10. Cf. the inscription from Khirbet el-Qom and from Kuntillet ʿAjrud.

11. There are occasional inscriptions at the end of the eighth century in Athens and at the second half of the seventh century for Laconia; cf M. Guarducci, *Epigrafia Greca* (Rome, 1967), I, pp. 135ff., 279ff.; C.W. Fornara, *Archaic Times to the End of the Peloponnesian War* (Baltimore, 1977), pp. 13ff.

the writing material for administrative texts, other than for simple notes. Under the predominant climatic conditions, however, papyrus findings are improbable. The absence of ostraca could confirm the common experience in archaeology, namely, that only those objects are found that originate from a building's last phase before its destruction.[12] Objects which demonstrably originated from a time period of more than three generations before the destruction are exceptionally rare.[13]

The epigraphical findings from the Assyrian cities Ashur, Kalakh and Nineveh of the ninth century illustrate this fact. Ostraca belonged to the daily administrative process; putting them into archives may have been just as unusual as filing dispatch notes for goods would be today. Destructions over wide areas that could have contributed to the preservation of ostraca, such as those of Samaria and Arad, are not known to have occurred in the tenth century with the exception of Philistine Gezer. Moreover, the sparse early Hebrew or proto-Canaanite inscriptions that have been found from this period are scratched inscriptions.[14] This fact could indicate that ink writing on the ostraca was either easier for the excavator to miss, or that ink writing has been lost due to weather. The absence of royal seal impressions up to the eighth century is no proof for the non-existence of a state's economic activities in earlier times. The amassed evidence of royal seal impressions only suggests that during this time the state's need for contributions had increased considerably. In view of the Assyrian campaigns to Palestine during the second half of the eighth century—which increased the expenditures on armaments and later on for due tributes to Assur—the stamped jar handles prove that during this time period a centrally oriented reorganization of Judah's economy took place.

In my opinion, it is not up to archaeology to decide an essentially theoretic debate, whose course until now has demonstrated only that the so-called hard facts are determined by the discussants' perspectives.

12. A considerable number of the ostraca found on the Agora in Athens come from the period between 487 and 480 BCE. This period is clearly over-represented, a fact that most probably is connected to the destruction of the city by the Persians; cf. R. Meiggs and D. Lewis, *A Selection of Greek Historical Inscriptions to the End of the Fifth Century B.C.* (Oxford: Oxford University Press, 1969), pp. 40ff.

13. Cf. Millard, 'Assessment', p. 305.

14. ʿIzbet Sartah, Tel el ʿAsi, Gezer, Ahiram-sarcophagus. This fact is in accordance with the findings of regions in Greece.

1. *The Notion of the State as a Form of Political Organization*

It is questionable whether applying the term 'state' to the forms of political organization of ancient communities addresses their factuality. The state, and hence our preconceived notion of it, is a manifestation of modern times. In my opinion, it is no coincidence that historians prefer the terms 'dominion/monarchy/rulership' over 'state' when describing the political structure of Israel. Terms like 'dominion' or 'rulership' appear to imply indistinct notions about the sociopolitical organization, whereas, to a good number of researchers, the idea of a rigid socio-structural organization is inherent in the term 'state'.

Furthermore, two contradictory paradigms influence the conceptualization of the state: according to one paradigm, the state is the result of conflicts, and of the perpetuation of the victory of the groups that came to power; according to the other, the state is the result of a consensus between the ruler and the ruled. The use of the term and the idea of 'state' as heuristic devices increasingly determines the debate on Israel's political constitution during the first half of the first millennium BCE, without further scrutiny of the theoretical concepts employed. The suspicion arises whether the discussants have not replaced the concept of the state with one of the two paradigms. At any rate, it is conspicuous that each side of the issue would differ not just in evaluating the biblical records, but also according to the implicit use of each paradigm.

It appears useful to me, first of all, to discuss various conceptualizations of the term 'state' which have influenced the discussion on the Old Testament. As a second step, I would like to utilize ethno-sociological studies on early states; this examination of the plausibility of the biblical record is based on the combination of sociological theory with empirical ethno-sociological data.

The theoretical discussion of the term 'state', that is, its organizational characteristics, is often intermingled with two other issues: the search for historical conditions for the emergence of the primary state, and researching the historical conditions in the formation of a certain historical state. In our case, however, we are only interested in the first and third issues, since Israel belongs to the category of secondary state formations. It needs to be considered that the formation of a secondary state is, in part, the response to qualitatively different conditions than those in the formation of a primary state. This becomes evident by the simple fact that secondary states always develop in the environment of another state-formation. That is why a society which consists of a narrow and possibly unstable socio-structural differentiation can become a state due to the modeling effect; and such a state-formation is unlikely under the conditions of a stateless environment.

The discussion on the definition of 'state' ranges from normative to regulatory conceptions.[15] The state is either identified with the organized and monopolized political power, or it is seen as a form of rulership which, being the highest authority, exerts influence on the distribution of power and the shaping of the society.[16] An intermediate position, a determination commonly used in international law, originates from Georg Jellinek. He attempted to develop an external definition of 'state': 'Der Staat ist die mit ursprünglicher Herrschermacht ausgerüstete Verbandseinheit seßhafter Menschen.'[17]

According to Jellinek, three dimensions have to be present for a political organization to function as a state: a state-territory,[18] a state-population,[19] and a state-power. Externally, the political union is based on the spatially circumscribed territory, but it is constituted by the intentional accordance between the rulers and the ruled within a temporal and spatial continuity.[20] State-power is a form of organized rule designed

15. Cf. M.H. Fried and F.M. Watkins, 'State', *IntEncSocSc* 15 (1968), pp. 143-57; M. Drath, 'Staat', in *Staatslexikon* (Freiburg, 7th edn, 1989), V, pp. 3305-53.

16. The latter position originates from Heller, who claims that the state is an operative system constituted by action- and effect-correlations. Cf. H. Heller, *Staatslehre als politische Wissenschaft*, III (ed. M. Drath, O. Stammer, G. Niemeyer and F. Barinsky; Tübingen, 6th edn, 1983 [1943]). I give no further consideration to this position since such an understanding of the state is derived exclusively from the abstraction of present conditions of the state. Under historical as well as archeological aspects such an understanding seems to be operational only when other concepts are consulted for a more accurate determination, as for instance the specific pattern of the correlation between the ruler and the ruled.

17. Jellinek does not consider the normative conception when describing the state; he characterizes the state as a specific political state of affairs; cf. G. Jellinek, *Allgemeine Staatslehre* (Darmstadt, 3rd edn, repr. 1960), pp. 174ff. esp. 180-81.

18. State-territory is defined as a geographically distinguished part of the earth's surface under exclusive sovereignty. The geographical area is determined by the associative unity of the people settled there.

19. The state-population is an association of people settled permanently.

20. Cf. Jellinek, *Staatslehre*, p. 177. Membership of a modern state is commonly acquired by permanent residence, but such was not the case in the ancient Greek and Roman states. In Athens as well as in Rome the community of citizens was identical with the state; cf. Jellinek, *Staatslehre*, pp. 129ff.

for permanence, and, due to power, predominant over other political forces within the state-territory.

This determination does have the merit of being generally accepted, but it is too abstract to serve as a heuristic yardstick for measuring the political constitution of historical individuals.

The notions about the state's normative functions lead to internal definitions of the state. Keeping up law and order becomes a state's main purpose.[21] Within the framework of a normative concept of 'state', the centralization of the political organization goes hand in hand with the monopolization of force and the systematization of the law. The state constitutes not only the supreme level of decisions but, in its manifestations, the state penetrates all elements of society.

The definition of 'state' from this perspective which has been most influential historically is Max Weber's contention of the modern state as an 'institution' (*Anstalt*). According to Weber, the state as 'institution' is a thoroughly organized political rulership-association with statutory rules and a specific administrative staff, that has the monopoly of the legitimate physical force for carrying through the rules.[22] Weber's contention of the modern state with its three essential characteristics, 'legislation'/'administration'/'monopoly on power', seems to have influenced the discussion of the Old Testament substantially.[23] State-power, in all its appearances, envelops society completely. This model suggests coherence and consistence of the state's constitution which—if it is supposed to be archaeologically proven—can hardly be excavated in reality.[24] The orientation toward an idea of state which includes a hierarchically-authoritarian total organization of a closed society under political aspects

21. This understanding leads to the thesis of the existence of a single law-maker or sovereign whose decisions are ultimately binding, regardless of opposition.

22. M. Weber, *Wirtschaft und Gesellschaft* (Tübingen, 5th edn, 1976), pp. 821-24; Weber deliberates on the state by analyzing its means and its reasons for legitimation which are rooted in each state's order. This conception of the state represents a maximized definition, inasmuch the state, theoretically and in reality, is understood as a monopolist of power. Weber assumes a specific configuration in the politics of domestic rulership.

23. A normative understanding of the state according to Weber forms the basis of the studies mentioned above.

24. From the perspective of Weber's definition of 'state', the archaeological hypothesis—which is geared toward reification—has yet to find a correlatory material substratum as the indicator for rulership-conditions of a state.

is more obstructive than yielding to the view on an ancient Near Eastern society.

Weber's distinction between the modern state and state-organizations of the pre-modern era received less attention. According to Weber, the pre-modern states belong to the category of patrimonial states. The organization of the patrimonial state follows the model of *oikos*, and not the one of *Anstalt*.[25] The ruling power is based on a commonly accepted agreement between the ruler and the ruled, the traditionally exerted authority of the lords is regarded as a legitimate right by the ruler.[26] This understanding of the state is more a regulatory, rather than a normative, conception. The ruled are obliged to pay taxes and to render services only for political purposes. The fact that the means for rulership remain in the possession of the lord is typical of the patrimonial state.[27] Personal relations between the ruler and the officials dominate rationalizing tendencies typical of every administration. The officials do not make up their own strata; instead they are ministry officials who are personally dependent on the ruler. Patrimonial administration serves primarily to provide for the ruler's household.[28] The political administration is a personal matter of the ruler, and it is first of all an occasional management. The appointment of tasks and offices is predominantly dependent on the relationship between the considered person and the ruler. The ruler's household is in charge of providing for the officials. Entitlements for supplies from the ruler's storehouse and land allocations are given only in case of extending the appointed tasks locally. The hereditary appropriation of prebends by the officials introduces their independence from the ruler's household. Characteristic for the patrimonial administration of the area state is a move toward permanent decentralization. The governing power of the ruler becomes limited by the executive power of the officials, who actually become independent by the appropriation of their prebends.

The patrimonial state, according to Weber, can pass through three phases.[29] Under given circumstances, a certain persistence of structures

25. Weber, *Wirtschaft*, pp. 133-35, 583-624.

26. Cf. Weber, *Wirtschaft*, pp. 590-92.

27. The keeping of bodyguards or of a mercenary force, which is paid by the ruler's income, is notable.

28. A distinction between the 'private' and the 'official' sphere cannot be established.

29. Cf. Weber, *Wirtschaft*, pp. 594-624.

takes place at each stage. The first phase is characterized by occasional administration.[30] Essential here is the absence of military threats and a sufficient basis for subsistence of the regional settlement units, making the central distribution of consumer items superfluous.[31] The second phase is marked by the transition toward a prebendal economy. The officials still belong to the royal household, but they have already acquired entitlements of continuous supplies for themselves. During this phase, it becomes possible for officials to found and own households outside the capital.

Traffic conditions, the extent of contributions necessary for keeping up the royal household, the character of the allocated prebends, as well as the subsistence-conditions of the region, are among the factors introduced by the independence of the officials' households. The contributions to the ruler—which by now have become regular—are furnished by leiturgical associations.[32] At any rate, a complex correlation of various factors can be assumed.

In the third phase of the patrimonial state, the officials establish their positions, and pass them on within their families as their own and not the ruler's entitlement. The appropriation of administrative powers by the officials leads to the corporate type of patrimonialism.[33] A new political stratum emerges, which not only mediates between the ruler and the ruled—as was the case in the occasional management—but actually regulates admittance to the ruler. The commonly accepted agreement between the ruler and the ruled may collapse in this phase, as evidenced by the patrimonial state's increased need for legitimation. As a result, a complex relationship of dependence emerges between the ruler and the aristocratic stratum of officials.[34] The conception of the patrimonial state,

---

30. Under favorable environmental conditions, the phase of the primitive patrimonial state can outlast the founder generation.

31. Archeologically, the stage of the primitive patrimonial state leaves only few traces outside the capital. The capital is supposed to have undergone a certain extension during this phase. The structure of the regional settlements would not necessarily indicate any changes. The few presently available literary records from and about these beginnings indicate that the theme of legitimacy of the ruler-position may have played a prominent part.

32. Cf. Weber, *Wirtschaft*, pp. 592-94.

33. Cf. Weber, *Wirtschaft*, pp. 596-602.

34. Archaeologically, the phase of the transition to the corporate patrimonial state may probably be evidenced by archive material, and perhaps by decentralized complexes of new representational buildings in some regions as well. The stage of

in my opinion, allows for a more distinctive interpretation of the ancient Near Eastern societies than the orientation toward the concept of modern state as a guiding principle. The notion of the patrimonial state still requires modifications through the insights from recent ethno-sociological research.

A model which has substantially preformed the Old Testament argumentation and which has been developed by ethno-sociological research is that of chiefdom.[35] The stage of chiefdom has been conceptualized by Elman Service as the evolutionary pre-stage of the primary state.[36] Two factors are to be considered when using this concept heuristically. 1) The chiefdom, as conceptualized by Service, is endogenous, and it is a necessary transitional phase leading to the primary state. 2) The data on which Service's model is based are almost entirely derived from the observation of insular societies in the Pacific. Carneiro[37] demonstrated that, under the conditions of geographical and/or ecological environmental circumscription of agricultural land, chiefdoms and states generally emerge. The nature of the environmental circumscription must be such that the population cannot spatially evade political pressure and has to be subject to the dominant political power. The purely endogenous emergence of a centralized authority takes place only when political conflicts have to be resolved within a clearly circumscribed area.

corporate patrimonialism may have found its archaeological expression not only in archives and in some representational buildings, but also in the phenomenon of an even distribution of so-called manor houses throughout the entire country, the emergence of super-regional markets outside the capital, and the development of socioeconomic strata within and between the settlements, so that four categories of settlements become evident: the previously existing type of settlement—which may have been a city or a village—a regional market center, and a capital.

35. Flanagan was the first to adopt this concept, and he interpreted the rulerships of Saul and David as chiefdoms; cf. J.W. Flanagan, 'Court History or Succession Document? A Study of 2 Samuel 9–20 and 1 Kings 1–2', *JBL* 91 (1972), pp. 172-81.

36. According to Service, this stage is characterized by the following features: a centralized leadership, a chief's hierocratic position and function, a monopoly in regard to the redistribution of consumer goods, an inherited status hierarchy, and primogeniture. Cf. E. Service, *Origins of the State and Civilization* (New York, 1975).

37. R. Carneiro, 'A Theory of the Origin of the State', *Science* 169 (1970), pp. 733-38; *idem*, 'From Autonomous Villages to the State. A Numerical Estimation', in B. Spooner (ed.), *Population Growth: Anthropological Implications* (Cambridge, MA: Harvard University Press, 1981), pp. 64-76.

Service's accumulated data are based entirely on the observation of such spatially restricted and circumscribed societies. The insular societies which formed the basis of Service's studies resemble furthermore the extreme case of this type.[38]

In my opinion, both elements are constitutive of Service's conception of 'chiefdom'. They only permit its use as an interpretative category for stereotypical ruling conditions if the requirements are met within the analyzed society as well: that is, 1) the primary formation of the state and 2) a living environment circumscribed by natural areas.

Chiefdom, as a permanent form of political association, is hardly probable in the immediate vicinity of primary states. Conditions of geographical isolation, comparable to an island or a river valley enclosed by deserts, are not present in Palestine. The development of state-conditions in this geographical region does not occur on grounds that are politically uncultivated.

Even if reckoning with attempts at conscious dissociation from the earlier state-organization in parts of regions of the Israelite settlement area, this earlier organization definitely correlates with the counter-movement's renewed organization. The pre-Israelite culture of city-states had not disappeared from the inhabitant's consciousness when the economic decline occurred. Besides, they appear to have continued to exist in a few cities belonging to Israel.[39] Likewise, the Egyptian provincial system lasted, at least in parts of the country, until the beginning of the tenth century.[40]

The influence of the great ancient Near Eastern empires, and their exemplary effect in regard to the formation of political associations in the border regions, did not disappear together with the temporary military retreat. The notion of chiefdom, devised by Service, is not able to sufficiently describe the formation of political associations in tenth-century Palestine.[41]

38. Cf. also N. Yoffee, 'Too Many Chiefs? (or Safe Texts for the 90s)', in N. Yoffee and N.A. Sherratt (eds.), *Archaeological Theory: Who Sets the Agenda?* (Cambridge: Cambridge University Press, 1989), pp. 60-78.

39. Such as, for instance, the Gibeonite tetrapolis, Jerusalem, Megiddo, Thaanach.

40. Probably in Gezer, presumably in Bethshean.

41. The regionally differing course of settlements' histories permits the conclusion that certain factors, varying from region to region, have contributed to the general formation of political associations.

2. *The Model of the Early State*

On the basis of empirical studies, the team of researchers around Henri Claessen, Ronald Cohen, and Peter Skalnik has established the thesis that a complex form of political and economic organization, such as the state, develops when several factors simultaneously modify and influence each other.[42] The driving forces which promote the emergence of the early state are made up of: population growth and pressure, war and the threat of war, conquests and raids, advances in production and the emergence of surplus, tributes, a common ideology and concepts of legitimation, and influence from states already in existence.

The research of Claessen and others includes the analysis of the early state-stages of more than twenty societies distributed all around the world. Consequently, their results are more reliable than the theories which have been derived from the studies of single African or Oceanic societies. According to the analyses of Claessen and others, the empirical early forms of the state reveal the following typical characteristics:[43]

1. The population is so numerous that socioeconomic stratification and specialization may set in, and with it an established need for coordinating daily activities. The minimum lies at 500 individuals.

2. Early states have a definite territory, which is regionally distinct, but whose outer borders are loosely marked.[44]

3. An early state has its own political organization and central government. The keeping up of civil order is largely based on authority. There is one governmental center and one royal court. Specialists exist only at the highest administrative level, provided that an administrative hierarchy has established itself. Codified law, a professionalized justice system, and a police corps are the exception.

4. The state is *de facto* independent; the government is in control of the power for preventing the permanent separation of territorial regions,

42. H.J.M. Claessen and P. Skalnik (eds.), *The Early State* (Den Haag, Paris, New York, 1978), pp. 15ff.

43. Cf. Claessen and Skalnik, *Early State*, pp. 586ff; furthermore H.J.M. Claessen and P. Skalnik (eds.), *The Study of the State* (Den Haag, Paris, New York, 1981); S.L. Seaton and H.J.M. Claessen (eds.), *Political Anthropology. The State of the Art* (Den Haag, Paris, New York, 1979); H.J.M. Claessen and P. van der Velde (eds.), *Early State Dynamics* (Leiden: Brill, 1987).

44. With few exceptions, all people permanently living on this territory are regarded as citizens, i.e. they are subordinate to the central power.

and for counteracting outer threats. The sovereign is the supreme military leader and has a bodyguard. The population is liable to military service.

5. The population shows a minimum of social stratification: the group of rulers is distinct from the majority of the population—which is the group being ruled.

6. The level of production is high enough to attain a surplus regularly, which is supposed to serve the maintenance of the state organization. The main income of the sovereign consists of taxes which are imposed on specific occasions, of services and of presents. The imposition of regular taxes appears first in the fully developed early state, but in general it is not common. The state's function of redistribution is ordinarily limited to the distribution of the surplus to the administration, and to the furnishing of sacrifices. The individual social units are economically autonomous. Normally, taxes are delivered to the state-administration by the kinship units liable to taxation, and each authority, beginning with the local collector's office, keeps its share before passing on the tax. In the majority of the cases, the right of land-ownership lies with bigger social units such as clans and villages. There are groups without the right of land-ownership, such as artisans, servants, slaves, and traders. Market economy, private ownership, and general social antagonism do not appear until the transition toward the fully developed, mature state.

7. Rulers base their positions on explicit ideas of legitimation, which are derived from an existing ideology of reciprocity. State ideology, especially of legitimation, is are evident in all states under analysis.[45] Not in all cases is the ruler the supreme law-maker and judge. In his function as the military commander-in-chief, he presents himself to the people as a protector. He compensates his servants, and he distributes presents and rewards among them; but he also rewards the people by providing celebrations and public buildings.[46] Ordinarily the ruler bears the expense for the periodic sacrifices to the gods. The state-ideology is supported and spread by the priesthood. In general, access to the priesthood is not yet closed.

---

45. The ruler can legitimize his position mythically by the reclamation of descent, or by the employment of deities. He conducts sacred rites himself, and he guarantees to keep law and order; cf. moreover Claessen and Skalnik, *Early State*, pp. 555ff; *idem*, *Study*, pp. 475ff.

46. Cf. Claessen and Skalnik, *Early State*, p. 564.

Further typical characteristics of the early state cannot be verified, as for instance the urbanization or documented writings of all administrative levels. The early state distinguishes itself from the chiefdom by permanently preventing the separation of territorial regions, and by a pronounced ideology of legitimation. As a rule, the concepts of legitimation of the early state are more distinct than those of the chiefdom. The ideology of reciprocity, and the sacral safeguarding of the ruler's position as well as the state's order itself, correlate in an explicit state-ideology; the genealogical legitimization of the ruler's position becomes less important, though the kinship system still prevails over the society.

According to Claessen and others, the ethnological data suggest distinguishing of three development phases at the stage of the early state: 1) the inchoative early state, 2) the typical early state and 3) the transitional early state.[47]

The inchoative early state is characterized by the following features. Kinship and community-ties dominate the political structures. Common ownership of land is the rule. Trade and market are of inferior significance. Taxes consist of occasional labor for the state, which is effected *ad hoc*, voluntary contributions, and tributary gifts. With regard to their subsistence, the sovereign and the ruling stratum are dependent on the income of their own land. The dominance of the ruling stratum is shaped more politically and ideologically rather than economically. There are few full-time specialists. For their duties, officials receive compensations that generally consist only of natural produce and land allocations. The succession to political offices is hereditary. The judicial system is informal, there are no codifications of law or full-time judges. The social differences between the ruling stratum and their subjects are reduced by the practice of reciprocity, and, ideologically, they are denied. Communal and tribal ideologies of religion exist parallel to the rise of the state ideology. The influence of the pre-state ideology is considerable. The emerging state ideology revolves around the problem of justifying the difference between the ruler and his subjects, and of perpetuating the state beyond its immediate cause. The legitimation of the state as a social establishment is largely carried out by religious specialists. The priests manufacture and spread creation-myths about the royal dynasty.

The second phase, the typical early state, has the following characteristics: Kinship relations are counterbalanced by local relations. Trade

---

47. Cf. Claessen and Skalnik, *Early State*, pp. 589ff, 640ff

and markets have developed on a supra-local level. Regular taxes are imposed in the form of natural produce and obligatory services. Competition and appointment become essential in filling administrative posts rather than descent. Besides customary compensation, officials start to receive pay. Redistribution and reciprocity determine the relationships between the social strata. Private ownership of land is still limited, but the state is slowly growing into the role of an influential landlord.

The third phase, the transitional early state, is characterized by the following features. Kinship-relations affect only marginal aspects of political actions. Private ownership of the means of production is asserting itself as well as the market economy, and an open antagonism of classes arises. The administrative machinery is controlled by appointed officials. Officials listed on the pay-roll are more numerous than those receiving remunerations. The governmental machine slowly develops into a relatively independent political force. The tax and contribution system is fully developed, and is maintained by a complex apparatus to ensure the continual flow of taxes. The codification of the law is completed, and the law is primarily carried out by the authority of full-time judges.

The essential features of the model of the early state, as devised by Claessen and others, exhibits remarkable resemblances with Max Weber's conception of the patrimonial state. This is demonstrated by the distinction of three developmental phases, by their rationalizing tendencies, and by the conceptualization of each phase. The examples of the late phase of the primitive patrimonial state and of the inchoative state respectively point out the characteristics common to both conceptions: no market economy, autonomous economic units, communal ownership of land, occasional management, tributary- and self-financing of the royal court, consensus between the ruler and the ruled, ideology of reciprocity, compulsory legitimation for the state-system of government.

The assessment of Claessen and others deviates from Weber in the description of the parallel developments of the relative status of the ruler and the group of officials. According to Weber and Claessen, the stratum of officials develops to become the political counterbalance to the ruler, and, as political mediators, they become the agency between the ruler and the ruled. According to Weber, the officials are appointed to their offices initially, and later they appropriate their offices by descent. Claessen and others, on the other hand, reconstruct the reverse development from their data; the officials inherit their offices after the second generation and, in the third phase, appointments become predominant. The difference in the materials analyzed may be the cause for this difference. Weber's assessment is largely based on descriptions of the conditions in ancient and medieval states of the northern hemisphere; Claessen's analysis, on the other hand, is based on data about ancient and modern states that lie predominantly in the southern hemisphere.

A further variation lies in the evaluation of the emerging contribution- and tax-system. According to Weber, the existing tributary system is displaced by a regular leiturgical system. Claessen and others, on the other hand, argue that a tributary system changes into a regular administrative system. This disagreement may be based not so much on the data but rather on Weber's preferred ideal type of the Roman imperial state and its refinancing system. In respect of the heuristic value of each concept, the notion of Claessen and others appears more open than Weber's. In the following, I will try to analyze the biblical record on the early state by applying the criteria used by both Weber and Claessen. The criteria used here are:

1. population size
2. territory
3. centralized government
4. political independence
5. stratification
6. productivity of surplus and tributes
7. common ideology and concepts of legitimacy

3. Biblical Records

Biblical records illustrate the development of several conceptualizations of the state. Without a doubt, the most interesting is recorded in Deut. 16.18–18.22, namely the critical reflection of the Israelite or Judaic state seen from the perspective of the sixth century.[48] The authors of this conception regard the development of the state's monarchical variant as unnecessary. The state, as outlined by Ezekiel, anticipates a prominent ruler whose functions are, however, narrowly limited; furthermore, Ezekiel carefully avoids the title 'king', designating the ruler always as

---

48. Cf. moreover C. Schäfer-Lichtenberger, *Josua und Salomo. Ein Studie zu Autorität und Legitimität des Nachfolgers im Alten Testament* (VTSup, 58; Leiden: Brill, 1995), pp. 69-106.

נשיא. Memories of the emergence of the monarchical state are not included in these concepts, notwithstanding the implication of the authors of the law on the king (Deut. 17.14-20); they regard the monarchy—as a form of political organization—to be a latecomer in Israel's societal history.

Another perspective is taken by the books of Samuel and of Kings. 1 Samuel 8–1 Kings 11 offers a portrayal of the emergence and extension of the monarchy which does not question the monarchical state as such. Both content and form of these records presuppose the state as a facilitating institution.[49] Their emergence within the setting of non-state conditions is hardly probable, as indicated by the themes 'legitimacy of governmental system of the state', 'continuity of the leadership', 'legitimacy of Saul's succession by David' and 'political enemies'. These themes go beyond the scope of a genealogically oriented family history. Such a record is improbable under societal conditions that are structured purely on family relations.[50] The image of the monarchy's emergence portrayed by these texts is, from a sociological perspective, very complex. The contrivance of the themes in the late post-exilic time-period, the appropriate description of their structures in the early stages of a state, and their projection back into the eleventh–tenth centuries BCE are, from a sociological point of view, extremely improbable.

The comparison of the traditions about Saul and David in the books of Samuel and Chronicles reveals that the problems of the 'legitimation of the new constitution', and of the 'succession' do not appear in Chronicles. Likewise, the problem of 'continuity of political leadership',[51] typical for the beginning phase of the state, is no longer

49. Cf. N. Lohfink, *Rückblick im Zorn auf den Staat. Vorlesungen zu ausgewählten Schlüsseltexten der Bücher Samuel und Könige* (privately published: Frankfurt am Main, 1984), pp. 19-34.

50. Particular characteristics of state records are: yearly accounts, the branding of the king's political opponents as rabble-rousers and the reflection on the legitimacy of the governing system of the state. The personalized depiction of structural conflicts and political differences is a means of state ideology, which allows for the toning down of reported confrontations, and for the disguise of the apparent failures of the political leadership.

51. With regard to the problem of the succession under monarchical conditions, cf. Schäfer-Lichtenberger, *Josua und Salomo*, pp. 107, 219-27, 356-64. A theoretical discussion on the problem 'continuity of the leadership' is presented in the portrayal of the relationship between Moses and Joshua and in the stylization of the Joshua

contemplated. Comparing the records of Chronicles with those of the books of Samuel and Kings proves, in my opinion, that the portrayal given in the latter is not a retrospective projection from a later era.

Even when assuming that the historical books reflect history in general but err in the particulars, their record still contributes to historical knowledge about the tenth century; it does so when sociological analysis demonstrates a correspondence between the structural development described in the record and the logic of the early state's development. The literary construction of a conception of the early state, with all of its typical problems and structural shortcomings, under conditions of the fully developed state, is not plausible. This hypothesis, occasionally contended in research, assumes that the analyzed authors have taken an objective-distancing position toward their subject, a position hardly conceivable in ancient times. Moreover, this hypothesis insinuates that the biblical authors had sociological knowledge which has been established only since the second half of the twentieth century.

a. *The Records of Saul's Rule*[52]

Population size. We can only estimate how many inhabitants of the hill country and the bordering areas accepted Saul as the sovereign. The smallest account given for his army (600 men—1 Sam. 13.15) allows of the assertion that the minimum of 500 persons required for the early state has been exceeded.

Territory. The territory governed by Saul is regionally differentiated, as indicated in 2 Sam. 2.9.[53] The outer boundaries are contested by Israel and its neighbors to the west, the Philistines, as well as the neighbors to the east (Moab, Ammon). Saul exerts his claim on a certain territory both defensively (1 Sam. 11.13) and offensively (1 Sam. 14). Toward the

figure. The distinction of the line of thought of both arguments exposes the difference between speculative (Joshua figure) and historically oriented (Solomon figure) reflection.

52. In the following illustration of Saul's rule, only those biblical texts that are attributed with historical or sociological plausibility according to the current level of research are analyzed. That is why accounts such as Samuel's rejection of Saul (1 Sam. 13.7-15; 15.10-35) and the Goliath episode (1 Sam. 17) are not under consideration.

53. In regard to the extent of the territory of Saul, cf. D.W. Edelman, 'The "Ashurites" of Eshbaal's State', *PEQ* 117 (1985), pp. 85-91; and G.W. Ahlström, *Who Were the Israelites?* (Winona Lake, IN: Eisenbrauns, 1986), pp. 88-96.

south, the boundary becomes frayed. There appear to be groups in the Judaic mountain range which accepted Saul's territorial claims when enforced, as in the cases of Keilah (1 Sam. 23.7-13) and of Ziph (1 Sam. 23.19ff.).

Centralized government. Israel has a government center in Gibeah under Saul's rule. The government essentially consists of the king and members of his royal household. The royal household is paraphrased as עבדי שאול (1 Sam. 16.15; 18.5, 23-24, 30; 22.9; עבדי המלך in 22.17) or עבדיו (1 Sam. 16.17; 19.1; 22.6; 28.7, 23, 25). Clearly assigned functions for military (1 Sam. 14.50b; 16.21; 18.5), for economic (21.8; 22.9; 2 Sam. 9.2), and for ritualistic purposes (14.3; 22.11-19; particularly 22.15) are discernible. The text does not reveal the existence of a civil administration and a regular tax-system. Only gifts are recorded as contributions (10.27). Next to the income of his own household, Saul possibly had shares of the booty, in the form of moveables as well as immovables, at his disposal (14.32-35; 22.7). The king may request qualified personnel to serve at the court (1 Sam 16.19-22). Various groups are distinguishable in court service: the closest male relatives take on military offices; furthermore the עבדי שאול and the נערים appear in serving as well as in advising functions, some of them being responsible for the management of the royal household (21.8; 22.9). The composition of the personnel at court—relatives and personally dependent persons—corresponds with the composition of the patrimonial *oikos* and the inchoative state respectively.

The political administration is an occasional one. Saul sends messengers (רצים, מלאכים) with obligatory commands (16.19-21; 19.11, 14-16), and he employs a messenger system to keep him informed (16.2; 23.27). The messengers may also carry out police tasks (19.11; 22.17). Saul's commands are generally obeyed. Domestic affairs in Saul's rule are essentially carried out by keeping warriors employed at the court (10.26; 13.2; 14.52), by keeping the control over the Yahweh-temple and over the priesthood of Nob which is regarded as Elide (14.3, 18-19; 21.2-10; 22.9-19). The ban against certain groups of soothsayers (28.9), which is attributed to Saul, could have been one of the controlling measures of domestic politics.

Lodging and food at the court (16.22; 18.2; 20.25) as well as land allocations (22.7) are cited as remuneration for the officials. The king probably passed on part of the spoils of war purposefully, as attested by the corresponding prize in the lamentation of the dead (2 Sam. 1.24). Saul's economic activity corresponds to that of the extended *oikos*.

Political independence. Political independence becomes evident in the building up of a military organization (13.2, 15; 14.52). Saul is the supreme commander: he has an army leader (14.50), he has commanders over regiments of 1000 and battalions of 100 (22.7), he has his own bodyguards (מִשְׁמַעַת, 22.14), and he has armor-bearers (16.21; 31.4). Saul also has a standing corps (אַנְשֵׁי הַמִּלְחָמָה, 10.26; 18.5) at his disposal. He demands military service and his request is respected (13.2-4; 14.52; 24.3). He appoints relatives to significant military positions. This practice, too, corresponds to that of the inchoative state and the early patrimonial state, respectively. Saul bases the sovereignty of his territory on the successful warding off of the Philistine claim for dominance (1 Sam. 13.1-7, 15-23; 14), and he also defends the territory against neighbors (1 Sam. 11.1-11, Ammon; 1 Sam. 15.1-9, Amalek; 1 Sam. 14.47-48, Moab, Zobah, Edom), and is active in preventing looting crowds (14.48). The political association would have dissolved immediately after Saul's definite defeat at Gilboa and his death, if his sovereignty was constituted as a chiefdom. The succession to the rule of the only surviving son of the king, Eshbaal, indicates that the rulership association was not being held together solely by loyalty toward the supreme commander.[54] The keeping up of the common political organization, in spite of the defeat and the death of the king, is an indication that the political structures were established to a degree that was independent of the person and the ruler-position of the commander. The association was advanced beyond the era of chiefdoms. Under the conditions of chiefdom, Abner would have had been elected the ruler, being the politically most competent leader from Saul's clan. It is Eshbaal, and not Abner, who becomes king, because only Eshbaal has an appropriately efficient *oikos* at his disposal to finance the political organization. Choosing Eshbaal rather than David at this point in time can be regarded as a demonstration of political independence from the Philistines.

54. It can be assumed that the identity of interests of the regions of Gilead, Asher, Jezreel, Ephraim and Benjamin has found its expression in existing institutions; their continued existence seemed indispensable to a political group of officials gathered around Abner.

Stratification. All political acts are initiated by Saul. Saul has the final say in political affairs.[55] Officials acting on their own behalf are guilty of high treason (16.2; 22.6-19, 22). Within the political sphere, Saul is regarded the highest authority, and he requires obedience toward him. Saul uses force where his authority fails (22.6-19; 23.7-13). The opposition between Saul and David is described as a political one.[56] The differentiation between the ruler and the ruled is established.

Productivity of surplus and tributes. The texts contain only a few statements about the financing of the political organization, and they contain almost nothing about the socioeconomic sphere outside the state. It is inconsequential to speculate on this. Four different sources of income can be identified: gifts (10.27), booty (13, 14), income of Saul's own household, and services (14.54; 18.19). The existence of a standing army can be considered an indication of a surplus economy.

Common ideology and concepts of legitimacy. The establishment of the monarchy requires legitimation, as pointed out in the accounts of 1 Samuel 9–11. Saul's kingdom is legitimized in three ways: by calling on the will of the deity, by the choice of the people, and by success. The expression of Israel's unity is manifested by the king's position and the king as a person. The person of King Saul is considered sacrosanct (24.7-8; 26.11, 16; 2 Sam. 1.14-16). The priesthood is under the control of the king (1 Sam. 22.9-19).

On balance, we may say that Saul's rulership is characterized by the typical features of an inchoative state.

b. *The Records of David's Rule*
2 Samuel 2–1 Kings 1. I do not intend to analyze the earlier period of David's career in more detail since it is less significant for the evaluation of the established political structures.

Population size. The texts allow of the unmistakable conclusion that during the era in Hebron, the population under David's rule already consisted of more than 500 persons.

---

55. 1 Sam. 13.4—Saul is regarded the person responsible, and not Jonathan; 14.16-23; 18.5, 13.
56. 1 Sam. 18.16; 20.31; 23.7-13; 23.19-28.

Territory. From Hebron, David rules over a circumscribed territory which is considerably increased by the later political union with Israel. He wins sovereignty in the wars with the Philistines (2 Sam 5.17; 8.1), and he defends it in fights against the Aramaeans (2 Sam 8.3-8). During the battles against the neighbors, the borders of the territory are shifted toward the east (2 Sam 8.2, 12-14). Everyone living in that territory is subjugated to his rule (2 Sam 8.2, 6, 14).

Centralized government. The governmental center is at first in Hebron (2 Sam. 2.3-4) and later on in Jerusalem (2 Sam. 5.6ff.). David's personal following settles down in the respective capital. At first the government consists of the king and the members of his royal household. At least two phases are evident in establishing the political organization, the time in Hebron and the time in Jerusalem. There are indications that a reorganization of certain administrative areas took place after the Absalom rebellion.[57]

To David's following in Hebron belong his men (אנשיו, 2 Sam. 2.3; 5.6, 21; 16.13; 19.42);[58] the leader of this group is always David. The men are settled in villages around Hebron. This procedure accommodates the personal following, and at the same time is a control device for domestic affairs. Another group is led by Joab on military campaigns; to this group belong נערים (2 Sam. 2.14; 2.21; 18.15) and the עבדי דוד (2 Sam. 2.17; 3.22, 38). The עבדים and נערים are at the court in Hebron. The latter serve David as a police force (2 Sam. 1.15; 4.12). Another group of functionaries, מלאכים, are mentioned (2 Sam. 2.5; 3.14) who deliver political messages to David. A harem, consisting of six women and a corresponding group of children, reside at the court. The details given about the harem may be an indication of David's purposeful politics of marriage (2 Sam. 3.2-5). The size of the harem presupposes an adequate economic capacity on David's part. There are, however, no indications about a contributory system. The court in Hebron is supplied by booty (2 Sam. 3.22); further income sources are not evident in the texts. Since a contract between David and his men founded David's rule over Judah, it can be assumed that mutual services had been part of the

57. Cf. C. Schäfer-Lichtenberger, 'Exodus 18—Zur Begründung königlicher Gerichtsbarkeit in Israel-Juda', *DBAT* 21 (1985), pp. 61-85.

58. David's following plays a more eminent role during the time before Hebron; cf. 1 Sam. 18.27; 23.3, 5, 8, 13, 26; 24.4-5, 7-8, 23; 25.13, 20; 27.3, 8; 29.2, 11; 30.1, 3, 31.

agreement.[59] During the time period in Hebron, it appears that, with the exception of messengers, there was no differentiation among the officials within David's following. The classification אנשים, נערים and עבדים was used for designating the social-legal status of the people.

David's government in Jerusalem offers a more diversified picture. The group labeled as 'David's men' disappears almost entirely after having followed David to Jerusalem. The group only appears as David's following at the beginning and after the Absalom rebellion (2 Sam. 16.13; 19.42).[60] The נערים as a military group continues to be assigned to Joab (2 Sam. 18.15; 20.11); single members are deployed as guards (2 Sam. 13.34) or as servants to a prince (2 Sam. 13.17). The news-delivery by the מלאכים remains intact. As a collective designation for the people at the court who do not belong to David's clan phrases containing עבד are frequently used.[61] Subsuming of the people at court under this term indicates their closeness to the ruler, as well as their dependent position in the relation between the ruler and the ruled.[62]

David's governmental transactions become more diversified and so, accordingly, does the political organization of his rule.[63] The texts make

59. Cf. the negotiations between Jephthah and the elders of Gilead (Judg. 11.9-11).

60. 2 Sam. 21.17 mentions 'David's men' one more time in the form of a narrative account. The 'list' reflects the conditions at the time of the Philistine battles; in regard to the difficulty in determining dates, cf. H.J. Stoebe, *Das zweite Buch Samuelis* (KAT, 8.2; Gütersloh, 1994), pp. 465-66.

61. Such as עבדי דוד (2 Sam. 10.2; 12.18; mercenary 2 Sam. 11.17; 18.7, 9), עבדי המלך (2 Sam. 11.24; mercenary 15.15; 16.6; 1 Kgs 1.9), עבדי אדוניו / אדוניך (2 Sam. 11.9, 13; mercenary 2 Sam. 11.11; 20.6), or simply עבדיו (2 Sam. 10.2-3; 12.19, 21; 13.31, 36; 15.14, 18; 16.11; 24.20; 1 Kgs 1.2; mercenary: 2 Sam. 11.1; 21.15; 21.22). The title עבד המלך is no longer found in records about Solomon's time in 1 Kings 2–11, and nor is the term עבד שלמה. Jeroboam is called עבד לשלמה (1 Kgs 11.26). The disappearance of the relations-term עבד in the record of Solomon may indicate structural changes at the court.

62. The use of the relational term עבד for David's officials also indicates that the court does not yet consist of a stratum of notabilities and representatives.

63. In regard to terms of offices, cf. T.N.D. Mettinger, *Solomonic State Officials. A Study of the Civil Government Officials of the Israelite Monarchy* (ConBOT, 5; Lund: Gleerup, 1971). On the basis of comparing data from Alalakh and Ugarit, H. Donner arrives at the conclusion that Canaanite models laid the foundation for David's administrative system; cf. H. Donner, 'Studien zur Verfassungs- und Verwaltungsgeschichte der Reiche Israel und Juda' (ThD dissertation, Leipzig, 1956), pp. 8-10, 61-97.

a task-oriented administration evident; military-, civil-, and cult-offices are combined in separate departments.[64] The list of David's ministers in 2 Sam. 8.16-18 mentions two military and three civilian positions.[65] Appointment to the positions takes place according to qualifications. The establishment of the civil administration (recorder, priest, secretary) and the employment of advisers (Ahitophel, Hushai) allows of the conclusion of a more complex organization of governmental practices. The ministers' list can be understood as an indication of the existence of more subordinate administrative levels. It is not determinable whether or not and at which point in time a contributory system was introduced for the entire empire under David. 2 Sam. 24.1-9 refers to clashes as the result of a census ordered by David. A census is the prerequisite for establishing a common contributory system.[66] The ethno-sociological data indicate that states on this level of structuredness are in no need of a locally positioned administration outside the capital since this function is fulfilled by the kinship organization. The administration of the conquered provinces requires its own system.[67] It cannot be determined which chief minister was assigned to the provinces' administration.[68]

The second ministers' list of 2 Sam. 20.23-26 contains changes in the sequence of offices, and a new position is noted, that of the minister of forced labor. The newly created position is third in rank, after that of the army commander and that of the commander of the mercenary force. The order of rank of the civilian officers' list (recorder, secretary, priest) shows a change too, the priest position being last in rank now. Notable is the mentioning of a priest—designated to David—after the names of both of the main priests. This documents the monarch's claim to the right of appointing priests, regardless of the religious tradition, and

---

64. The absence of a commonly designated term for offices in the list of David's ministers, such as שׂר, may be an indication that these lists originate from the early period of the monarchy, when the monarchical administration was constructed and not yet established. Cf. U. Rüterswörden, *Die Beamten der israelitischen Königszeit. Eine Studie zu śr und vergleichbaren Begriffen* (BWANT, 117; Stuttgart: Kohlhammer, 1983), pp. 92-95.

65. Regarding the ministers' lists, cf. U. Rüterswörden (Beamten, 1985), pp. 71-91.

66. Joab undertakes the census accompanied by שׂרי החיל (2 Sam. 24.2, 4). The title is found only in this context. חיל can also have the meaning of wealth.

67. 2 Sam. 8.2: Moab became David's עבדים; 8.6: David elevated נצבים over Damascus; and Edom likewise, 8.14.

68. According to 2 Kgs 12.10, the *sōpher* is in charge of finances.

independently of the position's hereditary structure. The new order of rank reflects the changes in the political structures. The exercise of power and control becomes predominant. The north had tried in vain to secede from David's political union. After a failed secession attempt, it is likely that a political controlling authority was introduced which was independent from the kinship system. Setting up the superintendence of forced labor may indicate an increased need for construction and an altered income situation, but in part it may also indicate the exercise of political control. The admission of a priest from eastern Jordan into the ministers' list could suggest the increased significance of the east Jordanian regions, but at the same time a form of subtle political control.

The legal system of the Israelite cities and clans was not affected by the monarchy. The case of the woman from Tekoa (2 Sam. 14.1-11), and Absalom's anti-propaganda (2 Sam. 15.2-6) prove that the king was consulted as an arbitrator in instances which could not be resolved by traditional law. Non-Israelite cities, such as Gibeon, had to consult the king when Israelites committed offenses that were punishable by death (2 Sam. 21.4). A legal system that was largely informal and based on authority is typical of the early state. The Absalom rebellion could have resulted in a reform of the informally practiced legal system as a late consequence.[69] The establishment of a central cult (2 Sam. 6) may have been of considerable influence on the societal structures, and, likewise, the hierarchical annexation of non-Israelite cities, the demand for services, the recruitment of the army, the existence of a standing military force, and the substantial strata of officials called עבדי המלך.

Political independence. The state's independence is gained and defended by war against the Philistines. David's state successfully wards off external threats (2 Sam. 5.17-27; 10). The state can prevent the secession of parts of the country (2 Sam. 15.7-22). The monarch is the supreme army commander (12.28-29; 18.1-2), and the people are obliged to serve in the military. At first the military organization only distinguishes between the army and David's entourage (2 Sam. 11.1). At the beginning of the Absalom rebellion, a reorganization of David's troops takes place, which introduces the commanding ranks of general, commander over regiments of 1000, and commander over battalions of 100 men (2 Sam. 18.1). The king has a mercenary troop at his disposal which is designated

---

69. An indication may be the reference to Exod. 18.13-27; cf. Schäfer-Lichtenberger, 'Exodus 18', pp. 77-85.

to him, and which always remains under his command (2 Sam. 11.11b; 18.1, 9; 23.8ff.). David's state shows the *differencia specifica* as against chiefdom: the forcible defense of the territorial unity of his dominion.

Stratification. The distinction between the ruler and the ruled is evident. The group of the so-called עבדי המלך is placed between the ruler and the ruled. David is the central decision authority, and he is regarded the supreme authority which demands obedience in borderline cases.[70] Political opponents are eliminated (Saul's sons, 2 Sam. 21.1-9) or put under arrest at the court (Meribaal ben Jonathan, 2 Sam. 9). Rebels such as Sheba ben Bichri are denounced as standing outside the social order (2 Sam. 20.1), are persecuted by David's mercenaries (20.7) and executed. Influential families are forced to be represented at court (2 Sam. 19.32-40). David decides on his succession independently from the authorities which had brought him to the throne (1 Kgs 1.28-35).

Productivity of surplus and tributes. The texts contain almost no information about the socioeconomic area outside the state. The existence of a standing army and the accommodation of an extensive court and of the centralized cult is indicative of an economy producing surplus. The regularly demanded army recruitment and conscription of labor are only conceivable against the background of a corresponding economic basis. A supra-local trade is not evident in the texts; this, however, may be due to the specific interests behind the messages given. Trade over long distances appears to be the exception as well, as indicated by the mentioning of contacts with Tyre (2 Sam. 5.11). It can be assumed that the tributary contributions from conquered provinces and the establishing of a state cult has led to the founding of regional markets.

Various income source are evident: gifts (8.10; 16.27ff.), booty (2 Sam 8.4, 7-8; 12.30), tributes (8.2, 6), crown estate,[71] forced labor (12.31; 20.24), and services (1 Kgs 1.4). Expenditures included construction,[72]

---

70. Cf. the following instances: the request for Bathsheba, 2 Sam. 11; deciding positively on the case of the widow of Tekoa, 2 Sam. 14; the handing over of the Saulides, 2 Sam. 21; requesting Abishag of Sunem, 1 Kgs 1.1-4.

71. The following are indications of the existence of crown estate: 2 Sam. 9: returning Saul's belongings; 2 Sam. 13.23: Absalom's sheepshearing at Baalhazor; 2 Sam. 14.30: Absalom's and Joab's field close to Jerusalem.

72. The extension of the acropolis, 2 Sam. 5.9, and the building of the palace, 5.11.

the employment of bodyguards (עבדי המלך), the foreign legion (Kreti and Pleti), the harem, the state cult, and the officials. The officials are accommodated by boarding at the court and by land allocations. Natural prebends are not recorded; in view of the tributary income, however, they are probable.

Common ideology and concepts of legitimacy. The establishment of the monarchy is no longer in need of legitimation, as the accounts in 2 Sam. 2.4 and 2 Sam. 5.1-3 indicate, without further commentary. David's kingdom is based on a contract with the men of Judah (2 Sam. 2.4) and the contract with the elders of Israel (5.3), the latter acting in agreement with the tribes of Israel. The marriage of Saul's daughter, Michal, may give the impression of a hereditary succession practice of David's ruler-ship. The legitimacy of David's rulership over Israel is contested by the Benjaminite clans. David's counter-propaganda is intended to portray him as a faithful, yet unrecognized follower of Saul (1 Sam. 24; 26), and as a blood-feud avenger of his father-in-law and his brother-in-law (2 Sam. 1.1-16; 4). David's election to the throne is portrayed as an expression of divine predestination (2 Sam. 5.2b), and it leads to the development of a religious leadership ideology, which culminates in the divine promise of an enduring dynasty (2 Sam. 7.11-16).

Cult and cult personnel are conformed according to the state's inter-ests. David adopts the existing non-Yahwistic cultic places (Gibeon, Jerusalem) and personnel (Zadok, Nathan). The priesthood is under the control of the king. The bringing of the ark to the temple of Jerusalem (2 Sam. 6) marks the beginning of an established public cult of the state. By leading this inaugurating procession with the sacrifices, the king demonstrates his right of having the cult at his disposal (2 Sam. 6.5, 14-19).

On balance, in areas such as population size, territory, political inde-pendence and ideology, David's state is—as evidenced in biblical texts—in its third phase, namely on the level of the transitional state; whereas in the areas of centralized government, stratification and surplus economy, the stage of the inchoative state has been reached, and some charac-teristics of the typical early state established.

FROM PATRONAGE SOCIETY TO PATRONAGE SOCIETY

Niels Peter Lemche

At a meeting of the Nordelberische Arbeitsgemeinschaft in the spring of 1993, as I presented the first draft of what was to be the article 'Is It Still Possible to Write a History of Israel?',[1] Klaus Koch correctly drew the conclusion that after having removed most if not all of Israel's pre-state history, it was only natural and logical to direct the shooting towards the so-called United Monarchy. There is no longer any reason to consider this a period that from a historian's point of view should be accepted as it is presented in the Old Testament.

At this conference several contributors have already addressed the question of how Israel became a state. The sophistication of their approach may differ from scholar to scholar, but the general outcome is that a naive acceptance—paraphrase, if you wish to put it thus—of the biblical story as history cannot and should not be accepted anymore. Scholars—especially scholars—should no longer let themselves be dragged around by the nose by pietistic colleagues, nor even by biblical story-tellers who, much better than modern readers, knew the importance of an entertaining story, and who were probably never interested in presenting us with historical facts from days of old.[2]

As I write this paper, I cannot, however, have more than a vague idea of the other contributions to the volume, and accordingly, I will have to refer to what has already been published. The two studies of David Jamieson-Drake and Michael Niemann are of special interest as they have both reached almost the same result—although by different approaches—asserting that there was no state on Judean territory in the

---

1. Now published in *SJOT* 9 (1994), pp. 165-90.
2. Here I have hardly moved since my settlement with Abraham Malamat, 'On the Problem of Studying Israelite History—Apropos Abraham Malamat's View on Historical Research', *BN* 24 (1984), pp. 94-124.

tenth century BCE.[3] It has been interesting, and at the same time rather depressing, to be a witness to the almost total silence about Jamieson-Drake's study in scholarly literature; it would also be wrong to say that Niemann's study has so far attracted the public interest which it deserves, and as Niemann's approach is seemingly traditional—biblicist—I can see little reason for this, except that the language of the publication may nowadays be an obstacle to readers outside Germany. However, another explanation may be more correct: that whereas quite a few colleagues have accepted—after more than thirty years of discussion—that there was nothing like the biblical early Israel, the dismissal of the biblical United Kingdom of David and Solomon would bring havoc upon Jews as well as Christians. The pain threshold has so to speak been crossed, because of the theological consequences of the possibility that there never was a David of history. So people instinctively react against any such suggestion with a hostility that was never displayed (at least to the same degree) when we started demolishing the early history of biblicist Israel.

At a seminar in Copenhagen in April 1995 on 'Jerusalem in Archaeology',[4] it became evident that Jamieson-Drake's book is not a major piece of work. Not so much because of its methodology, which is faultless, but because of the material on which he based his theories. Seemingly, Jamieson-Drake is dependent on material of low scholarly value, dated archaeological reasoning, wrong or simply bad archaeology, misleading conclusions, and so on.[5] However that may be, it is still an obvious hypothesis that so far as the material evidence from Judea in the Iron Age is concerned, there are few traces of anything which can be compared to a state organization before the eighth century—which was in fact also the conclusion reached by Niemann.

3.   D. Jamieson-Drake, *Scribes and Schools in Monarchic Judah: A Socio-Archeological Approach* (The Social World of Biblical Antiquity, 9; JSOTSup, 109; Sheffield: JSOT Press, 1991); H.M. Niemann, *Herrschaft, Königtum und Staat. Skizzen zur soziokulturellen Entwicklung im monarchischen Israel* (Forschungen zum Alten Testament, 6; Tübingen: Mohr, 1993).

4.   Among the participants were Margreet Steiner from Leiden, Patrick McGovern from Philadelphia and John Strange from Copenhagen.

5.   Although to an outsider this must sound almost ridiculous: there is hardly a territory in this world which has been dug so extensively as Palestine. How can it be that after more than a hundred years of excavations several experienced archaeologist are forced to admit that hardly any safe opinion about the status of the Judean territory at the beginning of the first millennium BCE can be reached, that we still have a long way to go before any safe and enduring reconstruction can be presented?

Now it is sometimes maintained that this is immaterial, as we are not looking for a modern state but an ancient one, which was certainly otherwise organized than modern states.[6] So Judah may have been a state after all, in spite of the fact that its organization was, to say the least, embryonic—rudimentary—in comparison to anything that would merit the name of a state in the present world.

Although it is certainly true and not to be disputed that the states of the ancient Near East were not modern states, the argument *per se* is irrelevant, as we—when deciding for statehood in an ancient Palestinian society—are not discussing an ancient theory of states but are presenting our reasoning on the basis of a modern definition of a state. It is rather immaterial whether we accept one scribe as the sole and lonely administrative officer in ancient Jerusalem and maintain that an ancient state did not need more scribes to run the business. The important thing is whether this scribe fulfils the duties and obligations which are parts of a society properly called a 'state', and here Niemann is absolutely right: the few scattered references to administration to be found in the Hebrew Bible hardly make up for the presence of a state. They are only vestiges of a rudimentary administration system which might one day have developed into a proper administrative system of a more complicated society.

Any state definition must perforce contain a number of elements and graduations, as there is of course a very long way to go from the primitive, or rather traditional, organization to be found in tribal societies to the fully developed bureaucratic systems of state societies. From this perspective nothing from Judah in the tenth century BCE indicates that more than the vestiges of a state organization was present at that time and place. This fact cannot be overcome by the argument that if people simply accepted their community to be a state (but how should that be?), then it was a state. This is of course not true. From a sociopolitical perspective a state can only be so called if it fulfils the requirements of organizing and administering society, including the protection both of the citizens and itself as a state organization.

It is on the other hand obvious that the biblical narrative leaves us

6.   This argument was used against my idea of a Hellenistic origin for the Old Testament (cf. N.P. Lemche, 'The Old Testament—A Hellenistic Book?', *SJOT* 7 [1993], pp. 163-93)—especially against my view of the kingdom of David—by F. Willesen, 'Om fantomet David', *DTT* 56 (1993), pp. 249-65. Cf. my answer to this criticism in my 'Det gamle Testamente, hellenismen og David. Svar til Eduard Nielsen og Folker Willesen', *DTT* 57 (1994), pp. 20-39.

with the impression that Jerusalem was the centre of a mighty state and, thanks to Niemann, that the author of the narrative about the United Monarchy in the days of David and Solomon did not know much about what a real empire would demand. Here the biblical narrator is not very different from other ancient authors who, with the exception of Aristotle and perhaps also Plato and a few other Greek philosophers, never display any deep comprehension of how societies are organized and ruled. It is in this connection a truism that if the ancient authors were right in maintaining that almost every Roman emperor was mad and incompetent, it is hardly understandable that this huge political structure could survive for centuries. None of these so-called historians—whether the gossip-monger Suetonius or the supposingly more serious historian Tacitus—has really provided an explanation for the durability of the Roman Empire. However, the orientation of such writers is personalized. Suetonius and Tacitus see history as a series of events pertaining to individuals: to rulers or other persons in direct contact with the ruling few. This is the mode of narration to be found in the Greco-Roman world, and it is certainly the same mode to be encountered in the Hebrew Bible, not least in its description of the history of the United Monarchy.

The harshest criticism to be levelled against Niemann's study on administration is that the authors are not likely to present such facts as will allow a proper reconstruction of the central administration of the period of a David or a Solomon; what we have is in fact merely chit-chat, remarks torn out of context. On this basis it could be argued that Niemann's study is simply inconclusive.

However, he is probably right—as is also Jamieson-Drake—in maintaining that there was no state in ancient Judah before the end of the eighth century BCE at the earliest. Even though Jamieson-Drake's pins and columns may have to be moved around, corrected, or eliminated as one goes along, statistics are on his side, and some of his conclusions may eventually survive even a major revision of the single components of the statistics. Niemann's problem is different, as his conclusions are based on a rather historicist reading of his textual material. However, his narrator did not show any awareness of what a state is all about. That is, the biblical story offers us no evidence of a state.

There is however, another way of entering this debate about the kind of society to be found in the central highlands—especially its southern parts—in the tenth century BCE. That is to discuss the nature of the society supposed to be around in those days.

The normal method would be to discuss the progression from a tribal society to a state: *Die Staatenbildung der Israeliten*, as Albrecht Alt phrased it.[7] This would require that we had a tribal society at one end of the continuum, and at the other a state. Neither of these points of departure is evident. Because of this I decided as an intermediary stage to discuss the progression from a tribal society to a patronage society; but again, what do we really know about tribal societies in Palestine in the period, say, 1300–800? 'Tribe' is such a meaningless word, because it embraces all kinds of traditional—primitive—societies, and because no conclusive definition can be reached as to what a tribe really is—except the conclusion that a tribal society is not a state.[8]

To avoid this problem I have introduced the concept of a *patronage society* as more likely to cover the societal varieties of Syria and especially Palestine in the LBA period. I am at the moment preparing a series of studies on the nature of such societies, some of which are already published; others will appear in the near future.[9] The general idea is that political power structures are personalized because the society is divided into only two groups, the 'haves' and the 'have nots', the first being the so-called 'full citizens' known from the Hebrew Bible, the other part the many destitute to be cared for, the *dalim*, *ebyonim*, or whatever they may be called in Hebrew. This model—often called the 'Mediterranean social system'—seems to be almost ubiquitous in—to

7.   Cf. his article of the same name 'Die Staatenbildung der Israeliten in Palästina' (1930), in his *Kleine Schriften zur Geschichte Israels*, II (1956), pp. 1-65 (ET, 'The Formation of the Israelite State in Palestine', in *Essays on Old Testament History and Religion* [trans. R.A. Wilson; Sheffield: JSOT Press, 1989], pp. 171-237).

8.   Cf. my *Early Israel: Anthropological and Historical Studies on the Israelite Society before the Monarchy* (VTSup, 37; Leiden: Brill, 1985), pp. 231-44 and the literature quoted there.

9.   See my 'Kings and Clients: On Loyalty Between the Ruler and the Ruled in Ancient "Israel", in D.A. Knight (ed.), *Ethics and Politics in the Hebrew Bible*, *Semeia* 66 (Atlanta: Scholars Press, 1995), pp. 119-32; 'Power and Social Organization: Some Misunderstanding and Some Proposals: or Is It all a Question of Patrons and Clients?' and 'The Relevance of Social-critical Exegesis for Old Testament Theology' (both to be published in T.L. Thompson [ed.], *Changing Perspectives in Biblical Interpretation* [Sheffield: Sheffield Academic Press]), and 'Justice in Western Asia in Antiquity, or: Why No Laws Were Needed!', *Chicago–Kent Law Review* 70 (1995), pp. 1695-1716. A monograph devoted to this subject is in the stage of preparation (Sheffield). In New Testament studies the concept of patronage has been extensively used especially by Bruce Malina.

use sociological terms—societies of a certain degree of complexity, however not yet bureaucratic states. They should not be taken to be tribal societies, while on the other hand neither are they feudal societies, although they may at a certain point develop into feudalism proper.[10] Characteristic of a patronage society is its vertical organization, according to which at the top we find the *patron*, a member of a leading lineage, and below him his *clients*, ordinary men and their families. The bond between patron and client is a personal one, the client having sworn allegiance to the patron and the patron having sworn to protect his client.

Once diagnosed, the effects of the patronage system can be found on all levels of society. To mention just one example I may refer to my lecture at a recent conference on ancient law at the Robbins Collection, Berkeley University, in March 1995.[11] Here I traced the reason for the conspicuous absence of laws in Syria and Palestine in the Iron Age back to the existence of patronage systems, which made such laws super-fluous and unnecessary: nobody can really tell his Godfather how to judge.[12] It is also obvious from a closer juridical analysis that the

---

10. See E. Gellner and J. Waterbury, *Patrons and Clients in Mediterranean Societies* (New York and London: Duckworth, 1977). On the development towards feudalism in the LBA period, cf. M. Liverani, 'Communautés rurales dans la Syrie du IIe millénaire a. C.', *Recuils de la Société Jean Bodin pour l'histoire comparative des institutions* 41 (1983), pp. 147-85. Here Liverani describes how the independence of the village society is threatened by the donation of villages as fiefs to privileged members of the palace community.

11. Cf. 'Justice in Western Asia in Antiquity'.

12. The Book of the Covenant belongs, as has been effectively demonstrated by for example S.M. Paul (*Studies in the Book of the Covenant in the Light of Cuneiform and Biblical Law* [VTSup, 18; Leiden: Brill, 1970]), to the Babylonian tradition of law codes. Cf. among other studies, R. Westbrook, 'What is the Covenant Code?', in B.M. Levinson (ed.), *Theory and Method in Biblical and Cuneiform Law* (JSOTSup, 181; Sheffield: JSOT Press, 1994), pp. 15-36. It is certainly not old or part of 'early Israel's' heritage. Contrary to these authors, I would, however, argue that the Covenant Code is not an old collection going back to the early period of Israel's putative history; it is rather a literary recollection of the Mesopotamian literary law tradition as represented by the great codes of Lipit-Ishtar, Hammurabi etc. (On the non-legal character of these codes—which seems to be the current view among Assyriologists—see originally F.R. Kraus, 'Ein zentrales Thema des altmesopotamischen Rechtes: Was ist der Codex Hammu-rabi?', *Genava* ns 8 [1960], pp. 283-96. Modern statements: H. Klengel, *König Hammurabi und der Alltag Babylons* [Darmstadt: Wissenschaftliche Buchgesellschaft, 2nd edn, 1992], pp. 184-264; E. Otto, 'Aspects of Legal Reforms and Reformulations in Ancient

passages on law and the enactment of justice in Deut 16.18-20, 17.8-13, and 19.14-21 do not speak about a court and justice in the normal— western—sense of the word but about the instalment and function of an agent to act between the patron families belonging to one and the same local community.

The idea of a patronage society as distinct from tribal societies is a very important part of the argument for the absence of proper states in Judah in the Iron Age—or maybe in fact in greater parts of Syria and Palestine in antiquity. The state is supposed to care for its citizens, and this has been part of the ideology of ancient states from Sumerian times to Hammurabi and to the Assyrian and Babylonian kings of the first millennium. Famous in this connection are the social decrees from Urnammu to Hammurabi and the prologue to the Codex Hammurabi in which he programmatically states that he was introduced to kingship in order to make his subjects happy.[13] This concern is conspicuously absent from the biblical material, be this the outspoken anti-royalist tirades of Samuel (1 Sam. 8 and 12), the criticism of an unjust society in the prophetic literature, or the description of the juridical system itself, which did not allow for ordinary people to find help and justice in court if they did not belong among the land-owning so-called full citizens. Social security seems to have been utterly 'privatized' in those days.

When we are studying the development of political structure in the Palestinian world from the LBA society to the Iron Age, the period of the so-called Hebrew kings, it becomes obvious that social solidarity was not part of the original sociopolitical ideology. A number of studies of LBA society in Syria and Palestine have demonstrated that this system was formed around political centres which were organized as palatine states, with the king as the general director of the business or industry which was really the palace, and the rest of the society his slaves. It is, on the other hand, very clear that the palace state was not a welfare state, and was never understood to be such a thing; it was very much a

---

Cuneiform and Israelite Law', in Levinson [ed.], *Theory and Method*, pp. 160-96; and especially J. Renger, 'Noch einmal: Was war der "Kodex" Hammurapi—ein erlassenes Gesetz oder ein Rechtsbuch?', in H.-J. Gehrke, *Rectskodifizierung und soziale Normen im interkulturellen Vergleich* [Tübingen: Mohr, 1994], pp. 27-58.)

13. Cf. on the royal *misharum* act F.R. Kraus, *Ein Edikt des Königs Ammi-saduqa von Babylonien* (SDIO, 5; Leiden: Brill, 1958), and also his *Königliche Verfügungen in altbabylonischer Zeit* (Leiden: Brill, 1984). Cf. especially the passage from the Codex Hammurabi: '... at that time Anum and Enlil named me to promote the welfare of the people...' (*ANET*, p. 164).

patronage society on the brink of developing into a feudal system.

The ideology of the petty kings of Syria and Palestine in the Bronze Age has been extensively studied by Mario Liverani, who being an Italian has not overlooked what has almost always been overlooked: that the international political system of the Amarna Age was understood by these 'kings' to form a patronage system (the Egyptian Pharaoh seems to have seen it differently).[14] The political ideology of the kings of Palestine and Syria was, briefly, that Pharaoh was their protector, as they had been faithful to Pharaoh alone and had not been playing with other Gods (kings). Therefore Pharaoh was going to protect them and help them when in distress. Pharaoh on his side understood the system to be bureaucratic. The petty kings of Syria and Palestine were his servants, employees, whom he might promote or sack as he wished.

Pharaoh's understanding of political relations was therefore impersonal and state oriented: the petty kings were Egyptian officials employed by Pharaoh to carry out his orders and decrees; they were not to act on their own behalf. Loyalty to Pharaoh therefore meant being true to the orders given to you, not the more comprehensive feeling among people from Syria and Palestine of personal allegiance and loyalty.

The Egyptian system was in fact much closer to a modern concept of a state, although the idea of the almighty God being the incarnate ruler of his kingdom may seem foreign to modern citizens. However, this 'God' could provide security and welfare for his subjects in the impersonal way which is usually the case also in modern welfare states. In Syria, on the other side, things looked different as relations between individuals were always understood in a very personal sense. That meant that the subjects of, say, Abdi-Ḥepa of Jerusalem were in theory allied to their ruler in a personal way, being not so much his subjects as his clients. He was their protector (as was Pharaoh to his subjects) but not because he was the king but because he was the patron; and if dissatisfied with your patron, then you could switch patrons and find a better one—at least in theory, but sometimes also in practice as is shown by the burgeoning movement

14. Cf. M. Liverani, 'Contrasti e confluenze di concezioni politiche nell'età di El-Amarna', *RA* 61 (1967), pp. 1-18; 'Political Lexicon and Political Ideologies in the Amarna Letters', *Berytus* 31 (1983), pp. 41-56; and *Prestige and Interest. International Relations in the Near East ca. 1600–1100 B.C. History of the Ancient Near East/Studies*, I (Padua: Sargon, 1990), esp. pp. 187-96 ('The Ideology of Protection') and pp. 197-202 ('The Ideology of Brotherhood').

in this period of refugees, people without patrons, known as the *Habiru*. In Syria and Palestine this political system of allegiance was supported by the homogeneity of the population compared to the relative physical heterogeneity of the territory in question, two factors which at one and the same time created unity and discord. People of Syria and Palestine were more or less the same wherever they travelled, but they lived in different environments, and especially in Palestine in a country which by nature was divided into several very small self-contained units. Thus in this territory regionalism and internationalism could survive side by side.

Of course the societal layout worked differently in different places. In the spatially more affluent Syrian states such as Ugarit, the village structure which embraced 80 to 90 per cent of the population would probably encourage a system to be established, in which the king would be reckoned the head patron—the 'capo di capi'.[15] The village itself, however, formed a subsystem, which would be subject to a patron who could either be the king or some local potentate, eventually a high-ranking client of the king who was entrusted with this village as his personal fief.[16] However, on the local basis the village may at many occasions have functioned almost like an acephalous tribal system without officially appointed leaders,[17] where decisions were made on a

15. On village and city in Ugarit (and other Syrian states of the LBA period) cf. M. Liverani, 'Communautés de village et palais royales dans la Syrie du IIème millénaire', *JESHO* 18 (1975), pp. 146-64; 'Ville et campagne dans la royaume d'Ugarit. Essai d'analyse économique', in *Societies and Languages of the Ancient Near East in Honour of I.M. Diakonoff* (Warminster: Aris & Phillips, 1982), pp. 250-58. Another valuable study is M. Heltzer, *The Rural Community in Ancient Ugarit* (Wiesbaden: Reichert, 1976).

16. On this cf. Liverani, 'Communautés rurales' (cf. n. 10 above). On royal agricultural estates in Ugarit, cf. M. Liverani, especially his 'Economia delle fattorie palatine ugaritiche', *Dialoghi di Archeologia* ns 1 (1979), pp. 57-72.

17. From Ugarit three titles are known: the *hazanu*, the *rab*, and the *Shakin* (cf. Heltzer, *Rural Community*, pp. 80-83). The officially headman, eventually imposed on the village by the palace administration, need not be the real head of the village itself, but just some intermediary who could represent the village when in negotiations with the outside world, and to whom the palace would direct its instructions intended to be carried out by the villagers. A number of modern analogies demonstrate that this office is not very much sought after or respected; rather it is more likely than not given to a non-important or junior member of one of the leading lineages.

communal basis.[18] Some juridical documents point in this direction as in certain cases (the infamous cases of unsolved murders of merchants) they treat the village as a collective rather than looking for an individual offender.[19]

In Palestine, the village system hardly existed in the LBA.[20] Instead we encounter a system of small scale townships (the normal scholarly term 'city' is a most unfortunate one, as it directs our ideas in the wrong direction) ruled by so-called 'kings',[21] tiny political structures which probably allowed for a personal system of relationships between ruler and subject. No intermediary organization was necessary, and only a most rudimentary administrative system was needed. We hardly have sufficient information to provide a safe picture of the political system in the nooks and corners of Palestine in the LBA, but apart from Hazor— certainly not a typical 'Palestinian' city in those days—and a few other places especially on the plains in the north such as Tell Keisan—by all criteria a Phoenician city—the walled settlements are tiny, so tiny that it is seemingly impossible at the moment to find the Jerusalem of the LBA. Nothing comprehensive was needed to control these societies: a scribe and a few soldiers was sufficient. I remember that some years ago I referred to the petitions of the kings of Palestine to Pharaoh for military support: 'Send me—not a thousand or a hundred soldiers, but twenty or thirty'. Even though the political situation in the Amarna letters is often described as catastrophic to the loyal vassals of Pharaoh, the problems were limited to a scale where a dozen Egyptian troopers could establish order and peace again![22]

If we look for parallels to the physical structure of Palestinian society,

18. See on this Heltzer, *Rural Community*, pp. 75-77.

19. On this Heltzer, *Rural Community*, pp. 63-65; Liverani, 'Communautés rurales'.

20. Cf. T.L. Thompson, *The Settlement of Palestine in the Bronze Age* (BTAVO, 34; Wiesbaden: Reichert, 1979); cf. also A. Mazar, *Archaeology of the Land of the Bible ca. 10,000–586 B.C.E.* (New York: Doubleday, 1990), pp. 239-41. Generally, scholars have concentrated on the supposed reduction of urban culture in Palestine in the LBA period; cf. R. Gonen, 'Urban Canaan in the Late Bronze Period', *BASOR* 253 (1984), pp. 61-73. Her conclusions are, however, questioned by Mazar (*Land of the Bible*, p. 240).

21. The Egyptians very purposefully and realistically called these rulers 'mayors', *hazanu*.

22. *Early Israel*, pp. 419-20 including references to request for support from Abdi-Ḥepa, Rib-Adda, and Abimilku.

I would suggest that we leave out circumstances in greater Syria, as well as—of course—in Mesopotamia in antiquity. Instead I would suggest that better parallels could be found in medieval Europe, in what I would call the *Burg-Gesellschaft*, the 'fortress-societies' of the early Middle Ages. Here embryonic centralized organizations arose around the castles (really more strongholds than castles) of the patrons, later to develop into cities. Denmark provides fine examples not least because in those days it was a small-scale society, and the development is well attested from our history—to such a degree that it is part of the ordinary curriculum in primary schools. Around the fortress villagers settled to obtain protection from the lord of the fortress, their patron. And from this cities developed. The proof of this is the number of medieval Danish cities with names such as Nyborg, Faaborg, Vordingborg, Skanderborg, and Aalborg. The Danish word *borg* is the same as the German *Burg*. Other names would be compounds with Danish *hus* ('house'), such as the second biggest city of the kingdom, Aarhus, or *gaard* ('farmhouse', but often used also for royal houses), often in the form of the name *Nygaard* (the 'new farmhouse'), like the Russian Novgorod (which is a Scandinavian word as Novgorod was in fact founded by Viking chiefs as a stronghold). Even Copenhagen traces its origin back to such a development in the twelfth century CE, as the city arose around a fortress built by an archbishop (Absalon) in 1167 CE.

Well, the end of the LBA probably relates to a societal crisis. It was, however, a crisis that arose not so much because of internal structural problems in the small political communities of Syria and Palestine; it was rather occasioned by an international crisis such as the break-down of trade relations,[23] or by changing environmental circumstances such as drought and famine.[24] It is also well known that the effects of the crisis varied enormously from place to place and from region to region. Thus the major cities such as Ugarit or Hazor—to stay with these—succumbed: Ugarit to a combination of factors, dissolution of trade, destructions wrought by intruders and a natural catastrophe; Hazor to as yet unknown factors, but unlike Ugarit, which was abandoned, eventually to be substituted by a 'Burg-society'.

23. The general thesis of R.B. Coote and K.W. Whitelam, *The Emergence of Early Israel in Historical Perspective* (The Social World of Biblical Antiquity Series, 5; Sheffield: Almond Press, 1987).

24. As preferred by T.L. Thompson, *The Early History of the Israelite People: From the Written and Archaeological Sources* (SHANE, 4; Leiden: Brill, 1992).

Out of the patronage society of the LBA period in Syria and Palestine arose a tribal society—though we may question whether we are really speaking about a tribal society. Of course we know from the Hebrew Bible about the tribes of Israel, but how far does that description comply with reality? I argued several years ago that the description of the tribes of Israel is formalized to such a degree as to present a caricature of a living tribal society.[25] The biblical authors displayed very little understanding of how such societies were organized and how they functioned. The tribal system of the Hebrew Bible seems in fact to belong to what would in a modern community of anthropologists be called 'arm-chair theory', far removed from the real world.[26]

In modern times we are likely to be seduced by words, and nothing but words. In the Bible we read about tribes, and we are immediately let to believe in what we are told: Israel was a tribal society, and—well—then it was truly so. But we do not think about what this means. We compartmentalize our evidence: tribal society here, state society there, and even patronage society in the middle—somewhere. From a logical point of view we argue that we need a clear-cut borderline between the various definitions in order to establish a line of development between the different compartments. People move from a tribal society to something else, for example a political system governed by chieftains, later to become kings when they got matters of succession settled. We create the rules for this development from one system to the next without recognizing that there may be no development at all, or rather, many developments at one and the same time and in the same place and society.

The tribal society is only a metaphor for a society not organized as a state,[27] and by state I mean the state according to the modern definition. In the period leading from the LBA to Iron II, the so-called period of the Hebrew United Monarchy, we may find structures not very dissimilar from the ones pertaining to the preceding period and very much like the

25. *Early Israel*, p. 274.

26. Which did not prevent this author—like so many of his colleagues—from presenting another sophisticated but nevertheless speculative reconstruction of what an Israelite tribe might have been like; cf. *Early Israel*, pp. 274-90.

27. Cf. also—preliminary—the discussion in my *Ancient Israel. A New History of Israelite Society* (Sheffield: JSOT Press, 1988), pp. 98-99. A better definition would perhaps be to argue that 'tribe' is a metaphor that expresses the functions of a state in a non-state society.

ones to appear in the future. If we follow Finkelstein's reconstruction of
Early Iron I society in Palestine as—in the central region—mainly a
village society,[28] we may have a tribal society, but probably more likely
a mixture of tribal or rather *lineage* ideology and patronage systems.

This demands an explanation. Contrary to the opinion of many
scholars but well exposed in my *Early Israel*, the governing structure in
traditional Middle Eastern societies not yet totally embraced by a
centralized state is not the tribe but the lineage, defined as a patrilinear
descent group of some extension.[29] The lineage survives the political
changes of time, the shift from statehood to chiefdom and vice versa,
and it is dominant on all levels of society, or rather the ideology of
belonging to a certain lineage dominates. Reality shows things to be
different in that only the well-to-do lineages are politically important; the
rest have to adjust their political allegiance to one of the major lineages.
This is the basis of the patronage system according to which the members of unimportant lineages have to look for richer—more influential,
mightier—lineages for personal protection.

What may have happened in Palestine at the end of the LBA is that
the walled fortress of the patron, the 'city of the king', disappeared and
was substituted by local structures, 'villages', either organized without a
protecting substratum like the patron—the so-called 'king'—or with
local influential patrons, now impossible to trace in the remains of the
villages. The presence of regional patrons may be evidenced from the
distribution of clusters of villages in the central and Galilean highlands.[30]

In this way, the village culture in the central highlands of Palestine
simply represents an interval between two periods of more extensive and
well-formulated patronage systems, simply because what happened, say
between 1000 and 900 BCE, was in fact the re-establishment of a system
of 'Burg-civilisations', partly to be compared (but not identified) with
the system of the LBA to be found in the same area. It is guesswork to
present any kind of definite reconstruction of the history of this period
but several avenues of development are feasible. Here I shall point at
two. 1) The villages were part of a tribal society of some kind, the
correct nature of which is nowadays impossible to reconstruct. They

28. I. Finkelstein, *The Archaeology of the Settlement of the Israelite Tribes*
(Jerusalem: Israel Exploration Society, 1988).

29. *Early Israel*, pp. 223-31 and 245-74.

30. Cf. the charts in Finkelstein, *Settlement*, pp. 95 and 189. Mittmann's Gilead
survey may provide the same picture; cf. Finkelstein, *Settlement*, p. 115.

were governed by tribal ideology[31] according to the rules of such societies. However, at a certain stage and because of certain conditions— competition for dwindling natural resources, warfare, or whatever—they had to invent a more solid way of organization, reuniting into chiefdoms run by families or lineages best described as patronage families, and later to assume the language of kings and princes. 2) The villages were already from the outset part of small-scale patronage systems, which under the conditions mentioned (or others—nobody can really tell) were forced to be incorporated into a major patronage system, symbolized by the re-establishment of a centralized construction such as a fortress—a 'Burg'.

In the first case the system of government changed, but the ideology as well as life inside the lineage remained (almost) the same. In the second case almost nothing happened at all, except that a tendency towards centralized settlement may be the reason for the establishment of fortresses like Jerusalem and Beer-Sheba in the second half of the EI I period and at the beginning of the first millennium BCE.[32] The establishment of these centres has been related to the disappearance of village culture, or at least a reduction of the number of villages and minor townships at the same time. So probably we see a movement towards centralization, and a strengthening of the position of the village patrons (some of them) into a kind of regional patrons, the people we have been used to call kings.

In his 1995 *SJOT* article, Thomas Thompson directs his attention to

31. Perhaps reflected in traces of what is normally understood to be tribal ideology present in much later biblical writings. On this F. Lambert, 'The Tribe/State Paradox in the Old Testament', *SJOT* 8 (1994), pp. 20-44. It is, however, my opinion that this ideology is mainly part of the lineage system and that it does not necessarily reflect the previous or current existence of tribes.

32. The archaeological chronology of the LB and EI periods seems again to be in jeopardy. According to M. Steiner (at the conference in Copenhagen in March 1995, cf. n. 4 above), no evidence of a Jerusalem in the LB period has been found—apart from Abdi-Ḥepa's six letters (EA 285-290)—or it is at least still to be found. A fortress was built at this place in the twelfth century BCE, and some monumental structures were supplemented in the tenth century BCE. On this see M. Steiner, 'Re-dating the Terraces of Jerusalem', *IEJ* 44 (1994), pp. 13-20. Full evidence will be presented when her dissertation ('Jerusalem in de brons- en ijzertijd. de Opgravningen van de "British School of Archaeology in Jerusalem", 1961–1967', Leiden, 1994) is published, hopefully in 1995. On the relationship between Beersheba and its surroundings see Finkelstein, *Settlement*, pp. 37-47.

the notion of a 'house of David' as evidence of the presence of a patronage system organized around the descendants of the apical David, making the historicity of this David rather dubious and certainly unnecessary.[33] In this place I shall not repeat Thompson's arguments, but only supplement him by referring to the fact that the many dynastic, political names to be found in Western Asia in the Iron Age, reaching from the Mesopotamian Aramaic states of Bit Adini, over the Syrian Bit Gusi, down to Palestinian Bit Humriya and Bet David, may hardly be evidence of tribal societies which changed into kingdoms; it is much more likely that they testify to the fact that assumption of power was based not on single persons, but on major patron lineages that arose among the small-scale patron lineages of the previous period. And by changing the origin of the Judean 'royal' family from a single historical person into an eponymic ancestor of this lineage, we have happily escaped being entangled in the personalized mode of narrating history of the author of the books of Solomon. As is well known from general anthropology, apical ancestors are likely to attract all kinds of traditions without themselves being necessarily historical persons. A parallel to this would be the hero-kings of ancient Ugarit, Kirta and Danilu—again probably never living persons, who, however, seem to function as the ancestors of the reigning house of the kingdom of Ugarit in the LBA period. As Liverani many years ago pointed out there is a huge distance between the imaginary presentation of the king in the epics of Kirta and Aqhatu and the management-like royal organization in the state of Ugarit, but the king of Ugarit eventually needed such an ancestor to think of at the end of the day after having concluded the tedious business affairs of his industrial organization—like a modern business tycoon, going hunting for the weekend.[34] That is the kind of stuff dreams are made of.

33. '"House of David": An Eponymic Referent to Yahweh as Godfather', *SJOT* 9 (1995), pp. 59-74.

34. M. Liverani, 'L'epica ugaritica nel suo contesto storico e letterario', *La poesia epica e la sua formazione. Accademia Nazionale dei Lincei, Quaderno No.* 139 (1970), pp. 859-69; 'La royauté syrienne de l'age du Bronze Récent', in P. Garelli (ed.), *Le palais et la royauté (RAI)* (Paris: P. Geuthries, 1974), pp, 329-56, 338-41.

BARE BONES:
PUTTING FLESH ON THE ECONOMICS OF ANCIENT ISRAEL

David Hopkins

When excavators pried loose the stone sealing off the entry and stepped down into the rock-cut bench tomb on the eastern slope of Mount Zion, the dead did not rise up to greet them.[1] Five partial skeletons reclined on the two benches of the first chamber. Bones and grave goods rested in piles on the floor. A second chamber with its three benches and repository offered more bones and grave goods. Forty-three individuals—adults, juveniles, and infants—had spent the better part of three millennia encased by rock walls. Can we reconstruct the economy of their Late Iron period Jerusalem? What were the economic underpinnings of their existence?

For the purposes of the question of the formation of a state an additional question confronts us as we peer into the tomb: Were these people residents of an ancient Judean state? The economic basis of three state-defining attributes will shape the answer to the question. 1) States control, however imperfectly, the production and distribution of the material means of need satisfaction (to introduce Polanyi's definition of a the substantive economy).[2] 2) States attend to the maintenance of social structures linked to the management of the economy, creating and interpreting the symbols of legitimacy and status. 3) States exercise political

1.   D. Davis and A. Kloner, 'A Burial Cave of the Late Israelite Period on the Slopes of Mt. Zion', *Qadmoniot* 11 (1978), pp. 16-19 (Hebrew).

2.   K. Polanyi, 'The Economy as Instituted Process', in *Trade and Market in the Early Empires* (ed. K. Polanyi, C. Arensberg, and H.W. Pearson; New York: The Free Press, 1957), p. 248 and the expanded version of this article in *The Livelihood of Man. Studies in Social Discontinuity* (ed. H.W. Pearson; New York: Academic Press, 1977), p. 20. See the recent re-presentation of Polanyi's models by R.H. Halpern, *Cultural Economies, Past and Present* (Austin, TX: University of Texas Press, 1994), pp. 34-84.

power, notably through the coercive agency of military might. States exist at the confluence of economic, social, and political power.[3]

Constraints

Constraints on economic reconstruction face us in a variety of specific ways that make methodological issues a priority concern. Much economic behavior is materially invisible or its material correlates are ephemeral. The realia unearthed and handled by archaeologists eclipse perishable organics: even the staple foods are preserved in sparse quantities. Elements of the organization and the relations of production can only be 'invisible' in the archaeological record. The interests of the biblical literature and the rare inscriptional find hardly correct this imbalance of preservation. The very way archaeologists approach data collection, including the choice of 'testable' hypotheses, often imitates the ethnographer's fieldwork. But ancient historians cannot generally call upon the 'imponderabilia of actual life'[4] with which ethnographic fieldwork usually occupies itself. We may have learned to think like

---

3.   The literature on states and state formation is reviewed by F.S. Frick, *The Formation of the State in Ancient Israel* (The Social World of Biblical Antiquity, 4; Sheffield: JSOT Press, 1985), pp. 25-50. See also J.S. Holladay Jr, 'The Kingdoms of Israel and Judah: Political and Economic Centralization in the Iron IIA–B (ca. 1000–750 BCE)', in *The Archaeology of Society in the Holy Land* (ed. T.E. Levy: London; Leicester University Press, 1995), pp. 371-79; P.S. Khoury and J. Kostiner, 'Introduction: Tribes and the Complexities of State Formation in the Middle East', in *Tribes and State Formation in the Middle East* (ed. P.S. Khoury and J. Kostiner; Berkeley, CA: University of California Press, 1990), pp. 1-22; E.A. Knauf, 'The Cultural Impact of Secondary State Formation: The Cases of Edomites and Moabites', in *Early Edom and Moab: The Beginning of the Iron Age in Southern Jordan* (ed. P. Bienkowski; Sheffield: Sheffield Academic Press, 1992), pp. 47-54; H.T. Wright, 'Prestate Political Formations', in *Chiefdoms and Early States in the Near East: The Organizational Dynamics of Complexity* (ed. G. Stein and M.S. Rothman; Monographs in World Archaeology, 18; Madison, WI: Prehistory Press, 1994), pp. 67-84; and N. Yoffee, 'Too Many Chiefs? (or, Safe Texts for the 90s)', in *Archaeological Theory: Who Sets the Agenda?* (ed. N. Yoffee and A. Sherratt; Cambridge: Cambridge University Press, 1993), pp. 60-78.

4.   C.A. Gregory and J.C. Altman describe one aspect of the ethnographer's task as 'to record minute, detailed observations of the "imponderabilia of actual life", and, where possible, to participate in the daily life of the people' (*Observing the Economy* [ASA Research Methods in Social Anthropology; London and New York: Routledge, 1989], p. 12).

Diakonoff and Gelb and Braudel, but 'onionology' is beyond our data base.[5]

Quantification
There are few numbers, and fewer still are reliable; there are no statistics and no broad cliometric data. Quantification, the great desiratum of every economic historian, is beyond our reach for most aspects of the economy. There are some figures, of course, for example, in the biblical presentation of Solomon's achievements (1 Kgs 10.14ff.) or the tax levies of Jehoiakim (2 Kgs 23) or the tribute paid by Moab (2 Kgs 3.4). Even if the figures bordered on the reliable (which they don't), any calculations based upon them would be nonsensical because we simply lack the data necessary to relate particular numbers to any broad economic context, such as a Solomonic GNP. So we are little better off than the Deuteronomistic historian who asserts in Kings (1 Kgs 6.47) that the weight of newly cast bronze temple paraphernalia could not be calculated. We, too, cannot calculate the weight of the bronze, the volume of the grain or the olive oil, or the number of board feet of cedar. This inability to quantify our analysis extends to all ancient periods and includes such worthy endeavors as charting the balance between resource base and populations.[6] Historians of the economy of ancient Palestine confront data constraints, 'painfully aware of their inability ever to reconstruct a dead world in its completeness'.[7]

Mount Zion Tomb: Standard and Diversity
A dead world confronts us in the tomb excavated on Mount Zion. It belongs to the category of 'bench tomb' that has been described as the 'standard' or 'definitive' Judahite form of burial by the eighth century.[8]

---

5.   I.J. Gelb, 'Approaches to the Study of Ancient Society', *JAOS* 87 (1967), p. 8.

6.   For example, even the well thought through attempt of Baruch Rosen, 'The Subsistence Economy of Stratum II', in I. Finkelstein (ed.), *'Izbet Sartah: An Early Iron Age Site near Rosh Ha'ayim, Israel* (BAR International Series, 299; Oxford: BAR, 1986), pp. 156-85. See my fuller discussion in *The Highlands of Canaan: Agricultural Life in the Early Iron Age* (The Social World of Biblical Antiquity, 3; Decatur, GA: Almond Press, 1985), pp. 130-32.

7.   S. Schama, *Dead Certainties (Unwarranted Speculations)* (New York: Alfred A. Knopf, 1991), p. 320.

8.   Elizabeth M. Bloch-Smith uses these descriptive terms in her extremely helpful analysis of Judahite burial practices from which most of the mortuary data in

The generic plan of the tomb—rectilinear doorway, main chamber, peripheral benches and a repository—took shape in this instance as a pair of linked chambers. While the bench tomb may be the 'standard', even the narrow confines of Iron IIc (ca. 725–575 BCE) boasted a assortment of other burial types (jar burial, cave tomb, the Assyrian style 'bathtub' coffin and simple graves). The diversity of burial practices suggests that describing our bench tomb as the 'definitive' or 'standard' type means merely that it was the 'most prominent' type.

This diversity held for the economy as well. The most fundamental aspect of our approach to reconstructing the economic underpinning of Late Iron II Judean life is to recognize that there never was 'an ancient economy', but a set of economies. In Palestine, this multiplicity stands on a geographically complex, fragmented landscape. More or less favorable and reliable natural givens, more or lesser isolation from economically developed zones, caravan routes, and waterborne trade and greater or lesser sociopolitical stability; all these circumstances imposed economic variegation on this territory. Economic reconstruction demands dealings not so much with a socioeconomic system, but with intersecting economies and societies. This is true with respect to greater Palestine; true with respect to its sub-regions; true with respect to the territory of ancient Judah, home of our putative state.

Economic Zones

During the Iron Age as well as other periods of population growth, agricultural intensification, and, presumably, sedentarization, two economic zones emerged on this fragmented landscape. One encompassed the rural life of Palestine, where economic activity was confined within the radius of the small village and its near neighbors. This zone met tangentially with a zone of more fully developed and inter-regionally integrated town or urban-focused economy. These two economic zones were distinguished especially by the relative extent of subsistence versus market-oriented economic production.

The village zone produced almost exclusively for self-consumption, not excluding, of course, the production for rent and taxes. Village farmers entered the market—to the extent that such a price-fixing arena of buying and selling existed—but rarely. They were subsistence cultivators

this paper is derived: *Judahite Burial Practices and Beliefs about the Dead* (JSOTSup, 123; Sheffield: JSOT Press, 1992), pp. 23, 51.

who similarly went to the marketplace only for specialized goods. The vast proportion of their product comprised goods possessing limited ranges: grains, vegetables, and fruits were consumed where they were produced. Agricultural produce did leave home. It entered the urban zone as rent to landlords and taxes to support the royal administration, but not as produce destined for market.

Though the town offered small-scale workshops with manufactured goods (textiles, ceramics, tools) for sale, it was primarily a center of consumption, not manufacture. Thus the economy was not at all urban-based. In the urban zone, rulers ate from pantries supplied by taxes, while townspeople who lacked the ability to import produce from their own estates satisfied their dietary needs at the marketplace. The urban zone was never to any degree economically independent of its rural environment.

State as Economic Commander

To a large extent, these two zones owed their existence to extremely high transportation costs. Within the radius of ox cart and donkey transportation, the limited marketplace promoted investments in commodity production, for example, wine and olive oil. But the town's immediate hinterland was hardly a uniform canvas. Inasmuch as the overall weight of the urban population was small, demand was low and the volume of goods that flowed through markets was modest. Another factor intervened as well: poorly developed managerial techniques limited the extent to which the politically powerful urban world could dictate the life of the hinterlands. A conclave of officers living in the capital city or regional administrative center—whether one terms it a 'well-oiled bureaucracy' or not—was hard pressed to fashion an integrated regional economy. Doubtless, the king's men could not even have articulated a policy. States were, as Cowgill remarks, 'at best half-understood by the various people who made them, maintained them, coped with them, and struggled against them'.[9] What is true of states is doubly true of economies: there

9. G. Cowgill, 'Onwards and Upwards with Collapse', in *The Collapse of Ancient States and Civilizations* (ed. N. Yoffee and G. Cowgill; Tucson, AZ: University of Arizona Press), pp. 253-54, quoted by Yoffee, 'Too Many Chiefs?', p. 71. According to Postgate ('The Economic Structure of the Assyrian Empire', in *Power and Propaganda: A Symposium on Ancient Empires* [ed. M.T. Larsen; Mesopotamia: Copenhagen Studies in Assyriology, 7; Copenhagen: Akademisk Forlag, 1979], p. 214) the economic structure of Assyrian imperial rule '...consists

is absolutely no evidence that ancient administrators possessed any but the most commonplace notions about the 'economy', an abstraction that was itself unknown. The patchwork of the ancient Judean economic landscape was thus an ecological fact as well as a half-hewn artifact of human origination.

Late Iron Age Integration

Before the Late Iron Age, these limiting realities appear to have prevailed. There is hardly any compelling attestation of administrative re-casting of the Judean economic framework, certainly not in the tenth century in any region of the highlands, even if one accepts the Yadin trinity of building projects (Gezer, Hazor and Megiddo). Yet by the period of the Mount Zion tomb, a regional character did appear in a number of discrete aspects of material culture, suggesting the state's impact on the production and distribution of the material means of need satisfaction. The 'repetitive repertoire'[10] of pottery shapes that were manufactured in nearly identical fashion throughout Iron IIc Judah heads the list. The ceramics of the Mount Zion tomb shared this orange-red slipped, wheel-burnished style that Mazar suggests was mass-produced and distributed throughout the territory.

This homogeneous ceramic culture does not demand an interpretation as the correlate of the administrative management of economic behavior, however, and the general nature of pottery production and distribution discourages one. Pottery represented a low order commodity—low cost, high frequency of demand—with a small range. Low prices, but lots of transactions enabled producers to survive without shipping ceramics beyond a limited radius, while the consumer's regular need discouraged long trips to acquire pottery from any central source. Itinerant merchants may have taken up the middle ground in this stand-off. Yet in an economy dominated by bartering, it is difficult to imagine pottery purchases involving much movement at all beyond the local scene.[11] 'Sourcing' a

of the imposition of an administrative pattern upon underlying and largely unchanging economic realities'.

10. A. Mazar, *Archaeology of the Land of the Bible: 10,000–586 B.C.E.* (The Anchor Bible Reference Library; New York: Doubleday, 1990), p. 308.

11. See Bryant G. Wood's discussion of the 'expansion diffusion' of ceramics in *The Sociology of Pottery in Ancient Palestine* (JSOTSup, 103; Sheffield: JSOT Press, 1990), pp. 59-81. On the economics of low-order goods, see the essay of Stuart Plattner, 'Markets and Marketplaces', in *Economic Anthropology* (ed. S. Plattner; Stanford: Stanford University Press, 1989), pp. 171-208.

broad selection of this ware would elucidate the economic processes. Neutron activation analysis has shown that the renowned *lmlk*-type jars originated from the same clays, perhaps a signal of special royal initiatives in the wine industry.[12]

Nevertheless, the eighth century did see the emergence of distinct Judean material culture which suggests an integrating economy. The labelled dome-shaped stone weights for measuring of silver in seventh-century Judah imply a uniformity of trade transactions (one step removed from coinage) that penetrated even Ashdod, Ekron, and Timnah of Philistia. Recent analysis by Ronen has shown that a concerted and successful attempt was made to change the weight of the shekel at this time. Abandoning the Egyptian standard, the shekel's weight rose 20 percent (i.e., its value was reduced).[13] The bench tomb belongs also among these signs of regional material culture.

The concrete role of the state as a shaper of economic institutions appears graphically in the development of the Judean settlement landscape through the Iron Age. The region witnessed changes in both locational and appropriational movements, rubrics Polanyi used to delineate economic institutions. Appropriational movements address 'changes of hands': patterns in the organization of rights and obligations regarding economic goods.[14] Locational movements ('changes of place' analogous to the term 'mode of production') represent transfers and transformations of the ecological or technological kind.[15]

---

12. G. Barkay, 'The Iron Age II–III', in *The Archaeology of Ancient Israel* (ed. A. Ben-Tor; trans. R. Greenberg; New Haven, CT: Yale University Press, 1992), p. 349.

13. Y. Ronen, 'The Enigma of the Shekel Weights of the Judean Kingdom', *BA* 59 (1996), pp. 122-25.

14. According to Halpern (*Cultural Economies*, p. 59): 'changes of hands' consist of '(1) organizational changes, or (2) transfer of rights. Organizational changes involve changes in the principles allocating resources or goods, e.g., a shift from communal land tenure to private property.... Transfer of rights change people's access to and control over goods and resources'.

15. Again Halpern's definition is helpful (*Cultural Economies*, p. 59): '"Changes of place" or locational movements consist of one or more of the following: (1) transfers from one physical space to another, involving (a) physical transfers of goods or of people from one place to another, as in movements of work crews, or (b) physical transfers of productive resources, such as tools; (2) *physical changes* in the material stuff of livelihood, for example, changes in the physical condition of a foodstuff (raw to cooked, whole to divided, seeds to plants); (3) *energy transfers,*

Major shifts in locational movements are the most obvious and were necessitated by the demographic spiral that was uninterrupted until the Assyrian invasion. Population growth began with a burst in Iron I and accelerated through the Iron II when Judah's settlement landscape reached its Iron Age zenith at the end of the eighth century. At the same time, Jerusalem itself took on world-class proportions (150 ha). The institutional arrangements—that is, the locational movements—regarding settlement site sizes and agricultural operations had changed markedly: agricultural expansion and intensive investments in commodity production became prominent features of the Late Iron II landscape.

The settlement pattern shifted as well.[16] Jerusalem had emerged, in the tenth century, as the center of its region. Yet the site hierarchy still approximated the rank-size model. This suggests more parity among towns and the freer play of factors charting economic production and distribution. The beginning of the Iron II period showed a relative increase in the area of the largest sites. This trend continued for two centuries during which the middle of the site-size curve eroded and intermediate sites began to dwindle. Finally by the end of the eighth century, and certainly by the first part of the seventh after the destruction of Lachish, Jerusalem loomed as a primate site within its own circumscribed territory. The economy focused on a small number of regional administrative centers that commanded and commandeered production toward the center.[17] This constituted a system of finance used to mobilize goods from subsistence producers to pay for the activities of the elite government. Centralized control—basically the dictation of the terms of participation in the production system—displaced the economic decision-making of the rural zone. Taken together with other indicators of economic management noted previously, the reconfiguration of the settlement map reveals a pattern made by the movements of goods and persons in the economy, appropriational movements

such as the relocation of resources and storage facilities from one place to another or the relocation of a village vis-à-vis ecological zones.'

16. See A. Ofer, '"All the Hill County of Judah": From a Settlement Fringe to a Prosperous Kingdom', in *From Nomadism to Monarchy: Archaeological and Historical Aspects of Early Israel* (ed. I. Finkelstein and N. Na'aman; Jerusalem: Yad Izhak Ben-Zvi and IES; Washington, DC: BAS, 1994), pp. 92-121.

17. As Jamieson-Drake concludes, this alteration of the settlement pattern produced a configuration of settlement sizes matching the primate model, centered on Jerusalem.

that fit Polanyi's model of redistribution.[18]

It is worth pausing to consider a methodological difficulty associated with visions of state structure and a command economy shaping the lives of our tomb dwellers. It is crucial for analytical purposes to separate Polanyi's two categories of movements. What one observes in the rural-urban (town) zonation of the later Iron Age (i.e., in the settlement pattern) clearly represents a transformation of locational movements. It does not necessarily follow that there are also shifts in appropriational movements, that is, changes in land use rights. This situation can be compared with the more obvious case of inter-regional exchange: the principles behind the movement of a product, whether it is a wine amphora, a bag of wheat, or an ivory carving, cannot be determined by examining the locational movement only. Locational movements do not, in and of themselves, necessarily imply any change in the organization of rights and obligations vis-à-vis a particular item nor testify transparently regarding the relationships between the parties involved. Other evidence for the strength of the state's impact on appropriational movements, the *lmlk* impressions, for example, permit the primate status of Jerusalem to be read as indicative of its greater command of the produce of the field.

The State and Social Stratification

A second aspect of state definition focuses on social stratification, that is, the emergence of an elite class and the creation of symbols that project and maintain this hierarchy and its association with the welfare of the larger social universe. The Mount Zion tomb itself offers the clearest indicator of a social hierarchy. Rock-cut bench tombs are cogently associated with the burial practices of the wealthy by virtue of their limited numbers and intrinsic costs. At the same historical moment, others used simple or cist graves (though few have been found) or communal burial fields (e.g., Jer. 26.23). Moreover, the grave goods of the Mount Zion tomb included several items that may have marked the social status of the dead. Mourners contributed the usual assortment of ceramic vessels to the burial: lambs, jugs, jars, and bowls. The dead were

18. Polanyi formalized patterns in these movements as forms of economic integration (reciprocity, redistribution, market exchange, and householding). Halpern clarifies the point that the four forms of economic integration must be understood as formal models that can be thought of as diagrams (*Cultural Economies*, pp. 50-54).

interred as well with jewelry, three bronze arrowheads, a quartz crater, and a scaraboid seal. Jewelry is extremely common in all grave types, probably because of its apotropaic value.[19] Arrowheads are more exclusive in their appearances, belonging most typically to cave and bench tombs. The quartz crater adds further distinction to the dead of this tomb: craters were untypical of highland tomb contents but represent a lowland grave good, occurring in association with Phoenician and Cypriot forms. The scaraboid seal provides the strongest indicator of the elite status of these dead. While seals were placed in all types of burials throughout the Iron Age, only a meager number of seals has emerged from Iron IIc highland tombs. The seal depicts a fish. Above and below the fish, an inscription signals out the seal's owner: *lḥmyʾh bt mnḥm* 'belonging to Ḥamyohel daughter of Menaḥem', one of a small group of women making an epigraphic appearance. Seals belonged among the upper echelons of Judean society and played key roles in the administration of the kingdom. Many carry the symbolization of Judean royal power and prerogative: the winged beetle. The unique fish was chosen for Ḥamyohel's seal for some connotation other than a dietary one.[20] It was not a significant item on the everyday Judean menu.

Funerary ritual may have offered another public presentation of status, now represented only by the grave gifts left behind. Nothing exists to connect the *marzeaḥ* to this tomb, though it offers another indicator of state-level social power, functioning as a legitimizer of royal succession.[21] Despite the 'invisibility' of such ritual practices, the location of the tomb in the capital city Jerusalem cements its tie to the elite stratum of Judean society.

Missing from the tomb, as from nearly all of its type, are any tools. Even the most common grave tool found elsewhere, the blade, occurs in less than 10 percent of all the burial types, and most of these date to Iron I. Though classed as a tool, most blades typically served as weapons or eating utensils, not part of productive technology. The Iron IIc dead were envisioned as busying themselves with day-to-day chores, yet these elite dead did not reckon field labor (picking, hoeing, plowing, cutting) among their tasks. Requisitioning and distributing the labor product,

19. Bloch-Smith, *Burial Practices*, p. 81.

20. Fish were among the items of luxury trade mentioned in the Amarna letters as received by LB Palestinian lords.

21. Eleanor Ferris Beach ('The Samaria Ivories, *Marzeaḥ* and Biblical Texts', *BA* 55 [1992], p. 131) discusses the signification of the royal *marzeaḥ*.

however, was not beyond the reach of persons such as these equipped with bronze arrowheads and seals. Bloch-Smith documents divergent assemblages of tools for the wealthy and for the those who worked to survive.[22] Thus the grave goods manifest the social position as well as the political power of the tomb's inhabitants.

The existence of an urban-based elite hardly occasions surprise. It is as much a part of Palestine as the bench tomb itself. The Jerusalemite's choice of the bench tomb for an 'ancestral home'[23] was made available over a centuries-long period of evolution. All the elements of what blossomed into the most prominent Judahite burial practice were present already at the end of the Bronze Age in the coastal and lowland regions of Palestine.[24] Reconstructing the development of the bench tomb from these prototypes resolves the debate about the origin of the Judahite tomb on the indigenous side of the diffusion versus evolution divide.

The embeddedness of this tomb type in the cultural history of Palestine parallels the embeddedness of the fragmented Palestinian social scene in its social and political history. Late Iron II Judah was not a society so much as a constellation of 'plural societies'. The nature and structure of this constellation was inherited from Bronze Age urban-based polities (the 'city-states').[25] These consisted of a proportionately tiny urban-based aristocracy, a larger assortment of townspeople, a mass of rural agrarians and a segment of nomadic pastoralists.[26] This prevailing social structure had undergone a striking effacement during the Late Bronze Age–Early Iron Age transition period, but re-surfaced in the conduct of the Iron Age Palestinian monarchies. These replicated the

22. *Burial Practices*, p. 90.

23. Apparently, the rock-cut bench tomb type was dressed as a house. The tombs preserve skeumorphs of residential features, including probably decorative elements, rendering the tomb 'conceptually acceptable as a residence design' (Bloch-Smith, *Burial Practices*, p. 44).

24. The Bronze Age tomb reused at Gezer contained a central room with benches and two secondary chambers also with benches. A reused tomb at Lachish and a freshly cut, ca. 1200 BCE tomb at Tell el-Farah (S) offered benches on both sides of single chambers. The Bronze Age tomb reused at Gezer contained a central room with benches and two secondary chambers also with benches (Bloch-Smith, *Burial Practices*, pp. 46-48).

25. See especially N.P. Lemche's treatment of LBA urban culture in *Ancient Israel: A New History of Israelite Society* (Sheffield: JSOT Press, 1988), pp. 77-88.

26. Following J.H. Kautsky, *The Politics of Aristocratic Empires* (Chapel Hill, NC: University of North Carolina Press, 1982), pp. 314-27.

city-states of the Bronze Age to a far greater extent than they anticipated the nation-states of the European industrial age. The nationalistic ideology of the biblical literature projects a unity that simply did not exist. The import of this for economic reconstruction rests in its caution about the potency of this nationalistic ideology. Far too often it has skewed portraits of Iron Age economics.[27] The residents of the Mount Zion tomb were not citizens of an industrial democracy with its attendant market economy.

The Political Economy of the Judean State
The economic life of Judeans in their pre-industrial (agrarian), aristocratic world stands at a great remove from contemporary economic experience. This much economic anthropologists have convincingly established and encapsulated in the concept of 'embeddedness'.[28] The economy was 'embedded' in society. Economic relationships had non-economic, social, cultural and political parameters. Though part of the modern economic world as well, non-economic parameters had greater weight in the pre-industrial world.

The implications of this embeddedness for reconstructing the ancient economy have been played out as a debate on the nature of economic decision-making. Are there cross-cultural, transhistorical principles of economic decision-making as 'formalists' contend? Do the existence of non-economic parameters invalidate generalizations about decision-making, as 'substantivists' argue? 'Formal' economic theory was drawn from western, market-oriented capitalism and offered micro-economic laws: people make rational economic choices based upon a cost-benefit calculus that aims to maximize utility. 'Substantivists' observed totally different economic concepts at work in the non-market economies beyond the margins of capitalism. Reciprocity, redistribution, and house-holding, rather than the market, served as organizing principles for the

27. Gabriel Barkay ('"Your Poor Brother": A Note on an Inscribed Bowl from Beth Shemesh', *EJ* 41 [1991], p. 241) shows the effects of this when he asserts that 'in ancient Israelite society there was a bond of brotherhood between all of its members...'

28. Access to the enormous literature generated by economic anthropology's debate on the issue of 'embeddedness', that is, the substantive versus formal nature of ancient economic principles, can be gained through Stuart Plattner, 'Introduction', in Plattner (ed.), *Economic Anthropology*, pp. 1-20 and M. Granovetter, 'Economic Action and Social Structure: The Problem of Embeddedness', *American Journal of Sociology* 91 (1986), pp. 481-510.

ancient economy. The kinship group, and not the individual, provided the locus of economic decision-making. Taking this 'embeddedness' seriously means acknowledging that the dead of the Mount Zion tomb were not members of the modern species *homo economicus*.

Among the most salient aspects of ancient economic institutions is the practice of risk aversion. Especially in householding economies, economies marked by production for one's own use, whether the family or the village comprised the unit of self-sufficiency, risk aversion or risk-spreading eclipsed utility maximization as the key decision-making signpost. In concrete terms, this means that village life in Judah tended to produce a diverse base of foodstuffs, combining pastoral with agricultural pursuits, field crops with orchards and vineyards. There is bountiful data, however, to suggest that the Iron Age witnessed a progressive specialization of production that concentrated on wine production and olive oil manufacture. The data range from the seventh-century ostraca of Arad to *lmlk* impressions of the late eighth century, from scores of rock-cut presses in the hill country to a well-preserved isolated farmstead on the outskirts of Jerusalem, from the viticulture of Gibeon to the concentration of olive oil production facilities at Ekron.[29]

As previously noted in reference to the settlement pattern, this is one economic arena that did specialize, creating desirable goods with greater ranges. The development of these specialized industries was based on the success of diversified village agriculture. But there is a great jump from a balanced Mediterranean economy to the production of commodities requiring centralized institutions (i.e., exchange mechanisms for their conversion into items satisfying the material needs of those who produced them: humans do not live by wine alone, alas). The history of agricultural development makes it highly unlikely that large-scale, long-term intensifying investments were made by those rural elements whose appropriational movements were based on householding.

It is no surprise and certainly no coincidence that oil production and viticulture were precisely those areas that experienced the greatest amount of centralized direction: viz., the royal manufacture or management and supervision of wine (the *lmlk* jars). An intensification mechanism of greater weight but less visibility in the archaeological record relied on land grants to royal retainers for the purpose of vineyard and orchard

29. Much of this data is surveyed in my 'The Dynamics of Agriculture in Monarchical Israel', in *Society of Biblical Literature 1983 Seminar Papers* (ed. K.H. Richards; Chico, CA: Scholars Press, 1983), pp. 177-202.

development. It is likely as well that those families with access to capital would be more willing to risk investment in long-term plantings. Similarly, these same families would share a greater ability to recover (or the perceived ability to recover) should the investment prove disastrous. By the eighth century, the growth of the state administration and its extension into the rural zone would have produced a segment of farming families with ties to the state apparatus. As Harris writes, 'the cost benefits of intensification are not the same for peasants or workers as for members of the ruling class.'[30]

The growth of terrace systems boasting vineyards and olive orchards represented a change in appropriational and locational movements that was based on and reinforced the society's stratification. The Mount Zion tomb contained an abundance of jugs that likely held gifts of wine for the deceased.[31] Whether the family was itself invested in wine production, we do not know. Regardless, in the commodity development of Late Iron II Judah, connotations of wine would differ between the governmental elite who sponsored it and those whose grazing rights were abrogated as hillside pasture land was transformed into vineyards in the process of agricultural intensification. The view of vineyard development embodied in the Isaianic 'Song of the Vineyard' (Isa. 5.1-7) stands at a far remove from that concretized in the requiem of Job 24.

The State in Global-Political Context

Over half of all the Iron Age II Judean tombs gathered in and around Jerusalem.[32] Thus, the tenants of the Mount Zion tomb had lots of company in the capital city where they rested from their role as agents and beneficiaries of the royal administration of the productive hinterland. The popularity of the costly rock-cut bench tomb, not only in Jerusalem but throughout Judah, may have ridden the crest of demographic and economic growth as well as social differentiation across the Iron Age. Its

30. Harris, *Cultural Materialism: The Struggle for a Science of Culture* (New York: Random House, 1979), p. 103.

31. H.C. Brichto ('Kin, Cult, Land and Afterlife—A Biblical Concept', *HUCA* 44 [1973], pp. 1-54) has speculated on the role of tomb location in securing familial property. If so, the prominence of the tomb type may signal a significant shift in the land tenure system, whether the tomb is seen as operationalizing the shift or defending customary rights against new social pressures.

32. Barkay, 'The Iron Age II–III', p. 359.

initial adoption possessed temporal depth and must be located in Late Bronze Age Palestine, as we have seen. Just as vital, its rise in popularity possessed spatial breadth and must be situated in the larger geo-political context.

The Iron IIc period was the period of Assyrian hegemony. During the eighth century when the bench tomb began to emerge as the most prominent Judean burial style, the 'bathtub coffin' also began to appear at a few sites.[33] The Assyrian provenance of the tub-shaped coffin style as well as the moment of its appearance serve as reminders of the eighth-century penetration of Assyrian imperial forces into the heartland of Judah. The cultural landscape of ancient Judah was not an isolated landscape. The emergence of the bench tomb as a prominent mark of distinction for the highlanders of Judah cannot be understood merely as the blossoming of some inchoate identity.[34] The political dimension of state structures reminds us not simply of internal politics and the coercive dominion of royal authority, but the inevitable existence of foreign policy and the politics of state autonomy, dependence, and survival on a complex and dangerous world map.

It is commonplace to note Palestine's position on a strategically crucial commercial and military crossroads. Did this geo-political landscape constitute a 'world system'? How fully was ancient Judah integrated into it? 'Interaction' studies—how intersocietal contact affects socio-political change—have taken their cue from the 'world systems' theory by which

33. Bloch-Smith, *Burial Practices*, p. 36; and Barkay, 'The Iron Age II–III', p. 353.

34. E. Wolf, *Europe and the People without History* (Berkeley, CA: University of California Press, 1982), p. 9. Wolf has noted that many have conceived of society as 'a thing moving in response to an inner clockwork'. He writes of the propensity to 'conceive of the nation-state as a structure of social ties informed by moral consensus rather than as a nexus of economic, political and ideological relationships connected to other nexuses'. Archaeological research is beginning to make gains in wrestling with the question of ethnicity in the material record, in elucidating the local and regional landscape of Palestine. But concentration on the local scene can be a trap. It is a trap into which the prevalent pattern of anthropological research has invited archaeology by its offer of ethnographic analogies from studies of 'bounded' villages, of 'little communities' (Redfield). Research design limitations (real and in effect), whether of 'tell-based' archaeology or regional studies that venture into the 'catchment' within a certain radius of a site, tacitly impose a model of ancient life as 'microcosm'. Biblical scholars, likewise, have not wrested themselves fully free of the 'uniqueness of Israel' paradigm that tethers interpretation within a narrow circle.

Immanuel Wallerstein sought to understand the spread of capitalism in the modern world.[35] The view demands analysis of the 'world' or arena in which societies interact, attention to asymmetrical power relations among interacting societies, and examination of unbalanced exchange that takes place between more developed (or organized) dominant core regions and their less developed peripheries.[36]

Can 'world-systems' theory help clarify Judah's involvement in the larger world of the Near East and eastern Mediterranean? Was Judah periphery to the Assyrian core? The economic relations between core and periphery in the modern world certainly cannot be applied literally to ancient Judah. The unequal exchange that links together the developed and underdeveloped regions in the capitalistic world system entails the exchange of high-capital-intensive goods (manufactured goods) for low-capital-intensive goods (agricultural produce, natural and human resources). Trade networks in the ancient Near East did not comprehend such transfers. Trade networks passing through Palestine carried luxury goods ('preciosities'), metals, and military equipment (including horses). Sea-borne trade handled bulk goods like grain and timber more readily, but still the core was incapable of 'developing underdevelopment' according to the modern pattern.

Judah's position on the overland routes constituting 'a North-South political-commercial axis embracing Tyre–Israel–Sheba, with branches across the Mediterranean and Red Seas'[37] made possible both active

35. 'Diffusion' by any other name, but broken free of its tie to cultural uniqueness and its absolutist anti-generalizing bias. See the volume of essays edited by Edward M. Schortman and Patricia A. Urban, *Resources, Power, and Interregional Interaction. Interdisciplinary Contributions to Archaeology* (New York: Plenum Press, 1992).

36. When applied by anthropologists to the ethnographic enterprise, the 'world-systems' commitment to understanding the social processes in one region in terms of its relationship to a larger world system compels the realization that the ethnographic, bounded village does not exist. There are no peoples 'without history,' as Eric Wolf puts it, that is, peoples who lack connection with history as its products and agents (*Europe*, p. 23). For Wolf, history is 'an analytic account of the development of material relations, moving simultaneously on the level of the encompassing system and on the micro-level'. This realization implies that those who use ethnographic analogies in reconstructing the life of ancient Judah must carefully test for hidden assumptions regarding the relationship between their subjects and the larger world.

37. A. Malamat, 'A Political Look at the Kingdom of David and Solomon and its Relations with Egypt', in *Studies in the Period of David and Solomon and Other Essays* (ed. T. Ishida; Winona Lake, IN: Eisenbrauns, 1982), p. 191.

participation in trade as well as a profit from orchestrating and taxing the transit trade through Palestine. A number of recent works have emphasized the great value of this South Arabian trade in spices, gold, gems, and incense that entered the larger world of commerce via caravan across the Arabian desert and to the Mediterranean through the Wadi Zered–Beersheba depression.[38] Mercantile activity can be a major component in state formation and underwrites the state's economic power as well as its maintenance of an elite class through the status conferred by imports. As Yoffee notes, the luxury commodities acquired through trade 'represent burgeoning economic status [and]... The process of acquisition becomes an institution requiring organization and thus a means through which status is produced.'[39] Two crucial qualifications must be made. While the flow of goods along this Phoenicia–East Africa–Arabia route (as well as the rest of the international trade network) responded to economic forces of supply and demand, it paid heed to military-political coercion more acutely. The attempt to portray trade as instrumental in the early formation of the Judean monarchy must reckon with the reality that both stimuli (market forces as well as military muscle) remained dampened in the tenth century. In other words, there is a fundamental contradiction in asserting vast wealth gained through control of transit trade during an interlude in which the traditional coercive forces of Egypt, Mesopotamia, and Anatolia were quiescent. The severe paucity of imported items in the archaeological record of Palestine's tenth century—what was the cumulative value of the trade?[40]—puts teeth in this caution.

The imports known from biblical lists and the commodities known from the hulls of archaeologically excavated ships and witnessed in a variety of epigraphic finds include incense, spices, resins, chemicals, metals, ivory, bizarre animals—in short, preciosities and strategic goods with lofty value to weight ratios. The exchange of these commodities did

38. Notably, Holladay, 'The Kingdoms', pp. 383-86; and I. Finkelstein and A. Perevolotsky, 'Processes of Sedentarization and Nomadization in the History of Sinai and the Negev', *BASOR* 279 (1990), pp. 67-88.

39. 'Too Many Chiefs?', p. 69.

40. Holladay's calculation ('The Kingdoms', p. 383) of the value of the Arabian trade—$175,000,000-250,000,000 in 1960 US dollars—is both fantastic and nonsensical since the larger universe into which this number would fit remains unknown.

not enhance the life of the rural zone: they were destined for the court and military and circulated only within the circumscribed range of royal administration. They served to reinforce the legitimacy of royal rule, but had a negligible economic impact outside the palace sector.[41]

Whether or not this overland trade played a role in the early Iron Age history of the Judean highlands, Assyria's late Iron Age penetration of Judah aimed precisely at the control of trade with Egypt and Arabia. Assyria also aimed to extract tribute: Ahaz joined in on an Assyrian list of tribute providers; Esarhaddon's annals record Manasseh among vassals required to supply materials for royal building in Nineveh; and Hezekiah's post-revolt tribute included gold, silver, gems, ivory inlaid couches, elephant hides, African blackwood, boxwood, and human beings.[42] Assyria's domination of Judah was not the capitalistic exploitation of the 'underdeveloped world' but the surest, swiftest form of enrichment: the golden target strategy.[43]

These tribute payments held more consequences for the Judean economy than short-term impoverishment. Most of the tributary goods were not indigenous to Judah. They had to be procured elsewhere, on the international trade network. To enter this network, Judean monarchs turned to the few exportable products available: wine and oil. Intensive investments in these 'economic crops' multiplied. Heavy Assyrian demands for precious metals spurred the monetization of the economy, a development evidenced by the standardized shekel weights.[44] Thus the Assyrian tribute demands pushed and pulled the tiny Judean productive base quantitatively and qualitatively, short-term and long-term.

To accomplish both these ends, Assyria usurped Judean autonomy by imposing vassal status. However control was exercised typically, Sennacherib's punitive campaign leaves little doubt about the ultimate exercise of sovereignty; the tenants of the Mount Zion tomb lived their lives as vassals from the time of Tiglath-Pileser until the collapse of the empire.

---

41. As Moshe Elat has long held: 'Trade and Commerce', in *The Age of the Monarchies: Culture and Society* (ed. A. Malamat; The World History of the Jewish People, First Series: Ancient Times, 5; Jerusalem: Massada Press, 1979), p. 80.

42. *ANET*, p. 288.

43. Mentioned by T.F. Carney, *The Shape of the Past: Models and Antiquity* (Lawrence, KS: Coronado Press, 1975), p. 172.

44. Carney (*Shape*, p. 144) notes the increase in the scope and scale of the use of money in Europe after the Roman imposition of tribute.

The challenge to Assyria's heavy hand taken up by the Ashdod rebellion and the revolts of Hezekiah and Manasseh demonstrate resistance to the domination of the 'core'. This military resistance obviously had an economic component since it both reacted to impoverishment produced by Assyrian demands and further encouraged exports to raise funds for military hardware. Moreover, preparations for siege—for example, the hewing of waterworks—were costly. The most well-attested revolt, Hezekiah's gambit, failed, militarily and economically: Assyria assessed Judah a huge tribute payment, increased its annual tax, and lopped off a significant slice of its territory.

Hewers of Stone: Economic Resistance and National Identity

Both the tunnel of King Hezekiah and the tomb on Mount Zion were cut in the same era of Assyrian hegemony. Both indicate that some economic and ideological resources—viz., Judean nationalism—of the periphery were deployed in resistance to the domination of the core. While manifold and powerful influences on Judah's economic life emanated from the core, certain features represented resistance to the core, countervalent ventures of economic autonomy. The irony of this resistance was that it propelled the society into greater involvement in commodity production and inter-regional exchange. This both sharpened social stratification and rendered Judah more, not less, vulnerable to economic disruption. The archaeologically obvious devastation of the Judean countryside in the wake of Sennacherib's campaigning armies resulted only partly from direct action; much issued from administrative collapse. Yet Jerusalem was spared destruction in Hezekiah's day. The distinctive Judean bench tombs—salient indicators of the emergent national identity—sought security in the shadow of its stronghold. The repose of the dead was cut within a world historical context.

Considering the economies of ancient Palestine advances our understanding of the formation of the Israelite and Judean states by forcing us to come to terms with Palestine's diversity, with the embeddedness of its economies in a shifting constellation of societies, and with the region's place in a larger world system that it could resist but do little to control. We confront as well the unfathomable strangeness of life among the dead. When excavators pried open the entrance of the Mount Zion tomb, the dead did not in fact rise up to meet them.

SOURCES

SAUL BEN KISH IN HISTORY AND TRADITION

Diana Edelman

What can be known about the historical Saul ben Kish, reported founder of the kingdom of Israel? Or, put differently, how much of the testimony of 1 and 2 Samuel contains accurate facts that a modern historian can use to recreate the career of this individual? What kind or level of history can be written about this person?

Using the understanding of history developed by the *Annales* School, that changes take place at different rates over time, a modern historian would ideally like to write a history on the most detailed level, that of event. For such a history, texts are essential. The existence of the corpus of biblical texts, some of which deal with Saul's career, should theoretically permit the undertaking of such an endeavor. However, the purpose and perspective of the texts and the amount of evidence they provide about the historical Saul needs to be assessed before deciding whether his career can, in fact, be recreated on the level of event.

In addition, archaeological excavations and surveys provide material cultural remains that should allow for the writing of a history on the level the *Annales* School calls conjunction, or a socioeconomic and cultural history. Such a history does not encompass the history of the person of Saul directly, but provides background about the world in which he would have operated. Data provided by material cultural remains allow the historian to present an enhanced understanding of changes that take place at the level of event by placing them within the framework of slower-paced changes at the level of conjunction.

Can a history of Saul be written at the level of event, then? This is the main question that will be considered in this essay. The central issue that will be addressed is how to sort fact from fiction in the biblical version of the reign of Saul. The good news is that there might be factual data preserved in the biblical texts. The bad news is that there is no agreed method to accomplish the task of determining what are factual data.

There are no extrabiblical data available to verify the results of biblical critical analyses when it comes to the person of Saul. Since there are no independent texts against which to evaluate the biblical testimony, all argument must ultimately be based only on the biblical texts themselves.

Individuals will assess the historical reliability of 1 and 2 Samuel differently, being heavily influenced in the end by their understanding of the Bible as literature vs. history as well as by their understanding of the relationship between sacred scripture and religious belief. Clearly, the number and nature of statements that are deemed to be historically accurate information will determine what 'raw data' are ultimately linked together through chains of cause and effect by each historian to provide a meaningful creation of Saul's career. The more data that are included, the more convincing and coherent can be the proposed construction. The fewer the data, the more room there is for creative linkings of the available information. It is crucial to understand that no one can ever reconstruct and fully comprehend actual events in the past. Events take place in history, but they are always given meaning through interpretive frameworks. Given this situation, there can never be a definitive reconstruction of the past; there can only be a range of creative associations by individuals who have been influenced by their own life experiences as well as by the data they believe to be reliable and choose to link together in chains of meaning.

It is possible, but not necessarily preferable, to create a 'history by consensus', in which a majority of individuals agree that one creation of events best suits the evidence. Such a consensus cannot guarantee, however, that the creation accurately captures the actual events. Most histories are created by linking together individual data into chains of cause and effect based on logical processing; real life does not necessarily operate by the same neat, rational principles. What is plausible then, is not necessarily what actually happened. Ultimately, it is the meaning assigned to actual events rather than the events themselves that holds importance for humans and influences their lives. The attempt to establish a 'history by consensus', whose accuracy can never be verified, is a potentially dangerous goal. Such a consensus obscures the individualistic and creative nature of the historiographic enterprise, defining an unnecessary orthodoxy that discourages fresh investigations and creative imaginings and which results in a form of thought policing.

Methodological Considerations

The process by which biblical testimony can be converted to evidence for use in historical recreation will be the focus of the ensuing presentation, using the narratives involving Saul ben Kish as a case study. All claims and statements made in the biblical texts begin as testimony that may or may not provide accurate information about the subject matter they purport to describe. It is only by asking questions about the texts, questions that will vary from case to case but which address chronological and/or ideological issues, that that for which they serve as evidence can be deduced or inferred. The results of the ensuing case study on Saul will be used to answer the previous question: can his career, or aspects thereof, be recreated on the level of event?

In order to establish what will be deemed fact vs. fiction in the biblical account of the reign of Saul ben Kish, the historian needs to evaluate the biblical testimony, using the full range of old and new literary critical methods. The process should begin with textual criticism and the establishment of the critically evaluated text that will be used as the basis of testimony. In the case of 1 and 2 Samuel, the divergent readings found in the MT and the LXX provide an immediate challenge. Rather than harmonize the two traditions to produce a hypothetical text that has no known acceptance or existence within a given community, it would be better to analyze the two traditions separately and then compare the results. In this way, differences in rhetorical structure, audience, and received tradition can be taken into account and weighed accordingly in the final evaluation.

While there was an original text of the Samuel narrative, its author and date of composition are not known. LXX translations and other versions based on them provide evidence only of one or more versions of the text that existed and were used in the third–first centuries BCE. The Vaticanus MS and Old Latin MSS may well contain alterations from the original LXX translation(s), given the centuries of transmission involved. Similarly, the three 4QSam manuscripts provide glimpses of one or more versions of Samuel that were used within the Qumran community in the first century CE while the MT text, dating from the ninth century CE, seems to trace back to one version that was current in ancient Palestine in the first century CE and which became normative for rabbinic Jews after the Council of Javneh ca. 90 CE. The attempt by Jewish and Christian communities to establish a canonical version of

Samuel was a rather late development in the history of the book and different versions were canonized by different groups. Given the current collection of manuscripts and the long history of the book, it is impossible to recreate the original 'Ur'-text of Samuel. At most, the extant manuscripts can provide a set of texts of the book of Samuel that were used and deemed meaningful by different communities in different periods.[1]

The second step should be a close reading of the critically evaluated texts, with a focus on the patterns and literary devices that the ancient writer appears to have used to convey his message to his intended ancient audience. This step includes a host of theoretical issues and battlegrounds over which much ink has been spilled. To touch briefly upon the main ones, first is the debate over where meaning lies: in the author's intentions and words, in the interpretation by the reader or hearer, or in the text itself, which can take on a meaning independent of the one originally intended by the author. All three of these options contribute to the final reading of a text. By focusing on authorial intentionality, however, the modern historian is able to map out what appear to be highly visible milestones within the text that point the way toward the writer's vision and message. Even if minor devices and patterns are missed, the delimiting of the major patterns should provide a fairly clear indication of the major points of meaning to be conveyed.

Next is the issue of 'author'. Given the long period of transmission and reinterpretation of the biblical texts within the the post-monarchic Judean, Jewish and Christian communities, can the original intention of a single author even be articulated? After all, a reader encounters a final form of the text and so is really only understanding the view of the final redactional hand that worked on it. While this is true, I would argue that

---

1.   Thus, I espouse a different approach to the issue of textual reconstruction than some of the reviewers of my book, *King Saul in the Historiography of Judah* (JSOTSup, 121; Sheffield: JSOT Press, 1991); contrast the approach favored by for example S. McKenzie (*RSR* 19 [1993], p. 67), T. Mullen (*CBQ* 56 [1994], p. 101) and G. Knoppers (*JBL* 114 [1995], p. 132). Knoppers has provided a fuller discussion of the principles of textual reconstruction than the first two, indicating what some of the issues are. Unfortunately, in his comments he has failed to distinguish between the original actual audience that read the book when it was first produced and subsequent actual audiences that read the forms of the book reflected in the MT, Qumran and LXX versions. He argues that the variant forms can furnish important clues about how the original audience understood the text.

the changes that have been introduced within subsequent tradition represent probably only a very small portion of the text, so that the reader sees most of the text as it was structured by its original author. In my opinion, careful attention to structuring patterns and literary devices will permit a person to understand to a significant degree the intention of the original author, regardless of whether or not one can definitively say what is primary and what is secondary in a given sentence. By the same token, by focusing on the devices that are present, a reader should be better able to decide what is likely to be part of the writer's original composition and what might be a secondary expansion.

The third main theoretical issue in a close reading is that of audience. It is particularly helpful to distinguish three main levels of audience when analyzing biblical texts: the intended ancient audience, for whom the author wrote his work; the actual ancient audience(s), who read the work and may or may not have understood the author's intended meaning; and the actual modern audience(s), of which we are a part.[2] We are separated from the writer even further than his actual ancient audience and subsequent generations of audiences by different cultural frames of reference and vastly different world-views. As a result, we need to try to understand the world-view and literary conventions that were prevalent at the time the texts were written and not superimpose our own contemporary structural and literary devices on these ancient texts. Our best recourse, which is not foolproof by any means, is to search for recurrent patterns contained within the biblical texts themselves. In addition, we need also to study comparative ancient Near Eastern texts to help with the discernment of patterns that have only been used once in the biblical texts but which were widespread regional conventions.

Finally, the issue of dating both the original writer and his intended audience should be considered. As is well known, clues for dating have to be derived from the texts themselves; so all arguments for dating can

---

2.   For an excellent discussion of levels of audience, see P. Rabinowitz, 'Truth in Fiction: A Reexamination of Audiences', *Critical Inquiry* 4 (1977), pp. 121-41. He identifies four levels of audience: the ideal narrative audience, the imitation or narrative audience, the authorial audience, and the actual audience. While all four are valid distinctions, I think issues about the historicity of story details are adequately addressed by focusing on the authorial audience and the actual audience. However, for ancient texts like the Hebrew Bible, a further distinction between the actual ancient audience and the actual modern audience needs to be made in light of chronological and cultural distances and differences.

easily become circular. Let me only point out that I think that literary and structural conventions used within the biblical texts did not change appreciably from the eighth century through the end of the Persian era in the fourth century BCE. It seems that it is only with the spread of Hellenistic models and ideas that a major change is introduced into ancient Near Eastern writing conventions.[3] Thus, whether a text is dated to the late monarchic or early exilic period will probably not affect the types of patterns and devices used to structure it; it will, however, affect the message because of the different situations and life experiences of the intended audiences in each period.

The third step in converting biblical testimony to evidence should entail a consideration of the types of sources that might have been available to the authors as they constructed the biblical narratives, the likelihood and manner in which such sources might have survived to be used, and, where available, the likelihood that such sources were in fact used. The fourth and final step in the process would include a consideration of what information might have been derived from such sources. Such speculative reconstruction can only be done on the basis of prior reflection over how the narrative has been structured and what main message its author was trying to convey.

In order for a modern historian to determine the contexts or situations for which statements in biblical texts serve as evidence, an evaluative process must be undertaken. Beginning with textual criticism, the historian then needs to engage in a close reading of the critically evaluated texts, focusing on authorial intention as revealed through the use of structuring patterns and devices. In this process, he or she needs to try to read from the perspective of a member of the ancient intended audience by becoming familiar with ancient world-views and literary conventions. Next, the historian needs to consider the availability of possible sources to the biblical authors and their use of such sources to create an understanding of the past. Only after this process has been completed can the individual historian responsibly move on to the task

---

3.   Direct contact with Greek or Mediterranean literature by Judahites is a strong likelihood by the end of the eighth century BCE, when Greek mercenaries began to be used in Egypt and Cisjordan. Such contact may have been significantly earlier, introduced by the Sea Peoples who settled in the area at the end of the Late Bronze Age and during the early Iron Age. It is only with the spread of Hellenism, however, that such literature would likely have become a desirable norm to be emulated as part of the new dominant culture.

of using creative imagining to link together data deemed relevant to the topic under investigation to provide a historical recreation of the past.

The Literary Saul

In my publications on Saul, I have suggested that various structuring patterns and devices were used by the original author of the narrative on the career of Saul ben Kish in 1 Samuel 8–2 Samuel 1.[4] This is not an independent narrative but a segment of a larger history of the monarchic era, composed, I believe, by the so-called Deuteronomistic historian.

The major pattern derives from the ritual ceremony for the installation of the king. It contains three elements: 1) the designation of the king-elect through anointing; 2) the testing of the candidate's worthiness to serve as YHWH's earthly vice-regent through the successful completion of a test in the form of a military deed; and 3) the installation of the candidate as king at the completion of step 2. The elements within this pattern have been deduced from a review of both biblical and extrabiblical texts.[5] This pattern seems to have been used three times by the Deuteronomistic historian within the narrative devoted to the United Monarchy: to describe Saul's rise to power (9.1–10.16; 11.15), to explain why Jonathan would not succeed Saul on the throne (1 Sam. 13–14), and to describe David's rise to power (1 Sam. 16.13; 17; 2 Sam. 2.4; 5.1-6). In the case of Saul, the designation as king-elect through anointing occurs in Ramah in 10.1, the test by military deed in 11.1-11 in the account of Saul's rescue of Jabesh-Gilead from the Ammonites, and the final coronation as king at Gilgal in 11.14-15.

---

4. See especially 'Saul's Rescue of Jabesh-Gilead (1 Sam. 11:1-11): Sorting Story from History', *ZAW* 96 (1984), pp. 195-209; 'The Deuteronomist's Story of King Saul: Narrative Art or Editorial Product?', in *Pentateuchal and Deuteronomistic Studies: Papers Read at the XIIIth IOSOT Congress, Leuven 1989* (BETL, 94; ed. C. Brekelmans and J. Lust; Leuven: Leuven University Press, 1990), pp. 207-20; *King Saul in the Historiography of Judah*.

5. The anointing and coronation elements were noted by T. Mettinger (*King and Messiah* [ConBOT, 8; Lund: Gleerup, 1975], pp. 72, 79, 86-87) and B. Halpern (*The Constitution of the Monarchy in Israel* [HSM, 24; Chico, CA: Scholars Press, 1981], pp. 51-148). Both seem to have been aware that the testing element was an integral part of the ritual, even though neither explicitly included it in the coronation pattern. I proposed it as an integral step in my article, 'Saul's Rescue of Jabesh-Gilead'. For another reconstruction of the coronation pattern, see Z. Ben Barak, 'The Coronation Ceremony in Ancient Mesopotamia', *OLP* 11 (1980), pp. 55-67.

The second major pattern used to structure the account of Saul's reign is the standard regnal formula: the accession formula appears in 13.1; the account of selected deeds in 13.2–14.46; the summary of the reign in 14.47-48; and the death, burial, and succession notice in 1 Sam. 31.1–2 Sam. 5.3. The long delay between the summary of the reign and the death, burial and succession notice can be ascribed to the writer's desire to signal—on the literary level—that Saul's career as king was effectively over when David was anointed king-elect, but that he remained king in name until his death. The first two patterns have been interwoven in the present narrative.

A third structuring pattern divides Saul's career into his life 'under YHWH's good spirit' and his life 'under YHWH's evil spirit'. The pattern allows the writer to demonstrate that as YHWH's anointed, who has received divine spirit, the king will remain in office and possess some form of divinely bestowed controlling spirit throughout his lifetime. The same principle is evident in the previous period of the judges, where the term of judgeship lasts the rest of a chosen individual's life; once divine spirit is bestowed, it remains until death (Judg. 2.18). The same theological understanding remains in force for the subsequent era of the kingdoms of Israel and Judah. Nevertheless, possession of the divine spirit cannot guarantee success as a leader. Disobedience of God will lead to divine rejection and the individual's inability to continue to serve his nation effectively as YHWH's earthly vice-regent during the remainder of his term of office. The king will lose YHWH's guiding spirit, which will result in his failure to be able to discern the divine will and act appropriately. As a consequence, his nation will suffer. A similar structuring device has been used in the account of David's career.[6]

In addition, the author appears to have used the motif of Jonathan's personal covenant with David as a major structuring device within the Saulide narrative and beyond, into the story of David's career as Saul's successor. The covenant is used first to demonstrate Jonathan's acceptance of David as Saul's divinely chosen successor, illustrating his understanding of the guilty verdict rendered against him by YHWH in 14.42. After David kills Goliath, Jonathan makes a covenant with him, giving David his own robe, his armor, his bow, and his girdle (18.1-5). In this act, the heir-elect to the throne symbolically endows David, the

---

6. See R.A. Carlson, *David, the Chosen King* (Uppsala: Almqvist & Wiksell, 1964), pp. 24-25.

secretly anointed king-elect, with the formal instruments associated with the second 'testing' stage of the three-part kingship installation pattern.

The covenant between Jonathan and David is reintroduced regularly in the narrative[7] to chronicle Jonathan's willing acceptance of David as Saul's successor and to contrast it with Saul's refusal to accept the divine plan for succession. At the same time, however, it portrays Jonathan as an astute politician who uses the covenant as a means to force concessions from David that will guarantee the future and safety of the Saulide line. By supporting David, Jonathan is depicted as hoping to have him serve as a single interloper in the Saulide dynasty and see his family maintain control of the throne in future generations.

Finally, the writer has used the contrasting word pairs *ṭôḇ* and *rāʾâ* and *lēḇ* and *ʾênáyim* and the key word *yāḏ* to help focus the audience's attention on the precepts of royal power and its potential abuses through the course of the narrative.

Potential Sources Underlying the Present Narrative

The use of a three-part pattern derived from later monarchic-era royal installation ceremonies to describe how the first king of Israel was empowered raises immediate questions about the availability of sources to the author of the Saul narrative. Had details about Saul's actual rise to power been known to the author of 1 Samuel, is it likely that the ancient audience would have expected them to be narrated within the framework of the normative coronation pattern? If so, the practice should have continued for all subsequent kings, yet it occurs again only for David. In both of these cases, the testimony suggests the lack of underlying hard evidence, which in turn led the writer to improvize by essentially 'historicizing' main elements of the ritual ceremony. According to the norm, to become a king a person must be anointed, be tested, and then be crowned, so Saul must have gone through these steps, too, but in a hypothesized past, not just in a cultic ceremony. Using this logic, it then becomes clear that if Saul is designated as king-elect in 9.16 for the

---

7.   D. Jobling has noted that the motif is developed progressively through scenes that alternately focus on Jonathan and David or Saul (18.1-5; 19.1-7; 20.1-21; 23.15b-18) and ones in which David and Saul interact (16.14–17.58; 18.16-30; 19.8-25; 21.2–23.15a [with other material]; 23.19 onward [with much other material]) (*The Sense of Biblical Narrative* [JSOTSup, 7; Sheffield: JSOT Press, 2nd edn, 1978], I, p. 15).

purpose of delivering the people from the hands of the Philistines, his test by military deed cannot be against the group he is to fight when he becomes king, because he is not yet king. Thus, another enemy is brought in to serve as the testers—in this case, the Ammonites.

Is it possible that Saul in fact fought the Ammonites at some other point in his career, so that this story is based on actual fact, even if the writer has recontextualized it chronologically within Saul's career? The answer I would offer is 'yes'. It could be argued that the summary of Saul's career in 1 Sam. 14.47-48 is drawn from some sort of royal annal or a collection of military songs like the Book of Yashar, in which some of Saul's battles were commemorated. This cannot be proven, however, and these verses may simply represent a list of Judah's traditional enemies retrojected to the time of Saul.

The following is a list of what I consider to be materials drawn from various early sources by the Deuteronomistic historian to construct the present narrative about Saul:

1. The *māšāl* in 1 Sam. 10.11-12, 19.24, 'Is Saul also among the prophets?' Its twofold use in different contexts makes its original context and meaning uncertain.

2. The song fragment in 18.7 and 21.12, 'Saul has slain his thousands and David his ten thousands'. Taken in isolation, the statement need not indicate that Saul and David were contemporaries or successors; it could be based on legendary figures from the past, both of whom were renowned for their military prowess, with no personal connection whatsoever.

3. The lament over Saul and Jonathan in 2 Sam. 1.19-27. Whoever wrote the lament considered Saul to have been a leader of some importance, who was able to dress the 'daughters of Israel' in crimson robes covered with gold dangles or ornaments. The title *melek* is not used, and yet the portrayal of Saul seems to be on a royal scale when compared with the stories underlying the judges, for example. Perhaps this is due to the different genres more than reality, however, so caution must be used in drawing conclusions about Saul's royal vs. non-royal status from the lament.

A careful reading of the narrative account of Saul's demise in chs. 28–31 suggests that most of the information there is a creative imagining of events based on the information in the lament. There is a noticeable overlap in vocabulary and concepts between the prose and poetic versions: the use of the verbs *ḥll*, *npl*, *bśr*, and *ṣrr*, the last in an impersonal construction; reference to the participation of royal family members alongside the army; reference to the Philistines as 'uncircumcised'; the location of the final defeat on Mt Gilboa; and the reference to Saul's sword as his primary weapon. The only information in the prose account that cannot be derived from the lament is the role of Beth She'an in the final battle. This could have been derived from an independent source or it could be the contribution of the writer's own imagination in light of the location of the final confrontation in the vicinity of Mt Gilboa. The lament can also be the source of the naming of the Philistines as Israel's prime enemies who are to be eradicated by the first king in 9.16.

4. The fragment of an administrative district list in 2 Sam. 2.9 that reflects the Saulide holdings that became Davidide. The list distinguishes between two types of holdings through the use of two idioms: *mālak ʾel* and *mālak ʿal*. The first is a very unusual term not attested anywhere outside the Saulide narrative. While it is true that the prepositions *ʾel* and *ʿal* sometimes substitute for one another in later texts, it is less likely that such an interchange is at work here because the resulting expression *mālak ʾel* is non-idiomatic. Such an interchange tends to occur when the resulting expression can be idiomatic with either preposition. The use of the expression *mālak ʾel* seems to be an attempt to distinguish more loosely affiliated regions from those under centralized control.[8] A comparison with the list of so-called Solomonic districts in 1 Kings 4 shows direct continuity over time, with territories acquired subsequently being added in as new districts.[9]

5. The Saulide genealogy in 1 Sam. 9.1 and other information that served as the basis for the family summary in 1 Sam. 14.46. The first genealogy has introduced an unnamed ancestor simply as 'a Yimnite man' and has included a female, Becorath, in order to use the literary convention of seventh-generational birth to foreshadow Saul's destiny to

---

8.   For a fuller discussion of this verse, see D. Edelman, 'The "Ashurites" of Eshbaal's State (2 Sam. 2.9)', *PEQ* 117 (1985), pp. 88-89.

9.   It could also be argued that the so-called Solomonic list is earlier than the list attributed to Eshbaal and that the latter represents a loss of territory. To make this argument, however, a plausible historical situation that would account for the boundaries of Israel as delineated in 2 Sam. 2.9 would need to be set forth, as well as a cogent explanation for the difference between the *mālak ʾel* and the *mālak ʿal* districts.

greatness.[10] It should be noted that the latter summary functions literarily to introduce the roster of characters for the upcoming story events except for Abinadab, who appears unannounced in 1 Sam. 31.2. He may have been introduced subsequently on the basis of the Saulide genealogy now preserved in 1 Chron. 8.33-40; 9.39-44.

6. An old tradition that underlies the current form of 1 Sam. 9.1–10.16, which told how Saul took control over a segment of Mt Ephraim. Beginning with Saul's introduction as a man destined to greatness by virtue of his position as a seventh-generation male,[11] the story goes on to reinforce Saul's character as a future hero by emphasizing his beauty and physical height as traits that set him apart from ordinary men. It then continues by having Saul search for his father's lost asses, the symbolic mount of royalty. In this task, he traverses four contiguous areas of Mt Ephraim, before learning the significance of his action, which is revealed to him in Ramah by the famous local seer, who makes him the guest of honor at a prearranged banquet. The tour through Mt Ephraim appears to function as a foreshadowing of future plot developments. The story should go on to describe how Saul becomes ruler over the area he toured. Instead, it breaks off in 10.16 and develops new themes.[12]

10. For this literary convention, see J. Sasson, 'A Genealogical "Convention" in Biblical Chronology?', *ZAW* 90 (1978), pp. 171-85.

11. It may be that the seventh-generation conventional device was an original part of the old tale, or it could be a later addition to the story by the Deuteronomistic historian, as a further means of emphasizing Saul's destiny to greatness. If it is part of the original story, then this postulated old tradition would be its source. If it is an expansion by the Dtr H, then a separate source would need to be posited for it.

12. For the contiguous nature of the four areas, see my article, 'Saul's Journey through Mt. Ephraim and Samuel's Ramah (1 Sam. 9:4-5; 10:2-5)', *ZDPV* 104 (1988), pp. 44-58. I think the anointing scenes in 9.15-17 and 9.27–10.1 are secondary expansions of the original story, which used the banquet as a means of designating Saul as future ruler. The identification of Samuel as the seer may also be secondary, although it is noteworthy that Samuel's reported sanctuary circuit tour in 1 Sam. 7.16-17 corresponds to the same territory traversed by Saul in 9.4-5. It could be argued that the Dtr H 'created' Samuel's circuit tour based on information in this old story after he identified the unnamed seer with Samuel; the old story might have gone on to tell how Saul replaced the seer as ruler of this delineated territory, presenting irony by having the seer designate his own successor/usurper. Alternately, it is possible that the old story went on to identify the seer as Samuel, who then ended up designating the man who would take control over his own little fiefdom. In this case, the statement in 7.16-17 could be based either on this story, or on an independently preserved tradition that remembered the territory that Samuel had

7. There are a number of passages that point to traditions linking Saul with Gibeon, even though there seems to have been a deliberate attempt by the so-called Deuteronomistic historian to obscure these links.[13] Whether these are historical or not remains to be seen. The main units include 2 Sam. 2.12–3.1, 2 Sam. 21.1-14, and 1 Chron. 8.29-40, 9.33-44. After Saul's death and David's coronation as king in Hebron, Abner is said to have collected the remaining Saulide heir, Eshbaal, whom he then took to Mahanaim and had crowned king. The implication of the wording and circumstances is that Eshbaal survived the slaughter at Gilboa because he was too young to fight and that Abner retrieved him from the capital to be crowned before the troops that had also escaped and had regrouped at Mahanaim (2 Sam. 2.12-13).[14] Immediately after Eshbaal's coronation, the writer narrates the episode about the ordeal by battle between Eshbaal's troops and David's troops. Although no explicit reason is given for the battle, it is portrayed to have involved a fight to control the throne of Israel. The confrontation reportedly took place at

controlled. For other discussions of this early tradition, see for example L. Schmidt, *Menschlicher Erfolg und Jahwes Initiative: Studien zu Tradition, Interpretation und Historie in Überlieferungen von Gideon, Saul und David* (WMANT, 38; Neukirchen–Vluyn: Neukirchener Verlag, 1970), pp. 58-102; J.M. Miller, 'Saul's Rise to Power: Some Observations Concerning 1 Sam 9:1-10:16; 10:26-11:15 and 13:2-14:46', *CBQ* 36 (1974), pp. 157-74; and P.M. Arnold, *Gibeah: The Search for a Biblical City* (JSOTSup, 79; Sheffield: JSOT Press, 1990), pp. 89-93.

13. For a detailing and analysis of these passages, see esp. J. Blenkinsopp, *Gibeon and Israel* (SOTSMS, 2; Cambridge: Cambridge University Press, 1972). For an anti-Gibeonite tendency in the Deuteronomistic History, see P.J. Kearney, 'The Role of the Gibeonites in the Deuteronomic History', *CBQ* 35 (1973), pp. 1-19.

14. This fact tends to undermine the claim in 2.10 that Eshbaal was 40 years old when he was crowned king. To the contrary, he appears to have been a pre-teen or teenager. His status as a minor tends to be corroborated by the information provided in various passages about Saul's family. Jonathan, the eldest son, is the only male child who is reported to have produced offspring before dying at Gilboa. His son Meribaal/Mephiboshet was said to have been a child young enough to have been carried and accidently dropped by his nurse when Jonathan died (2 Sam. 4.4). The other Saulide heirs that are said to have been sacrificed by the Gibeonites in 2 Sam. 21.1-14 were reportedly Saul's sons by a secondary wife or concubine and the sons of Jonathan's sister, Michal. The writer or a later editor seems to have deliberately made Eshbaal into an older man who would make a more worthy opponent of David in the struggle for the throne; he did not want it to be known that David was fighting a minor.

Gibeon. Since neither David nor Eshbaal was situated at Gibeon in the narrative, there is no literary motive for the arrival there of the other for the confrontation. Whether or not such an ordeal by battle ever took place, the writer is strongly implying in this narrative that he knew an older tradition that named Gibeon as the capital of Saul. Such a tradition would account for the writer's decision to situate a confrontation between representatives of the two rival kings, Eshbaal and Davíd, at the city.[15]

It is noteworthy that the Saulide genealogy in 1 Chron. 8.33-40 has been grafted onto one detailing the history of Gibeon (1 Chron. 8.29-40). The Chronicler makes a specific point of mentioning that in the post-exilic community, some of those who 'returned' to Gibeon, their alleged ancestral home,[16] chose to dwell in Jerusalem instead. This singling out

15. It is possible that the old tradition does not reflect past reality, but instead is the result of an ideological dispute over which sanctuary would become the primary seat during the Persian period in Yehud. Gibeonite priests arguing for the supremacy of Gibeon might have fictitiously associated it with David's precursor Saul, in order to give it priority by associating it with an earlier founder of the state to counter the established link of the Jerusalem temple with David. If this argument is to be made, details that support it instead of the alternate view that the texts preserve a genuine association of Gibeon with Saul would need to be pointed out.

16. As noted by A. Demsky, the mention of the clans of Ner and Gedor among those who resettle at Gibeon would seem to indicate that some of those who moved into the Persian province of Yehud were indeed returning to ancestral homes. Jar handles from late monarchic Gibeon bear the names *nr* and *gdr* ('The Genealogy of Gibeon [I Chronicles 9:35-44]: Biblical and Epigraphic Considerations', *BASOR* 202 [1971], pp. 20-23). Thus, not all the Persian population of Yehud were simply newcomers who had no former connections to the area, as suggested by T.L. Thompson, *The Early History of the Israelite People: From the Written and Archaeological Sources* (SHANE, 4; Leiden: Brill, 1992), pp. 418-23, esp. 422, and private discussion.

Alternatively, it might be argued on the basis of the evidence above that the population of Gibeon was not deported by the neo-Babylonians but remained in place through the sixth century. The results of excavations conducted at Gibeon have not been published adequately to allow a decision to be made about continuous or discontinuous occupation during the sixth century. A clear pottery sequence for the sixth century does not yet exist so even with full publication firm conclusions on this point would not be able to be made from the material remains alone. No debris associated with a general destruction by fire is reported to have been found for the Iron I or Iron II periods and jar handles stamped with the name Mozah, written in Aramaic script, provide evidence for some sort of settlement in the fifth century BCE (J.A. Pritchard, *Gibeon, Where the Sun Stood Still: The Discovery of the Biblical City* [Princeton: Princeton University Press, 1962], pp. 161, 163).

of Gibeonites to move into Jerusalem is curious since it is not done for any other city in the genealogy. Theologically, the writer seems to be implying that Gibeon had been a rival to Jerusalem during the previous monarchic period, but that in the new era, Jerusalem would have no rival, as indicated by the voluntary association of the Gibeonites with the 'correct' sacred city. That the nature of the earlier rivalry was in part religious is suggested by the tradition in 1 Kgs 3.4 wherein Solomon offered sacrifice at Gibeon prior to the building of the temple in Jerusalem because the former had been the largest *bāmâ* sanctuary. The tradition in 2 Sam. 21.1-14 about the slaughter of members of the Saulide family in Gibeon (21.6 following the reading in Codices Vaticanus and Alexandrinus as well as Aquila and Symmachus) may also allude to the city's former status as an important cultic site.

8. The use of some sort of northern, that is, Israelite rather than Judahite source for creation of the Saulide narrative is indicated by the alternation between Gibeah and Geba as designations for the same site. As argued by P. Arnold,[17] it is likely that the two names represent dialectical variants. The Deuteronomistic historian appears to have derived the northern spelling, Gibeah, from a source and has alternated its use in the narrative with the southern spelling, Geba, so that his southern audience would know which site was being discussed.

Historical Recreation

Information drawn from these source materials provides minimal core data for the reign of Saul. Can a history of the career of Saul ben Kish be written on the basis of this scanty set of data? Yes, but not on the level of event. With so few data, however, a number of different scenarios can be postulated and chains of cause and effect drawn. In addition, motivations for territorial expansion can be postulated on the basis of archaeological and geographical data that relate to the slower changes over time associated with long duration and conjunction.

My own recreation posits that Saul emerged initially as a petty king of Gibeon. This is based on the assessment that the scattered texts that link Saul to Gibeon reflect a past reality. Although the title *melek* is not used for him in any of the early sources outlined, I would assign him this title because of his status as head of the palace state of Gibeon. It appears from the limited source material available that palace states in Cisjordan

17. So Arnold, *Gibeah*, pp. 37-38, 42.

in the Late Bronze period used monarchy as the standard form of government within a social structure built on patronage. The few instances in the Amarna letters where elders are writing instead of a king could well represent extraordinary circumstances during which a king had been deposed by the Egyptians, had died creating a period of interregnum, or might have been absent from the city. Continuing a long-standing tradition, kingship would have been the rule, not the exception, at Gibeon at the end of the Iron I or beginning of the Iron II period.

From his base as king of that palace state, Saul expanded into surrounding Israelite territory, creating a territorial state with different levels of centralization. At its core, the fledgling state included the central Ephraimite hill country and Benjamin. In loose affiliation with that core were the north Samarian hills, both sides of the Jordan valley, and part of the central Transjordanian hill country. The new territorial state assumed the name of Israel (2 Sam. 1.24), a designation that was particularly associated with the population of the core districts of Mt Ephraim and Benjamin. Saul apparently had Benjaminite roots (1 Sam. 9.1, 21; 10.21), which would explain his eventual decision to adopt the name of Israel for his new state, even though he began his career among the Gibeonites.[18]

As an economic basis for his territorial state, Saul would have striven to control local trade routes and find markets for the few natural resources he would have controlled: olive oil, wine, wool, iron ore, possibly red dye, and foodstuffs and spices from oasis areas in the Jordan valley. In this quest he would have found himself in competition, particularly with the Philistines to his west in the lowlands, but also with independent palace states in Cis- and Transjordan and other emerging fledgling territorial and palace states in both areas. He died trying to expand beyond the north Samarian hill country into the Jezreel–Beth She'an corridor. I can only use my imagination to posit why he began his career at Gibeon and the order in which certain events took place in his career that led to his control over the areas named in the

---

18. If 2 Sam. 21.4-5 is set beside 2 Sam. 2.8-9, the following inference and deduction can be drawn. During the process of initial expansion, Saul may have administered the Gibeonites and the Israelites as two independent entities. At some later point in his career, however, he appears to have decided to consolidate them into a single unit, and it was the Benjaminites who prevailed over the Gibeonites. The latter were incorporated into the centralized district of Benjamin.

administrative list in 2 Sam. 2.4. At this point I am really beyond the realm of the data.

A date for Saul cannot be firmly established on the basis of the limited information available. He was associated with Israel, so any attempt to situate him in time needs to be done in relation to other Israelite kings whose existence can be verified by extrabiblical documentation. Omri is generally recognized to be the earliest king of Israel who is mentioned outside the Bible. He is named on the Mesha stele, which is dated on palaeographic grounds usually to the first half of the ninth century BCE. Dates based on biblical quotes for lengths of reign would tend to place him in the first quarter of the ninth century: 885–874[19] or 879–869.[20] If G.W. Ahlström is correct, however, that the seal of Shemaᶜ that was found at Megiddo refers to the servant of Jeroboam I rather than Jeroboam II, as commonly assumed, then he would be the earliest king of Israel whose existence would be confirmed by extrabiblical evidence.[21] Jeroboam I is generally dated during the last third of the tenth century BCE.[22] Saul would probably precede him since the *māšāl* and song fragment relating to him cast him as a shadowy figure of the past more than as an established royal monarch in a fixed king-list. It would seem logical to place Saul sometime during the tenth century BCE.

Conclusion

More than one plausible recreation of factors that led to Saul's emergence as the first king of Israel can be made on the basis of the delineated data pool. How close to historical reality any picture comes, however, cannot be judged. Be that as it may, a scholarly consensus about the career of Saul ben Kish can perhaps be reached, in spite of our inability to determine its accuracy. But is such a consensus desirable? I do not think so. The creation of an orthodox understanding

---

19. So E. Thiele, *The Mysterious Numbers of the Hebrew Kings* (Grand Rapids, MI: Academie Books, rev. edn, 1983), p. 10.

20. So J.H. Hayes and P.K. Hooker, *A New Chronology for the Kings of Israel and its Implications for Biblical History and Literature* (Atlanta: John Knox, 1988), p. 24.

21. G.W. Ahlström, 'The Seal of Shema', *SJOT* 7 (1993), pp. 208-15.

22. Thiele dates his reign from 930–909 BCE (*Mysterious Numbers*, p. 10) while Hayes and Hooker date it from 927–906 BCE (*New Chronology*, p. 16).

of the past will undermine the creative enterprise called historiography and will introduce a form of thought control that will eliminate individualism and freedom of expression.

RE-READING SAMUEL (HISTORICALLY):
'ETWAS MEHR NICHTWISSEN'

Graeme Auld

1. Re-Reading Samuel

Notable work has been published in recent years on how to savour, to
appreciate the riches of the books of Samuel. My three examples will
suggest the international spread of this effort.

1. Robert Polzin

Robert Polzin's volumes on Samuel and David are the second and third
parts of his *Literary Study of the Deuteronomistic History*. He is in no
doubt that the account in both books of Samuel of the beginnings of
monarchy in Israel is shaped for a later age.

The balancing fates of Eli and Saul, at beginning and end of 1 Samuel,
warn that the future does not lie in the hands of priestly or royal families
north of Jerusalem. But, equally, the decision after Absalom's revolt
whether to bring back David across the Jordan (at Gilgal) resonates with
questions closer to the historians' times: whether to bring back contemporary sons of David from the east to a restored future in Jerusalem
(1993: 195).

The earlier story of the loss and return of the ark shows how the
Lord's power is not diminished by Israel's defeat or the plunder of its
shrine. But again the ability of the ark to return leaderless from captivity
is pregnant with foreboding for the descendants of that very David who
comes to meet it and make it a focus of his capital.

David has no part in Saul's death; he has a secure alibi at a safe
distance. And yet he is also compromised by his own generous battle-
field law: 'as his share is who goes down into battle, so shall his share be
who stays by the baggage; they shall share alike'. 'The king who hid
himself among the baggage when called upon to rule (1 Sam. 20.22) is

replaced by one who stays beside the baggage (30.24) as he waits for a chance to rule' (1989: 223).

Polzin's eye and ear for connections of sound and sense and situation across the text seem very sure. What he suggests most clearly to any would-be historical evaluator of the books of Samuel is the high artistry of those who wrote these books in and for their own postexilic times. He also tries to block access to a history behind the text—I will comment later on his discussion of the textual history of David and Goliath (1989: 259-61).

2. *Jan Fokkelman*

Jan Fokkelman's four monumental volumes are devoted to exploring narrative art and poetry in the books of Samuel alone. He is concerned even more than Polzin to explore the intimate detail of the writer's craft: Fokkelman's approach is 'close reading' that merits the name. His work eludes review in a short paper; and I simply mention three details I will pick up later.

He is clear that the 'military campaigns of David mentioned [in 2 Samuel 8] did not all take place at the same time, shortly after the receiving of God's word. Several of them must have been undertaken in the period covered by II Sam. 9–20' (1990: 156). Similarly Halpern describes 2 Samuel 8 elsewhere in this volume as a 'capstone narrative' whose position is determined thematically, not chronologically. While Fokkelman goes on to note the artistic merit in these 'moments of anticipation', we must observe that a literary-historical account of the matter is not excluded by his approach.

Despite mocking 'the strict and priggish schoolmasters of source criticism', he concedes that a 'genetic solution to the contradiction of the double ascribing of the victory against Goliath' is appropriate (1990: 296); and he goes on to argue powerfully that 'by not retracting the event [the editors of Samuel] put the reader onto the track of the origin and intention of I 17: that enormous chapter wants to celebrate the hero David in spite of the fact that (and whilst it is not disputed that) the victory against Goliath is "not historical"'.

He is similarly effective in his discussion of God as hero or villain of the census story (310); and on links between 2 Sam. 21.1-14 and 2 Samuel 24 which I shall also discuss below.

3. *Moshe Garsiel*

Moshe Garsiel brings us closer to David's city. I know his work only from English translation. His attention to word-play, demonstrated also in his *Biblical Names*, and to analogous situation, is very attractive. And yet, coming from Polzin and Fokkelman, I wonder if Garsiel on 1 Samuel does not read David too positively. He finds it unproblematic (1990: 135) that David's savagery to Amalek is more favourably viewed than Saul's pity, and suggests that the author has had to work hard to produce indirect apologies for David sharing Saul's crime of keeping some Amalekite booty. If Polzin is more attuned to resonances from a later period, the analogies Garsiel explores are with earlier—and, I suppose, he presumes familiar—episodes in biblical narrative: Samuel and Moses; the Ark and the Exodus; Saul and Jonathan at Michmash versus Gideon and Jephthah; and of course David and Saul.

2. *'Etwas mehr Nichtwissen'*

If the first words of my title suggest readers of Samuel in the last decade, its last words—pleading for rather more ignorance about the United Monarchy—cite Wellhausen, a doubly influential earlier student of the book: his study of the text of Samuel (1871) and his *Prolegomena* (1878) remain monuments of our discipline. It is widely acknowledged how many of his retroversions of the LXX have been confirmed by finds at Qumran. I want to underscore just two points here, and to ask a question.

In the first sentences of his Samuel study, Wellhausen commends to us with greater confidence his method than his results: what he was attempting was a comprehensive evaluation of the nature of the received text, and not just a series of individual improvements to it—he complained of textual critics proceeding too sporadically. Wellhausen proved a good guide to the LXX in itself, and its underlying Hebrew text—and of the relationship of that text to the Masoretic text. Comprehensive evaluation is what we find again in his *Prolegomena*, when he writes on Chronicles as a document of its late biblical authors' time. But is he not too credulous when it comes to evaluating Judges, Samuel and Kings? He recognizes that the final editing of these books belongs to the Deuteronomists, and so to the period after the collapse of Jerusalem. He is remarkably confident, using Jeremiah's striking image, that the readers of the Former Prophets can still taste the fresh waters of early Yahwism, rather than stale water from the later and leaky priestly cisterns represented by the Pentateuch and books of Chronicles. I am not concerned here with his depreciation of P and Chronicles; but I am worried at the idea that Samuel gives ready access to early Israel.

3. *Issues Left Open by* Kings without Privilege

I want in this paper to focus attention on some of the historical implications of a book I published in 1994. In a nutshell, I was arguing against the consensus which has held since de Wette, and which was strengthened by Wellhausen, that what the Chronicler rewrote was the books of Samuel and Kings much as we know them. I suggested instead that the text common to Samuel/Kings and Chronicles—often referred to as the synoptic portions of these works—was also their main immediate source. If I am right, then the source *and controlling pattern* of both great biblical narrative works was a report of the whole history of David's house: it began with the death of Saul (1 Sam. 31//1 Chron. 10), and it ended with the fall of Jerusalem. This base-narrative had been roughly half as long as either of the successor works we now know. However, in the case of the David story, the text common to Samuel and Chronicles is only some quarter of the length of 1 Samuel 31 and 2 Samuel (Auld 1994: 14). My argument was that both Samuel/Kings and Chronicles became what they are by large-scale expansion in different directions from the story of David's house which they held in common. In order not to complicate such a novel case, I concentrated in my book more on the problems it might solve than on difficulties it might have to cope with.

Craig Ho adopted some of this case in his Edinburgh dissertation (1994). But he also argued there against the suggestion that the shared source-text had begun only with Saul's death. In a related article Ho sought to establish a link between a shorter version of Saul's death, a version closer in wording to 1 Chronicles 10 than the more extended 1 Samuel 31, and 'the last prophecy of Samuel', who predicted through the witch at Endor the total demise of Saul and his family—'tomorrow' (1995: 98). Langlamet, to mention just one other recent contributor, has sought to attach 1 Samuel 31 to a source-narrative that had made its previous appearance in 1 Sam. 26.25 (1994: 327). Ho went on in his thesis to argue that the pluses about the 'blind and the lame' in the Samuel version of David's taking of Jerusalem 'are connected with a tendentious account of the story of the house of Eli ("the blind") and with the narrative of David showing royal hospitality to Mephibosheth ("the lame")'. Since many of 'the Samuel pluses and variants have links with stories in which blood guilt of David or his throne is involved', Ho then offered 'a thematic study of these materials—i.e. most of the History of David's Rise plus the Succession Narrative'. The strength of his case lies in the close links observed between the minor additions within Samuel to synoptic passages and large-scale Samuel pluses.

The usual view is that the Chronicler suppressed the story of Saul, or Saul and David, or at least reduced it radically into what we find in 1 Chronicles 8–9. Ho proposed in his thesis—though he hardly argued the case—a source narrative on Saul and David containing about half the material now in 1 Samuel. If I were persuaded by him, then I would have to ask: What else may have been omitted by Samuel/Kings or Chronicles? However, I am unwilling to concede too much too fast of my recently published study of David's line. Instead I want to give a further example of one of the gains we may enjoy if we remove from Samuel and Kings the privilege of being regarded as the text which the Chronicler rewrote.

4. Inciting David to a Census

Even in my more radical moments when working on *Kings without Privilege*, I had never questioned the universal—or at least very widespread—judgment that Satan was introduced into 1 Chron. 21.1 to spare the Lord's blushes over setting up his anointed to commit a crime for which he would then prosecute him, as reported in 2 Samuel 24. I had long been impressed by von Rad's remark that 'the Chronicler could no longer endure this theological tension' (1962: 318). Both Polzin and Fokkelman may have advanced far beyond Wellhausen in their reading of the last four chapters of 2 Samuel as a well-planned conclusion: he had described them as 'an appendix of very peculiar structure' (1885: 178). With most scholars, they underpin their reading of 2 Samuel 24 by reaffirming the judgment of Wellhausen (1871: 216-17) and his predecessors that its opening words resume 21.1-14, and noting how with that Gibeonite story it brackets the four concluding chapters. But did the Chronicler, as faint-hearted theologian, intrude a satanic 'adversary'? Or was he excluded from Samuel?

Successor commentators on Samuel have been remarkably silent on the immediate contextual evidence noted by Wellhausen (1871: 220) and Ewald which at the very least hints at the alternative villain of the piece. The verbs *hsyt* ['incite'] in 24.1 and *šwṭ* ['roam'] in 24.2 not only play on the sounds of the first two consonants of *śaṭan*, but appear together in only one other biblical passage. And there, in the prologue to Job, they are joined also by Satan. We should conclude at the very least that the beginning of 2 Samuel 24 has been rewritten to demonstrate knowledge of the alternative account in 1 Chronicles 21—but it is simpler to suppose that Satan was part of the source.

'And Yahweh's anger continued to burn against Israel' (2 Sam. 24.1) may resume the content of the Gibeon story; but you would expect of ויסף אף יהוה לחרות ('and Yahweh's anger continued to burn'), after a three-chapter gap, that it actually resumed the phrase ויחר אף יהוה ('and Yahweh's anger burned') from somewhere within 2 Sam. 21.1-14. Yet the only other mention of Yahweh's hot wrath in all of the books of Samuel relates to the fate of Uzzah when the ark was returning to Jerusalem (2 Sam. 6.7). It is not immediately clear that the fate of Saul's descendants and the story of the census were drafted together.

The very last words of 2 Samuel—ויעתר יהוה לארץ ותעצר המגפה מעל ישראל with their assonance ('and Yahweh hearkened to the land and the blow was held off from Israel') resumes ויעתר אלהים לארץ ('and God hearkened to the land') from 21.14b and ותעצר המגפה מעל העם ('and the blow was held off from the people') from 24.21b. The latter phrase appears also in the Chronicles parallel, 1 Chron. 21.22b, but it is not repeated a few verses later as in Samuel. Here again, I submit, if it were not for the dominant view that the Chronicler rewrote Samuel, we would naturally conclude that the last words of Samuel make a new editorial connection between separately drafted stories—only one of which, about David's census, was part of the common source.

Discussing the links between 2 Sam. 21.1-14 and 2 Samuel 24, Polzin documents the importance of ש-ב-ע to both narratives: in the Gibeonite story, the seven victims play off the importance of oath-taking; while, in the census story, the seventy thousand victims from Israel play off a triple mention of Beer-sheba (1993: 209). Good and well—fine evidence of literary artistry in an author of the books of Samuel, possibly even of Polzin's Deuteronomist! But, when we compare this account of the census with its synoptic relative in 1 Chronicles 21, we find that two of its three mentions of Beer-Sheba are Samuel pluses—just as Craig Ho nicely shows that several of the Samuel pluses in the narrative of Saul's death have been added to prepare for the Gibeon story in 2 Samuel 21. We should perhaps conclude that 2 Sam. 21.1-14 was drafted for—or at least redrafted within—the books of Samuel.

5. *Battling for David and Goliath*

Craig Ho and I have already cooperated in fighting one round in the contest to decide how the story of David and Goliath grew—or at least how MT and LXX in 1 Samuel 17–18 are related (Auld and Ho 1992). At the time we prepared our article, we were not familiar with Polzin (1989) on the subject; and some further comments are appropriate here.

Polzin is humorously dismissive of historical and textual concerns: such 'activity, so necessary in itself, tends to become addictive and can divert one's efforts out of all proportion to the preliminary task of getting a global picture of what a "book" even as textually corrupt as 1 or 2 Samuel is driving at' (1989: 1). When he comes to read in 1 Samuel 17 the mortal combat of the unequal champions, he skilfully treats the many repetitions as marks of the storyteller's art (162-63). He also devotes an extended footnote (259-61) to Tov's discussion of this issue, from which I extract just two points.

Tov's argument (1985: 115-18), that a Greek translator otherwise so faithful to his Hebrew *Vorlage* would not have so shortened the text before him, he finds self-defeating, because its mirror-image is equally plausible: why should a Hebrew copyist, otherwise so faithful in Samuel to the text broadly shared by MT and LXX, have suddenly turned 'egregious conflator'? He sportively suggests that a consequence of Tov's discussion is that 'like Solomon with the feuding mothers, readers are confronted with two texts, one apparently mutilated and the other not'.

Auld and Ho sought independently to answer his second point in two ways. They suggested that the shorter LXX had its own integrity—it had lost no limbs. And they argued that the pluses in the longer MT, far from being ugly growths or the result of egregious conflation, were designed to bind the story more closely to the book as a whole by adding to the comparisons and contrasts between David and Saul.

His first point—why this unique case of such large-scale modification of the inherited text?—we have to meet head on, like Fokkelman on Goliath's two opponents from Israel, Elhanan and David. Two texts of 1 Samuel 17 are available. Both texts are to be respected: neither has been mutilated by limbs lost nor spoiled by careless expansion. And they resemble two frames from close to the end of a moving film of the composition of the books of Samuel—or two snapshots from a once larger collection. The story of David which was added to that of Elhanan was itself also added to.

The earlier draft of this paper, as read in Jerusalem, went on to suggest that far from being a unique case of substantial lengthening, it was merely a uniquely well-documented case of such expansion within the books of Samuel. Re-reading Rofé's notes on the relative lateness of the language throughout 1 Samuel 17—and his examples are drawn from both the LXX *Vorlage* and the MT pluses—makes me wonder whether late language and large-scale textual diversity should not be recognized as rather more unusual (1987: 125-44). I am reminded of the late paragraph about the altar at Ebal which different versions of the book of Joshua appear to have positioned at three different points within its narrative (Auld 1995: 175-78).

Yet everything I have argued about Samuel/Kings and Chronicles as large-scale expansions of their common source would also render it far from unique within a wider biblical context. 1 Samuel 17 is in fact an excellent example of a big story grown from a very tiny seed. And the historicity of the kernel—Elhanan the giant-killer—would be very hard to argue. The case of Goliath offers good inner-biblical evidence for the sort of growth of the Solomon material from kernels such as 1 Kgs 8.12b-13 [MT] or 9.16-18, proposed at the Jerusalem meeting by Ernst Axel Knauf.

6. *Reading Historically*

I have been advocating that any historical reader of the biblical narratives must start by paying close attention to two features of these biblical books: the high artistry of their composition, and the clear evidence of the later stages in the development of the versions available to us. The stories about David and Solomon alone occupy almost equal space to those of the subsequent royal history. This is true in Samuel–Kings, in Chronicles, and also in the material they share: my—their!—'common source'. And it suggests to me that—as far back in the documentation as we can reliably trace—David and Solomon belong to the age of legendary beginnings rather than royal record.

In the *Eretz Israel* volume dedicated to Avraham Malamat, I noted some of the implications of my approach for our understanding of Solomon. I drew particular attention to Solomon's Egyptian wife and the building of his palace, and showed how both prominent topics in Kings had been developed from much less significant beginnings still evident in Chronicles. I do not want to claim that the Chronicler never omitted from his source. He may, for example, have sought to diminish the reports of Pharaoh's daughter because he wanted to portray Jerusalem as a female-free zone. However, external evidence is required to sustain such a suggestion, and not just the supposed 'fact' of his omissions from his source.

The portrait of David has been even more substantially rebuilt in both Samuel and Chronicles. The material they share is nicely framed by the taking of Jerusalem and return of the ark followed by a Philistine defeat at the beginning, and the matching episodes of the death of Goliath and the violent divine anger that culminated in the purchase of the site for God's altar in Jerusalem at the end. In between come the Nathan oracle and various victories in Transjordan and Syria, recounted with very little detail.

The unfortunate result for the historical optimist is that our historical re-reading leads back from apparent information to manifest ideology. The stories of David and Solomon shared by Samuel/Kings and Chronicles belong to a golden age, not a historical period. The implications for Solomon I have explored in the Malamat volume (Auld 1993). About the 'father of the line' we learn simply that he transferred his capital to Jerusalem, that he received a double divine promise, that he secured the site of the national shrine, and that he was victorious over Philistines, Aramaeans, and Transjordanians—no historical surprises there.

BIBLIOGRAPHY

Auld, A.G.
1993 'Solomon at Gibeon: History Glimpsed', in *Avraham Malamat Volume* (EI, 24; Jerusalem: Israel Exploration Society): 1-7*.
1994 *Kings without Privilege* (Edinburgh: T. & T. Clark).
1995 'Reading Joshua after Kings', in J. Davies, G. Harvey, and W.G.E. Watson (eds.), *Words Remembered, Texts Renewed: Essays in Honour of John F.A. Sawyer* (JSOTSup, 195; Sheffield: Sheffield Academic Press): 167-81.

Auld, A.G., and Y.S. (Craig) Ho
    1992   'The Making of David and Goliath', *JSOT* 56: 19-39.

Fokkelman, J.P.
    1990/93 *Narrative Art and Poetry in the Books of Samuel* III/IV (Assen: Van Gorcum).

Garsiel, M.
    1990   *The First Book of Samuel: A Literary Study of Comparative Structures, Analogies and Parallels* (Jerusalem: Rubin Mass).

Ho, Y.S. (Craig)
    1994   'The Troubles of David and his House: Textual and Literary Studies of the Synoptic Stories of Saul and David in Samuel–Kings and Chronicles' (unpublished University of Edinburgh thesis).
    1995   'Conjectures and Refutations: Is 1 Samuel xxxi 1-13 Really the Source of 1 Chronicles x 1-12?', *VT* 45: 82-106.

Langlamet, F.
    1994   ' "David—Jonathan—Saül" ou Le "Livre de Jonathan": 1 Sam 16,14–2 Sam 1,27', *RB* 101: 326-54.

Polzin, R.
    1989   *Samuel and the Deuteronomist* (Indiana Studies in Biblical Literature; Bloomington, IN: Indiana University Press).
    1993   *David and the Deuteronomist* (Indiana Studies in Biblical Literature; Bloomington, IN: Indiana University Press).

Rad, G. von
    1962   *Old Testament Theology. I. The Theology of Israel's Historical Traditions* (Edinburgh: Oliver & Boyd).

Rofé, A.
    1987   'The Battle of David and Goliath', in J. Neusner, B.A. Levine, and E.S. Frerichs (eds.), *Judaic Perspectives on Ancient Israel* (Philadelphia: Fortress Press): 117-51.

Tov, E.
    1985   'The Composition of 1Samuel 16–18 in the Light of the Septuagint Version', in J.H. Tigay (ed.), *Empirical Models for Biblical Criticism* (Philadelphia: University of Pennsylvania Press): 97-130.

Wellhausen, J.
    1871   *Der Text der Bucher Samuelis* (Göttingen: Vandenhoeck & Ruprecht).
    1885   *Prolegomena to the History of Israel* (Scholars Press Reprints and Translations; Atlanta, GA: Scholars Press, 1994).

SOURCES AND COMPOSITION IN THE HISTORY OF DAVID

Nadav Na'aman

1. *The Introduction of Writing in the Court of Jerusalem*

The date of the introduction of writing is a major problem for the evaluation of the sources regarding the history of David. The installation of the office of scribe in the courts of David and Solomon, and several lists that were possibly drawn from original documents, are usually regarded as indications of writing in the tenth-century courts of Jerusalem. Many scholars assume that the Deuteronomistic historian had before him original documents from the time of the two kings. Recently, however, some scholars have questioned this assumption. They suggest instead that (a) Jerusalem did not become the centre of a state before the eighth century BCE; and (b) that writing in the court of Jerusalem did not antedate that century. They conclude that the history of the United Monarchy was composed only on the basis of oral traditions and is devoid of historical foundations (Jamieson-Drake 1991: 138-45; Knauf 1991a: 39; 1991b: 172; Thompson 1992: 409-10; 1995; Davies 1992: 67-70; Lemche 1994: 183-89; Lemche and Thompson 1994).

No extrabiblical source mentions either David or Solomon. This is not surprising. Detailed accounts on first millennium intra-state events appear for the first time in the ninth century BCE. All Syro-Palestinian inscriptions of the tenth century refer to local affairs and shed no light on international affairs. Even if David and Solomon accomplished the deeds attributed to them in the Bible, no source would have mentioned their names. The silence of tenth-century sources neither proves nor disproves the biblical account of the United Monarchy (*contra* Garbini 1988: 16; Knauf 1991b: 171-72).

There is one exception to the local nature of tenth-century inscriptions: the topographical list of Shishak. The Egyptian king left a long list of places conquered in the course of his Asiatic campaign. An analysis of the topographical list indicates that the campaign was directed against

Israel and the non-Judahite parts of the Negev, avoiding almost entirely the kingdom of Judah.

Shishak's campaign is referred to in 1 Kgs 14.25-28. The text makes it clear that it deals largely with the handing over of Solomon's golden shields to Shishak and their replacement by copper shields. Details of the Egyptian campaign are minimal and its description is schematic. What might have been the source used by the historian for the description? In my opinion, it must have been a text in which appeared a datum that in the fifth year of Rehoboam golden shields were delivered to Shishak, king of Egypt, and were replaced by copper shields. The historian logically interpreted the datum to mean that Shishak's campaign, about which he had no other source, was directed against Jerusalem and that the treasures of the palace and the temple were then delivered to Egypt. He wrote long after the conclusion of the campaign he described and was therefore entirely dependent on his sources. His interpretation of Shishak's campaign may look incomplete and even misleading, but it does not conflict with historical reality: the campaign indeed reached the area of Jerusalem and a heavy tribute was paid to Egypt on that occasion (Na'aman 1992: 79-86, with earlier literature).

The account of Shishak's campaign in the book of Kings indicates that scribal activity took place in the court of Jerusalem in the late tenth century BCE. One would naturally assume that it was not introduced by a petty king like Rehoboam, but rather by one of his ancestors, either David or Solomon. Indeed, royal scribes are mentioned in David's and Solomon's lists of high officials (2 Sam. 8.17; 20.25; 1 Kgs 4.3). This accords with some records which are included in the history of Solomon and were probably drawn from old written sources. For example:

1. The list of Solomon's high officials (1 Kgs 4.2-6).
2. The list of Solomon's twelve officers and their districts (1 Kgs 4.9-19).
3. Details of Solomon's building activity in Jerusalem and elsewhere in his kingdom (1 Kgs 9.15, 17-18).

The list of David's officers (*šālīšîm*) (2 Sam. 23.8-39) is certainly drawn from a very old document. The lists of David's wives and sons (2 Sam. 3.2-5; 5.14-16) may have been extracted from an original list. The lists of his officials (2 Sam. 8.16-18; 20.23-26) may go back to an old document, but equally might have been drawn from the list of Solomon's officials, since most of the names in the latter were sons of those mentioned in the former.

I would like to suggest an epigraphic evidence which supports the assumption that scribal activity took place in Jerusalem already in the tenth century BCE. A widespread use of hieratic numerals and signs appears in Israelite and Judean ostraca and weights of the eighth– seventh centuries BCE. They do not appear in documents of Israel's neighbours, only in texts written in the Hebrew script. Egyptian relations with the Philistine and Phoenician kingdoms were much closer in the ninth–early eighth centuries than with Israel and Judah, and it is hardly conceivable that hieratic signs would then have entered only the Hebrew script. Moreover, no definite eighth–seventh century palaeographical parallels have been found in Egypt for many hieratic signs (Lemaire and Vernus 1983), and use of the so-called 'abnormal hieratic' was waning in Egypt at that time (Goldwasser 1991: 251 n. 2). It is clear that the hieratic signs entered the Hebrew script before the ninth century BCE.

Writing in hieratic is known from southern Canaan in the late thirteenth–twelfth centuries BCE. Goldwasser (1991: 251-52) has there-fore suggested that Egyptian, or Egyptian-trained, scribes, cut off from their homeland in the late twelfth century, educated local Canaanite scribes, who in their turn passed on their knowledge to the new court of Israel, probably in the age of the United Monarchy.[1]

The long gap in the use of hieratic between the twelfth and early eighth centuries is greatly narrowed by the assumption that scribes entered the court of Jerusalem in the tenth century BCE, gradually developed the Hebrew script and spread their knowledge to north Israelite centres. Canaanite centres like Gaza, Ashkelon or Gezer could have been the transmitters of the proto-Canaanite scribal tradition in the early Iron Age.[2]

We may conclude that the appearance of hieratic numerals and signs in the Hebrew script of Israel and Judah strongly supports the assump-tion that scribal activity was introduced in the court of Jerusalem no later than the time of Solomon, and possibly already in David's time.

1.   There is also a possibility that the borrowing of hieratic signs and numerals took place directly from Egypt during the tenth century BCE (Goldwasser 1991: 251 n. 2).

2.   A somewhat similar problem is involved with the migration of the script from south Canaan to south Arabia. The latest proto-Canaanite inscriptions date from the twelfth century, whereas the earliest Sabaean inscriptions are no earlier than the eighth/seventh century BCE (Knauf 1989).

It is commonly accepted today that historiography developed in Judah no earlier than the eighth century BCE and that the Deuteronomistic history was composed either in the late seventh or early sixth century BCE. The earliest Judean inscriptions are dated to the second half of the eighth century and the spread of alphabetic writing in the kingdom took place only in the seventh century. Writing in the tenth–ninth centuries BCE must have been confined to a small group of scribes in the court of Jerusalem and was mainly used for administration and for diplomatic exchange.

2. The Chronicle of Early Israelite Kings

The majority of the narratives about David's rise to power and his time on the throne are not susceptible to source analysis. These stories may be examined according to literary, ideological and theological criteria. Their use as historical sources depends mainly on the trust of a scholar in the authenticity of biblical literature, on the assumption that they rest on oral traditions and are not mere literary novels, and on the belief that they include at least some germs of truth.

There are other accounts which relate historical episodes in a way that enables us to try analysing them as historical sources. Since my subject is 'composition and redaction', rather than the history of the United Monarchy, I will concentrate on tracing the sources which could have reached the author and enabled him to describe the history of David in a fairly reliable manner. The historicity of the accounts will be discussed only sporadically and briefly.

a. David's Wars with the Arameans

David's rival in his wars with the Arameans is called 'Hadadezer *ben* Rehob king of Zobah' (2 Sam. 8.3, 12). Scholars have long recognized that '*ben* Rehob' does not refer to Hadadezer's father, but rather to his land of origin, and that he was a king of Beth-rehob and Zobah. Two biblical references (Num. 13.21; Judg. 18.28) indicate that Beth-rehob covered most of the Beqaᶜ of Lebanon, from the area north of Dan up to Lebo-hamath. Zobah is located in the northern Beqaᶜ and northern Anti-Lebanon region, south of the kingdom of Hamath.

Winckler (1895: 141-43; 1901: 150) was the first to note the parallel between Hadadezer's epithet and that of Ba'asa '*mār Ruḥūbi* KUR *Amanaya*' of the monolith inscription of Shalmaneser III. It is well known that the Assyrians referred to many kingdoms by eponymic or dynastic names, and that the combination *mār Ruḥūbi* should be rendered 'son of Bīt-Ruḥūbi' (Ungnad 1906). Forrer (1932a; 1932b) proposed to identify KUR Amana with the Anti-Lebanon mountain range and that the text refers to the kingdom of Zobah located there. Thus, Hadadezer and Baʾasa were natives of Beth-rehob and their kingdom encompassed the regions of Beth-rehob and Zobah/Amana.

I have recently discussed the two dedication inscriptions to Hazael from Samos and Eretria (see Bron and Lemaire 1989; Ephʿal and Naveh 1989) and suggested translating them thus: 'That which Hadad gave our lord Hazael from ʿAmqi in the year that our lord crossed the River' (Na'aman forthcoming). ʿAmqi, Hazael's place of birth, was a name for the Beqaʿ of Lebanon in the second millennium BCE and was mentioned in the Amarna letters and in texts from Ḥattusha. It seems to me that ʿAmqi was a geographical name for Beth-rehob, just as Amana was a geographical name for Zobah. I further suggested that Hazael was the son of Baʾasa of Beth-rehob (ʿAmqi), who seized Damascus and unified for the first time these two major Aramean kingdoms. According to my analysis, Hadadezer, Baʾasa and Hazael were all natives of Beth-rehob and their ancestral kingdom included two regions: Beth-rehob/ʿAmqi and Zobah/Amana.

It seems to me that the figure of Hadadezer, '*ben* Rehob, king of Zobah', was modelled upon the historical figure of Hazael, his most successful heir to the throne of Beth-rehob. Several distinct features are common to the two kings:

1. Both originate from Beth-rehob and their ancestral kingdom has a dual structure.
2. The area under their hegemony extended from Transjordan in the south to the Euphrates. The extent of Hadadezer's domain in the south is indicated by the dispatch of his troops to help the Ammonites against David (2 Sam. 10.6-7), and in the north by his ability to mobilize troops from 'Aram, which is beyond the River' (2 Sam. 10.16). *Ēber ha-nāhār* is identical to Assyrian *Ēbir-nāri*, which refers to the areas west of the Euphrates. Also, David conducted a surprise attack on Hadadezer when he was on his way 'to leave/erect his stela on the River' (2 Sam. 8.3; 1 Chron. 18.13). 'The River' is, of course, the Euphrates. Hazael's hegemonic power in all the areas west of the Euphrates

is indicated in several inscriptions and in the Bible (Lemaire 1992: 101-106, with earlier literature; 1993).

3. Both rulers headed a coalition of vassal kings. Thus according to 2 Sam. 10.16, following the Aramean defeat at Helam all the kings who were vassals of Hadadezer became Israel's vassals (2 Sam. 10.16). The list of Hazael's vassals is indicated by the stela of Zakkur, king of Hamath and Lua'th (see Lemaire 1993).

4. Both were able to recruit for battle an enormous number of chariots and troops.

5. Aram Damascus was under their power. As suggested above, Hazael took over Damascus and usurped its throne and was therefore called by an Assyrian scribe 'the son of nobody'. No king of Damascus is mentioned in the account of David's wars. The absence of a king is explained by the assumption that the author deliberately described Damascus as a conquered district in Hadadezer's kingdom which sent troops to support its lord after his defeat (2 Sam. 8.5-6). It was only after David's death that Damascus became the seat of its own king (2 Kgs 11.23-24).

Hazael reigned in the second half of the ninth century BCE. Details of his political and military achievements were hardly known in the time of the Deuteronomistic historian (the late seventh or early sixth century BCE). The triple designation 'Hadadezer *ben* Rehob king of Zobah' (2 Sam. 8.3, 12) is known only from the ninth century, and the elliptic form *mār* PN to designate kingdoms ('son of Bīt-PN') scarcely appears after the eighth century BCE. I therefore suggest that a 'chronicle of early Israelite kings' was composed in the eighth century BCE, when the historical achievements of Hazael were still very much alive. Details of David's wars with the Arameans must have been quite vague at that time and the author of the chronicle tried to fill in the gaps with details borrowed from the late history of Hazael's kingdom. This early chronicle must have been one of the main sources on which the Deuteronomistic historian based his work (see below).

Clearly, our source about David's wars with the Arameans is problematic. Only the name of David's major enemy, his kingdom, the names of his general (Shobach) and his allies, the location of the battlefields, and the ultimate Israelite success in battle, may date back to the time of David. Unfortunately, there can be no unqualified certainty due to the great antiquity of these historical events.

b. *David's Wars with the Philistines*

The point of departure for the analysis is the discrepancy between the accounts of the United Monarchy and the reality of the time of the Deuteronomistic historian. According to biblical historiography, five Philistine kingdoms, each headed by a *seren*, ruled in the pre-monarchic and early monarchic periods. They were united in a kind of confederation and fought against Israel, until David defeated them and broke their power. On the other hand, the Assyrian inscriptions and biblical prophecies (Jer. 25.20; Amos 1.7-8; Zeph. 2.4; Zech. 9.5-6) mention only four Philistine kingdoms: Gaza, Ashkelon, Ashdod and Ekron. The city of Gath, which in David's early career appears as *primus inter pares* among the five Philistine kingdoms, was a border city of Ashdod from the mid-eighth century BCE. One may ask, what could have been the source available to the historian that caused him to depict the Philistines in a way that differed from the reality of his own time?

To answer this question let me examine the words of Amos (6.2) about Gath.

> Pass over to Calneh, and see; and thence go to Hamath the great; then go down to Gath of the Philistines. Are you better than these kingdoms? Or is their territory greater than your territory?

Gath appears in the text alongside two other capital cities—Calneh and Hamath. It is evident that the text refers to the three kingdoms of Unqi/Patina, Hamath and Gath. Since Gath lost its power before the time of Tiglath-Pileser III, the prophet may have been recalling past events which were better known to his audience than to us. Scholars usually examine the available sources, namely, the Assyrian inscriptions of the second half of the eighth century BCE, and assume that the text refers to events in the time of either Tiglath-Pileser or Sargon II. They therefore attribute the verse to a later disciple or redactor of Amos (Wolff 1977: 275; Paul 1991: 201-204; Blum 1994: 32-34, with earlier literature). However, relying on these late sources is like searching under the lamp-post. Despite the paucity of sources, to interpret the prophecy properly we must look for events which took place before the prophet's time.

The history of Kullani (Kinalua) between its conquest by Dayyan-Ashur in 831 BCE and Tiglath-Pileser III's campaign of 738 is unknown (Michel 1955–56: 224-27; Hawkins 1974: 81-83). But it is evident that Arpad expanded in the late ninth–early eighth century BCE and that Patina/Unqi lost its former power and parts of its territories (Elliger 1947; Ponchia 1991: 91-96; Weippert 1993: 58-59). Amos could have been referring to the destruction and decline of Kullani in the course of the struggle for the hegemony of northern Syria during that time.

The capital of the kingdom of Hamath was transferred north, to the city of Hadrach (Ḥatarikka), during the late ninth century BCE. Hadrach remained the capital of the kingdom until its conquest and annexation by Tiglath-Pileser III in 738 (Sader 1987: 216-26, with earlier literature; Ponchia 1991: 96-97). The background for the transfer of the capital and the long decline of Hamath remains unknown (but see below). We may therefore speculate that it was the (possible) destruction and decline of Hamath that is alluded to in the prophecy.

According to the account of 2 Kings (12.17), Hazael king of Aram marched to Philistia and captured the city of Gath. It seems to me that this violent conquest put an end to the status of Gath as an independent state (see Hammershaimb 1970: 97-99). Later it was taken by Ashdod and became a border town within its territory (2 Chron. 26.6; Fuchs 1994: 134, line 250; 220, line 104). One may further suggest that Hazael likewise conquered and partly destroyed Hamath, Damascus's northern neighbour, an event which led to its long decline.[3] We may conclude that the warning words of Amos could be a reference to the destruction and desolation of three Syro-Palestinian capital cities in the late ninth century BCE.

The biblical scribe who described Gath as an independent kingdom governed by its own *seren* must have recalled the city's status prior to the time of Hazael. He must therefore have lived long before the time of the Deuteronomistic historian. The source available for the historian is again the chronicle of early Israelite kings, whose author lived in the eighth century BCE, not long after the time of Hazael.

According to 2 Sam. 5.17-25 (and 1 Chron. 14.8-16) David fought two decisive battles against the Philistines. The first was launched in the valley of Rephaim, and David won by a frontal attack. The second battle apparently took place near Gibeon and David launched a surprise night attack and smote the Philistines 'from Gibeon to Gezer' (1 Chron. 14.16) (Na'aman 1994: 253-54, with earlier literature). These two victories of David are referred to by the prophetic words of Isa. 28.21: 'For the Lord will rise up as on Mount Perazim, he will be wroth as in the valley of Gibeon'. Mount Perazim refers to Baal-perazim (replacing Baal by the

3. It is tempting to restore in the ivory inscription from Arslan-Tash '... in the year of the [captu]re of Ha[math]' (see Puech 1981). Unfortunately, the restoration cannot be verified.

common noun 'mount'), where David launched his first victory (2 Sam. 5.20; 1 Chron. 14.11); and the valley of Gibeon is the location of the second battle (1 Chron. 14.13, 16). Evidently, David's victories over the Philistines were still commemorated in the time of Isaiah (the late eighth century BCE).

2 Sam. 8.1 summarizes David's later wars with the Philistines thus: 'After this David defeated the Philistines and subdued them and David took *meteg hā-ammâ* out of the hand of the Philistines'. The opening words ('after this') may have appeared originally after 5.25; the sequential relationship of the two episodes is self-evident. It seems to me that 2 Sam. 5.17-25 is an expanded and elaborated description of the chronicle of early Israelite kings and that the text of 8.1 is a verbatim copy of the old text. It probably mentioned the five Philistine *sᵉrānîm*, and was the source for numerous narratives about the Israelite wars with the Philistines. The early chronicle must have been the main source for the historian. He used it in different manners: sometimes he copied it verbatim, or other times he expanded and elaborated it, and in still other cases it formed the narrow core around which a whole new story was built.

c. David's Wars against Israel's Neighbours
The text of 2 Sam. 8.1 may help us to reconstruct the early form of the chronicle. It first summarizes the results of David's wars with the Philistines, and then relates that he seized *meteg hā-ammâ* from them. Various suggestions have been made to decipher this enigmatic term (see e.g., Driver 1913: 279-80; Mittmann 1983: 327-32, with earlier literature; Kobayashi 1992: 800). It seems to me that *meteg hā-ammâ* refers to a distinct booty, similar to other distinct spoils mentioned at the close of episodes which describe David's wars against Israel's neighbours. Thus, following his victory over Zobah, David took the quivers of gold carried by the servants of Hadadezer (2 Sam. 8.7); and following the conquest of Rabbah he took the crown of the god Milkom (2 Sam. 12.30) (for discussion, see Horn 1973; Barthélemy 1982: 263-64). It seems to me that the conclusion of every war with a reference to a distinct booty is an original trait of the early chronicle and was adopted by the Deuteronomistic historian. A good parallel is offered by the Mesha inscription in which the capture of important towns culminates with the taking of a distinct spoil and its dedication to the god as his preferential share in the booty (*ʾrʾl dwdh*; the vessels of YHWH).

What could have been the text of the chronicle which served as the main source for the long narrative of David's war with the Ammonites? Isolating the old core in chs. 10–12 is impossible, and the first part of the early chronicle's account cannot be reconstructed. Its closing part was possibly copied verbatim in 2 Sam. 12.29-30aα: 'And David gathered all the people together and went to Rabbah, and fought against it and took it. And he took the crown of Milkom from his head.'

The core of the episode of the envoy from Hamath (2 Sam. 8.9-10) should also be attributed to the early chronicle. Only a scribe who was acquainted with the realities of the tenth–eighth centuries would have described so accurately the relations of Damascus and Hamath, and the common interests of Israel and Hamath vis à vis Aram. In the time of the Deuteronomistic historian, the former kingdoms of Damascus and Hamath were split into several provinces and the ancient situation was forgotten. The name of the king of Hamath, and possibly some details about the delegation, could have been derived from an old memory of the historical event, but this cannot be established with certainty.

Did the episodes of the wars against Moab and Edom (2 Sam. 8.2, 13-14) derive from the early chronicle? The two kingdoms were well established in the early eighth century BCE. Moreover, the episode of David's victory over the Edomites in the Valley of Salt (vv. 13-14) looks like a reflection of Amaziah's victory over them in the early eighth century (2 Kgs 14.7). In my opinion, this is another example of the device of borrowing military outlines of an actual event to depict an episode of the early history of Israel. Provided that this suggestion is acceptable, then the reign of Amaziah (about 799–771) provides a *terminus post quem* for the composition of the chronicle.

The depiction of David's extreme cruelty in his war with Moab (v. 2) is a reflection of the way that the Moabites treated Israel in the time of Mesha. It looks like a literary compensation for what the Moabites had done in their wars with Israel. In the framework of the literary revenge, the author attributed to David the subjugation of Moab and the killing of a large part of its population. The text must have originated from a time in which the desire for revenge was strongly felt in Israel. In the time of the Deuteronomistic historian, on the other hand, the memory of bloody wars between Moab and Israel had already faded, and the author had no account to settle with Moab. It seems therefore that the core of the two episodes of Moab and Edom should also be attributed to the chronicle of early Israelite kings.

3. *The Library of the Deuteronomistic Historian*

Few texts from the time of David and Solomon could have survived and reached the Deuteronomistic historian in their original form. They were all lists originally recorded for administrative purpose. Van Seters (1983: 4, 40-51, 195-99) noted that, as far as we know, historians of the old world did not consult archives when they wrote their histories (see Momigliano 1966: 212-17). He questioned the commonly held opinion that biblical authors consulted archives and retrieved information of great antiquity from old sources. It should be noted that documents are quoted in the books of Ezra and Nehemiah for determining rights, reflecting the use of archival sources at that time (Bickerman 1946; Momigliano 1977: 31-33). However, there is no evidence of a similar use of archival documents in earlier works. So, the assumption that the Deuteronomistic historian had searched in the archives of the palace and temple for source material for his composition cannot be sustained. Some other explanation must be sought for the lists which are included in the histories of David and Solomon.

I would like to suggest that these lists, and many other documents, originated from the Jerusalemite palace or temple library, where they were used for the education and training of scribes.[4] Redford (1986: 206-28) has examined the contents of temple libraries in Egypt in the second half of the first millennium BCE and concluded that they encompassed a wide range of materials with which the fully trained scribe was supposed to be familiar (e.g., king-lists, 'annals', inventories, letters, stories, ritual literature, reference compendia, etc.). This rich source material enabled Manetho to reconstruct the ancient history of Egypt in his *Aegyptiaca*. A Babylonian temple library (or libraries), which had a rich variety of texts (e.g., Sumerian and Akkadian myths and epics, king-lists, chronicles, ritual literature, etc.), likewise enabled Berossus to write the history of the country in his *Babyloniaca* (Komoróczy 1973; Drews 1975; Burstein 1978; Kuhrt 1987: 32-48).

The contents and scope of private libraries in Assyria in the seventh century BCE were studied by Parpola (1983: 8-10). He noted that they

---

4. Jamieson-Drake (1991: 148-49, 151) made the plausible suggestion that scribal training took place primarily if not exclusively in Jerusalem and that all professional administrators were trained exclusively in Jerusalem. For a different opinion see Lemaire 1981: 46-54; 1984: 274-81.

existed in considerable numbers in this period and could be quite comprehensive, containing hundreds of tablets. He further suggests (1983: 10) that 'the libraries of specialists in a given field by no means consisted of only their professional material but could include hundreds of works outside their field of specialization. This certainly indicates the broad education and, in some cases, deep learning of the individuals in question.' It may further be noted that about one-fifth of the 30,000 tablets and fragments in the private library of Ashurbanipal (see Lieberman 1990) are non-literary texts (e.g., legal and administrative texts, letters, reports, etc.) (Parpola 1983: 6; see Oppenheim 1964: 15-24). The library also contains the so-called 'epic literature', fables, proverbs, etc. This indicates the wide range of texts that may be found in a royal library in the late Iron Age period.

The range of texts in the library of Jerusalem was certainly narrower than the rich palace and temple libraries of Mesopotamia and Egypt, but included all that was necessary for the education of scribes and for their manifold functions in the kingdom (see Lemaire 1981: 72-82, with earlier literature; for a different opinion see Haran 1993). We may assume that sign-lists, letters, judicial texts, inventories, cultic texts, literary and historical works, all of which were essential for the education and function of royal Judean scribes, were part of the Jerusalem library.

Jerusalem was the capital of Judah for four centuries, and the contents of its library must have reflected this long continuity. Old texts of an archival character were apparently used for educational purposes and copied many times, and so survived until the destruction of 587/86 BCE. Some of those texts might have been attributed—correctly or not—to prominent past figures like David and Solomon, and been transferred with this attribution into the stream of scribal learning. The chronicle of early Israelite kings and king-lists must have been part of this educational corpus. Likewise stories, such as the pre-Deuteronomistic narratives of King Saul and David's rise to power, might have been included in this corpus. Thus, when the historian composed his work he used this corpus as his main source for writing the history of Israel, just as Manetho and Berossus were able to use temple libraries for composing their respective *Aegyptiaca* and *Babyloniaca*. The attribution of texts to particular rulers may go back to old scribal traditions; their attribution by the historian may reflect his trust in the words of his sources. This may explain why his work was accepted by the scholarly elite of Jerusalem. Since he collected all the available sources and integrated them in his work, his description of the past did not conflict with what was known to other scholars. His competence as a historian and the clear and coherent picture that he drew made his work an authoritative source for all future study of the history of Israel.

Are we free to attribute the lists of David's officers and officials, and of his wives and sons, to his time? Certainty cannot be achieved in this matter. All that can legitimately be said is that the lists of names and the toponyms mentioned therein are very old and belong to an early stage of the Judean monarchy; and furthermore, that the historian could have had textual indications which caused him to attribute these lists to the era of David.

The chronicle of early Israelite kings was the major source from which the historian extracted details for the reconstruction of the chain of events in the time of the United Monarchy. The brief descriptions of Saul's kingship (1 Sam. 14.47-48) were perhaps extracted verbatim from that source. The passage about the coronation of Ishbaʿal, the son of Saul (2 Sam. 2.8), was possibly drawn from it. The episodes of David's reign in Hebron (2 Sam. 2.1-3), his struggle with Ishbaʿal, the conquest of Jebus (2 Sam. 5.6-9), the wars with the Philistines (2 Sam. 5.17-25), and his wars with Israel's neighbours—all these could have originated in the chronicle. Also, the episodes of the uprisings against Solomon (1 Kgs 11) were possibly drawn from the same source. The Deuteronomistic historian sometimes cited the chronicle verbatim, and in other instances used it according to his literary, ideological and theological objectives. Thus, in certain episodes we are able to reconstruct the original source, whereas in others it is worked into a whole narrative and cannot be reconstructed.

This evaluation of the source material shows plainly how complicated is the task of modern historians when they try to reconstruct the history of David. I will conclude my discussion with one example: the problem of the great kingdom attributed to David in biblical historiography.

According to the biblical account, the great kingdom was short-lived and fell apart after David's death. Since we are dealing with an episode that lasted perhaps for only a few years, and since there are no contemporary documents either to support or invalidate it, a clear-cut decision cannot be achieved. Let us compare it, for example, with the successive great kingdoms established by Yaḥdunlim, by Shamshi-Addu, and by Zimrilim in northern Mesopotamia in the late nineteenth–early eighteenth century BCE. Each of these kingdoms lasted for a few years and then disappeared. We are fortunate in having rich documentation for the three kingdoms, because otherwise their memory would have fallen into oblivion. They indicate the dynamic of changes at the stage of early state formation, and one can easily add many other examples to illustrate the phenomenon of the rapid growth and decline of states at that stage. In such a fluid situation, a talented and successful leader may conquer vast areas. It was not even necessary to have a permanent urban basis for such an achievement. The historical test is whether the conqueror and his heirs were able to keep the conquered areas and establish a permanent administration.

The opinion expressed by some scholars, of the impossibility of a Davidic great kingdom administered from Jerusalem (Garbini 1983: 1-16; 1988: 21-32; Jamieson-Drake 1991: 136-45; Knauf 1991b: 170-80; Thompson 1992: 331-34, 409-12; Davies 1992: 69), is, in my opinion, too rash. There is nothing impossible about the account of David's conquests—the only problem is whether or not it really happened. Unfortunately, the sources for this episode are of such nature that we are unable to answer the question with a definite 'yes' or 'no'.

BIBLIOGRAPHY

Barthélemy, D.
    1982   *Critique textuelle de l'Ancien Testament*. I. *Josué, Juges, Ruth, Samuel, Rois, Chroniques, Esdras, Néhémie, Esther* (OBO, 50.1; Göttingen: Vandenhoeck & Ruprecht).

Bickerman, E.J.
    1946   'The Edict of Cyrus in Ezra 1', *JBL* 65: 249-75.

Blum, E.
    1994   ' "Amos" in Jerusalem. Beobachtungen zu Am 6.1-7', *Henoch* 16: 23-47.

Bron, F., and A. Lemaire
    1989   'Les inscriptions Araméennes de Hazaël', *RA* 83: 34-44.

Burstein, M.B.
    1978   *The Babyloniaca of Berossus* (Sources from the Ancient Near East, 1.5; Malibu, CA: Undena Publications).

Davies, P.R.
    1992   *In Search of 'Ancient Israel'* (JSOTSup, 148; Sheffield: JSOT Press).

Drews, R.
    1975   'The Babylonian Chronicles and Berossus', *Iraq* 37: 39-55.

Driver, S.R.
    1913   *Notes on the Hebrew Text and the Topography of the Books of Samuel* (Oxford: Clarendon Press).

Elliger, K.
1947   'Samʾal und Hamat in ihrem Verhältnis zu Hattina, Unqi and Arpad',
         in J. Fück (ed.), *Festschrift Otto Eissfeldt zum 60. Geburtstage* (Halle:
         Max Niemeyer): 69-108.
Ephʿal, I., and J. Naveh
1989   'Hazael's Booty Inscriptions', *IEJ* 39: 192-200.
Forrer, E.
1932a   'Aram', *RLA* 1: 134.
1932b   'Baʾasa', *RLA* 1: 328.
Fuchs, A.
1994   *Die Inschriften Sargon II. aus Khorsabad* (Göttingen: Cuvillier Verlag).
Garbini, G.
1983   'L'impero di David', *Annali della Scuola Normale Superiore di Pisa*
         13: 1-20.
1988   *History and Ideology in Ancient Israel* (London: SCM Press).
Goldwasser, O.
1991   'An Egyptian Scribe from Lachish and the Hieratic Tradition of the
         Hebrew Kingdoms', *Tel Aviv* 18: 248-53.
Hammershaimb, E.
1970   *The Book of Amos: A Commentary* (Oxford: Basil Blackwell).
Haran, M.
1993   'Archives, Libraries, and the Order of the Biblical Books', *JANES* 22:
         51-61.
Hawkins, D.J.
1974   'Assyrians and Hittites', *Iraq* 36: 67-83.
Horn, S.
1973   'The Crown of the King of the Ammonites', *AUSS* 11: 170-80.
Jamieson-Drake, D.W.
1991   *Scribes and Schools in Monarchic Judah. A Socio-Archaeological
         Approach* (The Social World of Biblical Antiquity, 9; JSOTSup, 109;
         Sheffield: JSOT Press).
Knauf, E.A.
1989   'The Migration of the Script and the Formation of the State in South
         Arabia', *Proceedings of the Seminar for Arabian Studies* 19: 79-91.
1991a   'From History to Interpretation', in D.V. Edelman (ed.), *The Fabric of
         History. Text, Artifact and Israel's Past* (JSOTSup, 127; Sheffield:
         JSOT Press): 26-64.
1991b   'King Solomon's Copper Supply', in E. Lipiński (ed.), *Phoenicia and
         the Bible* (OLA, 44; Leuven: Peeters): 167-86.
Kobayashi, Y.
1992   'Methegh-ammah', *ABD* IV: 800.
Komoróczy, G.
1973   'Berosos and the Mesopotamian Literature', *Acta Antiqua Academiae
         Scientiarum Hungaricae* 21: 125-52.
Kuhrt, A.
1987   'Berossus' *Babyloniaka* and Seleucid Rule in Babylonia', in A. Kuhrt
         and S. Sherwin-White (eds.), *Hellenism in the East* (London: Gerald
         Duckworth): 32-56.

Lemaire, A.
1981   *Les écoles et la formation de la Bible dans l'Ancien Israël* (Fribourg and Göttingen: Universitätsverlag).
1984   'Sagesse et Ecoles', *VT* 34: 270-81.
1991   'Hazaël de Damas, roi d'Aram', in D. Charpin and F. Joannès (eds.), *Marchands, diplomates et empereurs. Etudes sur la civilisation Mésopotamienne offertes à Paul Garelli* (Paris: Editions Recherche sur les Civilisations): 91-108.
1993   'Joas de Samarie, Barhadad de Damas, Zakkur de Hamat. La Syrie-Palestine vers 800 av. J.-C.', *Eretz Israel* 24: 148-57.
Lemaire, A., and P. Vernus
1983   'L'ostracon paléo-hébreu no. 6 de Tell Qudeirat (Qadesh-Barnea)', in M. Görg (ed.), *Pontes atque Fontes. Eine Festgabe für Hellmut Brunner* (Wiesbaden: Otto Harrassowitz): 302-26.
Lemche, N.P.
1994   'Is it Still Possible to Write a History of Israel?', *SJOT* 8: 165-90.
Lemche, N.P., and T.L. Thompson
1994   'Did Biran Kill David? The Bible in the Light of Archaeology', *JSOT* 64: 3-22.
Lieberman, S.J.
1990   'Canonical and Official Cuneiform Texts: Towards an Understanding of Assurbanipal's Personal Tablet Collection', in T. Abusch, J. Huehnergard and P. Steinkeller (eds.), *Lingering over Words. Studies in Ancient Near Eastern Literature in Honor of William L. Moran* (Atlanta, GA: Scholars Press): 305-36.
Michel, E.
1955–56 'Die Assur-Texte Salmanassars III (858–824)', *WdO* 2: 137-57, 221-33.
Mittmann, S.
1983   'Die "Handschelle" der Philister (2 Sam 8,1)', in M. Görg (ed.), *Pontes atque Fontes. Eine Festgabe für Hellmut Brunner* (Wiesbaden: Otto Harrassowitz): 327-41.
Momigliano, A.
1966   'Historiography on Written Tradition and Historiography on Oral Tradition', *Studies in Historiography* (London: Weidenfeld and Nicolson): 211-20.
1977   'Eastern Elements in Post-Exilic Jewish, and Greek, Historiography', in *Studies in Ancient and Modern Historiography* (Oxford: Basil Blackwell): 25-35.
Na'aman, N.
1992   'Israel, Edom and Egypt in the 10th Century B.C.E.', *Tel Aviv* 19: 71-93.
1994   'The "Conquest of Canaan" in the Book of Joshua and in History', in I. Finkelstein and N. Na'aman (eds.), *From Nomadism to Monarchy. Archaeological and Historical Aspects of Early Israel* (Jerusalem: Yad Izhak Ben-Zvi and Israel Exploration Society): 218-81.
forthcoming 'Hazael of 'Amqi and Hadadezer of Beth-Rehob', *UF* 27.
Oppenheim, A.L.
1964   *Ancient Mesopotamia* (Chicago: University of Chicago Press).

Parpola, S.
1983   'Assyrian Library Records', *JNES* 42: 1-29.
Paul, S.M.
1991   *Amos* (Hermeneia; Minneapolis, MN: Fortress Press).
Ponchia, S.
1991   *L'Assyria e gli stati transeufratici nella prima metà dell'VIII sec. a.C.* (Padova: Sargon srl).
Puech, E.
1981   'L'ivoire inscrit d'Arslan-Tash et les rois des Damas', *RB* 88: 544-62.
Redford, D.B.
1986   *Pharaonic King-Lists, Annals and Day-Books* (Mississauga: Benben Publications).
Sader, H.S.
1987   *Les états Araméens de Syrie depuis leur formation jusqu'à leur transformation en provinces Assyriens* (Beirut: Orient-Institut der Deutschen Morgenländischen Gesellschaft).
Thompson, T.L.
1992   *The Early History of the Israelite People: From the Written and Archaeological Sources* (Leiden: Brill).
1995   '"House of David": An Eponymic Referent to Yahweh as Godfather', *SJOT* 9: 59-74.
Ungnad, A.
1906   'Jaua, mâr Ḫumrî', *OLZ* 9: 224-26.
Van Seters, J.
1983   *In Search of History. Historiography in the Ancient World and the Origins of Biblical History* (New Haven, CT: Yale University Press).
Weippert, M.
1993   'Die Feldzüge Adadniraris III. nach Syrien. Voraussetzungen, Verlauf, Folgen', *ZDPV* 108: 42-67.
Winckler, H.
1895   *Geschichte Israels in Einzeldarstellungen*, I (Leipzig: Pfeiffer).
1901   'Besprechungen zu Kittel, R. Die Bücher der Könige übers u. erklärt', *OLZ* 4: 141-52.
Wolff, H.W.
1977   *Joel and Amos* (Hermeneia; Philadelphia, PA: Fortress Press).

MONARCHY AND RE-URBANIZATION:
A NEW LOOK AT SOLOMON'S KINGDOM

Volkmar Fritz

The biblical description of the reign of Solomon in 1 Kings 1–11 presents us with two pictures of the king which are at variance with one another and based on differing traditions.[1] According to 1 Kings 1–2, Solomon comes to power through none of his own doing after a palace intrigue, but reveals himself subsequently as a man of power without scruples who brutally thrusts aside the old ruling elite and raises his own confidants to high public office. This constitutes a highly critical picture of David's successor, since his first measures to secure supremacy through the removal of his opponents are presented as an act of royal caprice.[2] By contrast, the subsequent description of his rule in 1 Kings 3–11 is not only devoid of all criticism but full of praise. Solomon combines all the virtues and capabilities of an ideal ruler in his personality; he rules with wisdom and justice, builds temple and palace, carries on trade and forms a company of charioteers. He also increases wealth and prosperity to an incomparable degree and secures his kingdom through the building of cities. As a result of his administrative measures, the Davidic kingship over the tribes evolved into a central rule over a state which included Israelites and Canaanites in its territory. This picture of Solomon's magnificence leaves no room

---

1. Cf. the analysis of E. Würthwein, *Das erste Buch der Könige. Kapitel 1–16* (ATD 11.1; Göttingen: Vandenhoeck & Ruprecht, 2nd edn, 1985).

2. Cf. L. Delekat, 'Tendenz und Theologie der David-Salomo-Erzählung', in I. Maass (ed.), *Das ferne und das nahe Wort. Festschrift L. Rost* (BZAW, 105; Berlin: de Gruyter, 1967), pp. 26-36; L. Rost, 'Die Überlieferung von der Thronnachfolge Davids', in *Das kleine Credo und andere Studien zum Alten Testament* (Heidelberg: Quelle & Meyer, 1965), pp. 119-253; E. Würthwein, *Die Erzählung von der Thronnachfolge Davids: theologische oder politische Geschichtsschreibung* (ThS, 115; Zürich: Theologischer Verlag, 1977).

for doubt about the greatness of his rule. The king has become, as it were, an idolized replica of himself—not only one of glittering perfection but one which shines forth as if covered in pure gold. It is the account given by the Deuteronomistic historian which has coloured our picture of the reign of Solomon to date. In his splendour, Solomon surpasses all the kings who came after him, and his magnificence was never attained again.

In order to create this picture, the tradition has been carefully composed and tailored. The focal point of the whole complex consists of the building and consecration of the temple in 1 Kings 6–8. Solomon's wisdom and justice are demonstrated by means of individual anecdotes, of which not a single one can lay any claim to historical credibility; in particular, mention should be made here of the story of the Judgment of Solomon (1 Kgs 3.16-28)[3] and the visit of the Queen of Sheba (1 Kgs 10.1-13).[4] The subjects of wealth, building activities and trade are mostly dealt with in short notes, the historical authenticity of which must be subjected to detailed examination. While some of the information, such as that which relates to the ivory throne in 1 Kgs 10.18-20 or horsetrading in 1 Kgs 10.28-29[5] is quite credible from a historical point of view, most of the notes such as those which deal with the journeys to Ophir, the land of gold, in 1 Kgs 9.26-28 and 10.11-12.[6] or another which mentions forced labour in 1 Kgs 9.15-24, are compositions of a later date, and hardly reflect the historical reality of the early period of the monarchy. Most of these short notes, written in a style similar to that of the annals, do not actually originate from official documents of the tenth century; rather, they represent a particular type of historical writing which, through its imitation of elements of annalistic style, was to be used to characterize and describe the special nature of the period of Solomon. By no means, therefore, should there be any indiscriminate acceptance of the potential usability of these pieces of information; each individual instance must be subjected

---

3.   The parallels were collected by H. Greßmann, 'Das salomonische Urteil', *Deutsche Rundschau* 33 (1907), pp. 212-28.

4.   Cf. W. Daum (ed.), *Die Königin von Saba* (Munich, 1988).

5.   Cf. Y. Ikeda, 'Solomon's Trade in Horses and Chariots in its International Setting', in T. Ishida (ed.), *Studies in the Period of David and Solomon and Other Essays* (Winona Lake, IN: Eisenbrauns, 1982), pp. 239-58.

6.   Cf. K. Galling, 'Der Weg der Phönizier nach Tarsis in literarischer und archäologischer Sicht', *ZDPV* 88 (1972), pp. 1-18 and 140-81.

to critical examination. Only two texts can be taken as original documents from the royal chancellery: the list of the royal officials in 1 Kgs 4.1-6 and the list of the administrative districts in 1 Kgs 4.7-19. In both cases official documents from the administrative offices were incorporated into the account of the rule of Solomon. These show that the kingdom ruled by him actually did exhibit features which were decisively those of a state; the exercise of the powers which emanated from the king was both delegated to others and subjected to supervision. Nor, after critical analysis of the sources, does Solomon simply disappear into the mists of the unknown: he remains identifiable as a king of an orderly, structured state even though not all aspects of this kingship can be described as tradition would have us believe.

There is one point on which the assertion of Solomon's power and magnificence can be examined, in order to obtain a picture of his kingship: the carrying out of building measures, as repeatedly asserted in the sources, can be seen as a reflection of Solomon's rule. However, it cannot be sufficient just to furnish evidence of the building of various cities as contended in 1 Kgs 9.15 and 19; it is rather more the nature of this building activity that must be discerned, so that the nature of Solomon's kingship can be understood. In other words, we should not just be concerned with demonstrating through individual pieces of evidence that building activity took place in settlement levels at the respective sites. Instead, an attempt should be made to relate innovations in the material culture to the introduction of kingship in Israel. Starting points here are the strata at Hazor and Megiddo, which date from the tenth century. Settlement remains from the early period of the monarchy at other sites are either absent or have not yet been adequately documented.

Hazor

Yigael Yadin has already dated Stratum XB in Hazor to the tenth century and, with reference to 1 Kgs 9.15 has declared it the city of Solomon, although this only covered the western half of the tell.[7] Of this settlement, an immense six-chamber gate with jutting towers, parts of the casemate walls and the remains of domestic architecture to the south-east of the gate as well as in the area of the citadel have been

---

7. Cf. Y. Yadin, *Hazor: The Head of all those Kingdoms* (London: Oxford University Press, 1972), pp. 135-46.

excavated.[8] These houses did not directly abut the wall, but were separated from it by a paved roadway. It is worthy of note that there were no official buildings in the area of the gate; the strong gate construction and the carefully built casemate wall provide a certain contrast to the remains of private houses inside the city, which do not conform to any identifiable building type.[9] Subsequent excavations carried out by Amnon Ben-Tor have not led to any modification of this contradictory finding,[10] but since only a few rooms of these houses have as yet been excavated, the possibility of definitive assignment to a particular type still cannot be excluded. It is clear, however, that the layout of these houses does not follow that of the four-room house. In the citadel area, building remains in Stratum X are even sparser, and the few walls (which are of one stone in width) do not permit any significant recognition of individual houses.[11] Thus this contradiction between planned and well-constructed fortifications and indiscriminate and unplanned private building must remain at present. This picture did not change in the subsequent Strata XA, IXB, and IXA, apart from the fact that small constructional alterations were made to individual rooms. It is only during the extension of the city in Stratum VIII that the small dwellings give way to a pillar-house with an annexe.[12] Although the six-chamber gate lost its function as such in this settlement layer, due to the fact that a new gate was built in the east of the city, the use of the construction for other purposes continued into Stratum VI. Notwithstanding this complicated situation, there is no doubt about the dating of Stratum XB to the tenth century. The gate and casemate wall are situated stratigraphically above graves in Stratum XI and meagre settlement remains from Stratum XII which both date to Iron Age I, to the pre-state period.[13] Thus Stratum XB marks the new foundation of a city, after only sporadic occupation of the site since the destruction of the final Late Bronze Age city in Stratum XIII at the end of the thirteenth century.[14] The pottery in Stratum X corresponds to that

---

8.   Y. Yadin *et al.*, *Hazor III-IV. Text* (Jerusalem: Magnes Press, 1989), pp. 1-122.

9.   Yadin *et al.*, *Hazor III–IV*, Plan VIII.

10.   A. Ben-Tor, 'Tel Hazor', *IEJ* 45 (1995), p. 66, Fig. 1.

11.   Yadin *et al.*, *Hazor III–IV*, Plan XIX.

12.   Yadin *et al.*, *Hazor III–IV*, Plan XI.

13.   Yadin *et al.*, *Hazor III–IV*, Plan XII.

14.   Yadin, *Hazor. The Head of all those Kingdoms*, pp. 129-34.

found in the material used as fill beneath the buildings of the oldest Iron Age phase of Samaria, which according to 1 Kgs 16.24 is attributable to Omri.[15] Since the pottery from this artificial deposit in Samaria must predate the ninth century, the dating of Stratum XB to the tenth century is at any rate certain. Thus Stratum XB of Hazor represents the new foundation of the city in the early period of the monarchy. Where its fortifications are concerned, the only explanation for the precise manner of their construction is that it was carried out in accordance with an already established building form.

In terms of architectural history, the origin of the six-chamber gate and the casemate wall cannot be explained. Both elements may have developed out of the Middle and Late Bronze Age type of fortification, although the gate complexes of these periods always consist of just three pairs of projecting piers opposite each other, so that a four-chamber gate was formed. The best example of this type is preserved in the Middle Bronze Age defence system at Dan (*Tell-el Qāḍī*).[16] The use of casemate construction is demonstrated in connection with the Late Bronze Age gate in area K at Hazor.[17] Even though the employment of the individual elements can already be attested in fortifications of the second millennium, questions concerning their transmission during Iron Age II have not yet been resolved.

In the light of the gate complex at Hazor Stratum XB, Yigael Yadin has also dated the six-chamber gates at Megiddo and Gezer to the period of Solomon.[18] The new investigations into the stratigraphy of Iron Age Megiddo by Yohanan Aharoni and David Ussishkin have revealed, however, that the six-chamber gate at Megiddo can only be dated to the ninth century at the earliest and thus cannot be described as dating from the period of Solomon.[19] The date of the six-chamber gate and adjoining casemate wall at Gezer is still under discussion. Other

15. Cf. the discussion (with a wrong conclusion) in G.J. Wightmann, 'The Myth of Solomon', *BASOR* 277/278 (1990), pp. 5-22.

16. A. Biran, *Biblical Dan* (Jerusalem: Israel Exploration Society, 1994), pp. 75-90.

17. Yadin *et al.*, *Hazor III–IV*, Plan XLV.

18. Y. Yadin, 'Solomon's City Wall and Gate at Gezer', *IEJ* 8 (1958), pp. 80-86.

19. Y. Aharoni, 'The Stratification of Israelite Megiddo', *JNES* 31 (1972), pp. 302-11; D. Ussishkin, 'Was the "Solomonic" City Gate at Megiddo Built by King Solomon?', *BASOR* 239 (1980), pp. 1-18.

gates of this type at Lachish (*Tell ed-Duwēr*) Stratum IV,[20] Ashdod (*Esdūd*) Stratum IX[21] and on *Ḥirbet el-Ġarra* (*Tēl ʿĪrāʾ*) were only built during the course of Iron Age II and attest to further use of this type of gate during the period of the monarchy.

Megiddo

Megiddo is among the few places in the country which was inhabited continuously in the twelfth and eleventh centuries, from the end of the Late Bronze Age to the recommencement of urbanization at the beginning of the period of the monarchy. The dating of the individual settlement layers between the final Canaanite city of Stratum VIIA and the Iron Age city of Stratum IV[22] with the six-chamber gate, city wall 325 and the large official buildings is hotly disputed. I follow the dates given by Aharon Kempinski and justified by him in his monograph on Megiddo.[23] Accordingly, the Late Bronze Age city of Stratum VIIA was finally destroyed shortly after the middle of the twelfth century, and neither the city gate nor the palaces (2041 and 5002) were rebuilt. Only the temple was re-used in Strata VIB and VIA. The subsequent settlements in Strata VIB, VIA and VB were unfortified, although entrance to them was effected via a gate structure situated between two buildings. Stratum VIB is to be dated to the second half of the twelfth century, Stratum VIA to the eleventh and Stratum VB to the end of the eleventh century and beginning of the tenth century. All three settlements are of a radically different nature compared with the final city of the Late Bronze Age in Stratum VIIA, although Stratum VIA does exhibit the reintroduction of elements of Late Bronze Age city culture. In contrast to Aharon Kempinski, I consider all three settlements to have been built and inhabited by Canaanites.

Subsequently, in Stratum VA, a basic modification of the structure of

20. D. Ussishkin, 'Excavations at Tel Lachish 1978–1983: Second Preliminary Report', *Tel Aviv* 10 (1983), p. 121, Fig. 11.

21. M. Dothan and Y. Porath, *Ashdod IV: Excavations of Area M* (Atiqot ES, 15; Jerusalem: Hamakor Press, 1982), Plans 6 and 12.

22. This stratum is also designated as IVA or IVB by other scholars; for the reason for the confusion cf. Z. Herzog, 'Settlement and Fortification Planning in the Iron Age', in A. Kempinski and R. Reich (eds.), *The Architecture of Ancient Israel* (Jerusalem: Israel Exploration Society, 1992), pp. 231-74 (250 n. 55).

23. A. Kempinski, *Megiddo. A City State and Royal Centre in North Israel* (MAVA 40; Munich: Verlag C.H. Beck, 1989), pp. 78-107.

the settlement is visible: the two-chamber gate was renovated, and the town was protected by a peripheral ring of houses. In addition to dwelling houses there were large public buildings: 'Palace 6000' to the east of the gate, building 1482 and palace 1723 in the south of the settlement as well as some other structures.[24] It should be noted here that Palace 1723 was not a *hilani*[25] and was situated within a large courtyard surrounded by a wall, accessible via a small gate structure.[26] At present, the function of building 1482 cannot be more closely defined, but it possibly consisted of residential units for royal officials. The existence and nature of the public buildings indicates a strong measure of centralized planning; domestic house building, where it occurs, does not exhibit any particular structuring or planning, owing to its irregularity. This settlement is to be dated to the tenth century, without a more precise date for its foundation being apparent. It was probably destroyed during the campaign of Shishak (Sheshonk) about 925 BCE and thus likely built during the rule of David or Solomon.

Only with the rebuilding in Stratum IV during the ninth century is Megiddo refortified by the kings of Israel as a military and administrative centre, and given a six-chamber gate. The large number of buildings for official use shows a careful planning of the city; the function of the pillar house as stables, store houses or barracks cannot be discussed in this context.[27]

---

24. Kempinski, *Megiddo*, Plan 11; cf. G.I. Davies, 'Solomonic Stables at Megiddo after All?', *PEQ* 110 (1988), pp. 130-41.

25. D. Ussishkin, 'King Solomon's Palace and Building 1723 in Megiddo', *IEJ* 16 (1966), pp. 174-86.

26. Cf. V. Fritz, 'Die syrische Bauform des Hilani und die Frage seiner Verbreitung', *Damaszener Mitteilungen* 1 (1983), pp. 43-58.

27. Cf. B. Pritchard, 'The Megiddo Stables. A Reassessment', in J. Sanders (ed.), *Near Eastern Archaeology in the Twentieth Century. Essays in Honor of Nelson Glueck* (New York: Doubleday, 1970), pp. 268-76; V. Fritz, 'Bestimmung und Herkunft des Pfeilerhauses in Israel', *ZDPV* 93 (1977), pp. 30-45; J.S. Holladay, 'The Stables of Ancient Israel', in *The Archaeology of Jordan and other Studies presented to S. Horn* (Berrien Springs, MI: Andrews University Press, 1986), pp. 103-65; Z. Herzog, 'Administrative Structures in the Iron Age', in Kempinski and Reich (eds.), *The Architecture of Ancient Israel*, pp. 223-30.

Gezer

In the case of Gezer, the excavators William Dever and John Holladay
have defended the dating of the construction of the six-chamber gate to
the time of Solomon.[28] This gate complex is connected to a casemate
wall but at any rate it predates the so-called outer gate. The question of
its assignment to the time of Solomon can only be resolved in
connection with the dating of the so-called outer wall, but this long-
discussed problem is still an open question.[29] According to finds made
up to the present time, however, the possibility of dating the six-
chamber gate into the ninth century cannot be excluded.[30] The gate is
assigned to the city of Stratum VIII. The remains of this settlement
level which have been excavated are expressly described by William
Dever as 'unimpressive'; they are probably those of modest private
houses, but have unfortunately not yet been published. Thus Gezer
exhibits a picture that is not clear so far.

Conclusions

Too little excavation has taken place at other cities which were founded
during the tenth century to enable any further conclusions. The city in
Stratum V on *Tell es-Seba*ᶜ was surrounded by a massive wall and
entered via a four-chamber gate. The complex of pillar houses to the
east of the gate was probably constructed during the period of this
stratum, so that the conscious planning of this city that is visible in
Stratum II was already established at the time of foundation. Owing to
a lack of publication of excavation results, details cannot be given at
the moment.

Even though only a few cities of the tenth century have been
excavated to date, the findings that have been reported do permit some
conclusions.

28. W.G. Dever, 'Late Bronze Age and Solomonic Defenses. New Evidence',
BASOR 262 (1986), pp. 9-34.

29. S. Bunimovitz, 'Glacis 10014 and Gezer's Late Bronze Fortifications', *Tel
Aviv* 10 (1983), pp. 61-70; I. Finkelstein, 'The Date of Gezer's Outer Wall', *Tel
Aviv* 8 (1981), pp. 136-45; W.G. Dever, 'Further Evidence on the Date of the Outer
Wall at Gezer', *BASOR* 189 (1993), pp. 33-54.

30. D. Ussishkin, 'Notes on Megiddo, Gezer, Ashdod, and Tel Batash in the
Tenth to Ninth Centuries B.C.', *BASOR* 277/278 (1990), pp. 71-91.

1. A re-urbanization took place during the tenth century, and there was a causal relationship between this and the establishment of the monarchy. At Hazor a new fortified citiy was founded after a period of only sporadic occupation. On *Tell es-Seba* the fortified city replaced the open settlement of the early Iron Age. At Gezer the previous, apparently open settlement was most probably fortified with a gate and a casemate wall. The construction of a new fortification was not undertaken at Megiddo Stratum VA, but public buildings were erected when it was taken over and palace 1723 was secured with its own encircling wall.

2. Seen against the history of domestic architecture over the preceding two centuries, no significant further developments took place in house construction at this time. The houses do not conform to any standard, and as yet there is no diffusion of the four-room type of house, with its clear ground-plan, in the cities.

3. The erection of public buildings at some sites is probably to be attributed to the issuing of royal decrees. These large buildings served an administrative purpose which arose from the establishment of the kingdom.

4. The building of fortifications is rooted in a tradition that cannot at present be closely defined. At any rate, it presupposes the existence of an organization of labour, which can only have been brought about through the new form of state—the monarchy.

Thus the foundation of new cities in the country was originally connected with the establishment of the kingdom. Even though hardly any change is discernible in domestic architecture, the existence of new large buildings indicates that, as a result of the establishment of the monarchy, a new situation arose. In order to meet its requirements, and to accommodate the administrative development of the state, the construction of suitable buildings had become a necessity. With the fortification of the settlements by means of walls and gates, the new state was put into a condition of defensive readiness, which first enabled the monarchy to carry on wars and thus make its presence felt. Accordingly biblical tradition has presented Solomon as a great builder; this he certainly was, according to evidence based on archaeological research, even though he may not have been the splendid ruler who appears in biblical tradition.

THE 'BAN' IN THE AGE OF THE EARLY KINGS*

Walter Dietrich

Setting out to search in the biblical narrative for information on the period of the early Israelite monarchy is nowadays to set foot on quicksand. The 'Young Turks of Copenhagen' merely clarify again what we all know: the Hebrew Bible found its final form only in the post-exilic period (or shall we say: in the early Judaic period?). Everything that precedes—not to mention the legendary early times of the first kings—must be sought underneath the surface of the present text.

Exegetes resemble archaeologists in this. They venture out on 'Tell Tenak', remove the top layer of debris caused by the history of the text—and happily discover right underneath layers of the Iron III period. Obviously, already before the turn of the age, the inhabitants of the area considered this hill a sort of a holy, untouchable place. Out of a pious awe they did not reinhabit it. At some distance three new settlements sprang up whose inhabitants all claim—though in quite different stories—that it was their ancestors who lived upon this hill and that they themselves, Jews, Christians and Muslims respectively, carry on their traditions.

Now, back to the exegetes on the tell. Many of them—almost all of the Jewish ones, but many Christians too—refuse to penetrate with the diachronic spade through the Iron III top layers. It is evident to them that not all that is found there bears the stylistic signs of the Hellenistic or Persian age. Much of it looks older, coming from the Iron II age. Still, these could be, as some suggest, elements consciously given an archaic flavor—a king's palace for example which was described in the exilic period according to ideas of how King David's or Solomon's residences may have looked. And—for that matter—those interested more in the

* I am deeply indebted to my student Christoph Schwarz (Bern, Switzerland) for translating, and to my colleague Steven L. McKenzie (Memphis, TN) for reading over my paper.

aesthetics of architecture consider the actual age of the respective elements from this biblical Iron III town irrelevant anyway. The only importance for them is to determine its final form and to reconstruct it accordingly.

It is mainly Christian Tenak-exegetes of a certain continental European sort who are willing to dig deeper. They assume that the Persian or Hellenistic urban engineers did much more than merely integrate single 'antique' elements of construction into their 'modern' town. Rather, they say that these engineers adapted or renovated or restored whole buildings, if not neighborhoods, erected in former times. Was 'Tell Tenak' already in the Iron II age a prestigious town? Do the oldest mansions of this king's palace derive even from the Iron IIA Age? (Luckily we are not pressed to consider Iron I.)

I will set my exegetical spade in a spot not apparently central. Let us call it the military compound of 'Tell Tenak'. And here I will not dig out the whole area but just one specific element of construction: the 'ban'. This is notably an institution that subjects an external enemy to total destruction under the cover of the will of a deity. Some variations concern the subject of such an annihilation: 'only' the armed troops of the enemy, or including women, children, and holy devices or even all material belongings.

1. *Conceptions of the Ban in the Post State Period of Israel*

The mass of the little less than 80 occurrences of the root חרם[1] are found in the Deuteronomistic writings. Its writers liked, as we know, to portray the taking of the land of Palestine by Israel as a victorious conquest and the alleged extermination of the native population as a 'consecration of annihilation'.[2] Victories in the Negev and in east Jordan form the prelude (Num. 21.2, 3;[3] Deut. 2.34; 3.6[4]). The next step is

1. The verb occurs 48 times, the noun 29 times; cf. the thorough article of N. Lohfink, 'חרם', *ThWAT* III (1978), pp. 192-213.

2. A later Deuteronomistic redaction has asserted that the taking of the land was not so rabid and radical (cf. R. Smend, 'Das Gesetz und die Völker. Ein Beitrag zur deuteronomistischen Redaktionsgeschichte', in *Festschrift G. von Rad* [Munich: Chr. Kaiser Verlag, 1971], pp. 494-509 = R. Smend, 'Die Mitte des Alten Testaments', *Ges. Stud.* 1 [BEvT, 99; Munich: Chr. Kaiser Verlag, 1986], pp. 124-37).

3. Cf. also the parallel tradition Judg. 2.17.

4. Looking back Josh. 2.10 refers to it.

Moses commanding Israel to do likewise west of the Jordan (Deut. 7.2).
Joshua fulfills this commission in his two great expeditions to the south
(Josh. 10.11, 28, 35, 37, 39, 40) and the north (Josh. 11.11, 12, 20, 21).
No human being, no נפש nor any נשמה, may remain alive in the
conquered cities, as the writers emphasize time and again.[5]

The Deuteronomic Torah was meant to give legal foundation to this
behavior. The so-called law of war presumably in a pre-exilic version
required 'only' the extermination of the men (זכור) of a conquered city
'with the edge of the sword',[6] while women, children, cattle and
movable property were to be considered as prey (Deut. 20.13-14). This
was later redefined in an addition: this was to be the rule only for cities
at a greater distance while those of the tribes of Canaan,[7] which YHWH
wanted to 'give as an inheritance' to Israel, were to be subjected to the
חרם. No human, not one נשמה, was to escape death (Deut. 20.16-17).[8] It
is quite obvious how a common rule of the law concerning behavior in
pugnacious quarrels was applied in a historicist way to the situation of
the conquest of the land. And this reveals the Deuteronomistic historian.
It is to be noticed that it was only he who carried the idea of the
extermination of the complete Canaanite population into the
Deuteronomic law of war. He did not get this idea from an older law!
Where he did get it from will be considered later.

A later, probably post-exilic edition changed the rabid picture of the
taking of the land in the Deuteronomistic book of Joshua: it says that
Israel did not succeed in creating a *tabula rasa*; on the contrary, foreign
tribes continued to live in the land.[9] This situation indeed had its benefits.
One could use the non-Israelite elements in the population for slave

---

5.   The ongoing existence of the Gibeonites (Josh. 9) is put forward as a great
exception.

6.   Note that the term חרם is not used here.

7.   They are described here by the conventional series of people who according
to Deuteronomistic conception lived in pre-Israelite Palestine: Hittites, Amorites,
Canaanites, Perizzites, Hivites and Jebusites.

8.   In this case I agree with the analysis of M. Rose (*5.Mose*, I [ZBK, 5.1;
Zürich: TVZ, 1994], p. 251): the Josianic core of the law must be sought in 20.10-
14, 19-20 while vv. 15-18 were added by a Deuteronomistic hand (or hands). Maybe
the reasoning given in v. 18 that Canaanites who remain alive might teach the
Israelites the worship of 'detestable things' is really to be regarded as tertiary; cf.
Josh. 23 which is assigned by R. Smend ('Das Gesetz') to DtrN, especially vv. 7,
12, 16.

9.   Cf. Josh. 23; Judg. 1-2 and above n. 3.

labor—as reportedly happened under Solomon (1 Kgs 9.21).[10] On the other hand, the situation held its dangers: through these foreigners Israel got to know foreign gods and threatened to be alienated from YHWH. Moses had already recommended extreme measures in such a case: against a city—that is, an *Israelite* city—which had become unfaithful to YHWH, the חרם was to be carried out; everything living in it was to be extinguished and all goods recovered from it were to be burned (Deut. 13.13-19).[11]

Both of these Deuteronomistic conceptions of the ban seem to be reflected in the Achan story, Joshua 6–7. Just before the assault on Jericho, Joshua declares the city 'and all that is in it'—except for the prostitute Rahab and her house—as חרם ליהוה (Josh. 6.17). The ban, then, is in fact executed 'on all that was in her [the city]': on men, women, children, elderly, even on the cattle (6.21). While this could be seen in line with Deut. 20.16-17,[12] the narration continues and reminds one of Deut. 13.13-19:[13] no silver nor gold, no utensils made in copper

10. Cf. on this W. Dietrich, 'Das harte Joch (1. Könige 12,4). Fronarbeit in der Salomo-Überlieferung', *BN* 34 (1986), pp. 7-16.

11. In the same spirit is the regulation in the Book of the Covenant—certainly added there—that everyone who sacrifices to gods other than YHWH is to be banned (Exod. 22.19). Because an exact definition of חרם is lacking here, Chr. Schäfer-Lichtenberger ('Bedeutung und Funktion von Herem in biblisch-hebräischen Texten', *BZ* 38 [1994], pp. 270-75) wants to conclude that exclusion rather than extinction is meant ('aus der Gruppe der JHWH-Kultteilnehmer ausgeschlossen', p. 274), and that this is a unique and, in the history of tradition, early linguistic usage. But one should not build so much on an *argumentum e silentio*. Deut. 7.26 alone is a warning against such an interpretation. There it is also idolatry which is at issue and a definition of חרם is also missing. Yet extinction is clearly demanded: of the cult-symbols not belonging to YHWH (how could these be excluded if not through extinction?) and of those who are handling them. If we enlightened and modern people perceive this claim as an unreasonable demand, we still cannot interpret it away.

12. It is striking, though, that vv. 17 and 21 contain the neutral expression כל, which would apparently include the cattle under the ban. This was explicitly not thought of in the law of war—at any rate not in its older form, which was also taken up by DtrH; cf. Deut. 20.14.

13. In my opinion not all statements about the ban aiming at extinction made in Josh. 6 lie on the same text-level (against V. Fritz, in his new commentary, *Das Buch Josua* [HAT, 1.7; Tübingen: Mohr, 1994], p. 66). Yet Deut. 13.13ff is talking about Israelite cities among which one can hardly count the Jericho of that time. But as is well known Jericho did not exist at that time, and later it lay very much within Israelite territory (1 Kgs 16.34).

or iron are the soldiers allowed to take with them. All of this is 'holy to YHWH' and is to be added to the 'treasure of YHWH'. In case of defiance the Israelite camp will itself be subjected to the חרם (Josh. 6.18-19). When the Israelite Achan actually takes from the 'banned' items (Josh. 7.1, 11, 21), Israel promptly loses its next battle and is only able to win again after having found and eradicated the delinquent, his whole family and his possessions. In this late Deuteronomistic didactic narrative[14] the term חרם has lost its unique cultic and military double meaning and has emerged as two concepts: the one of the assignment of valuables to the sanctuary of YHWH and the other of a total defeat brought about by YHWH.[15]

There are further examples of both elements in the exilic and post-exilic literature. The texts under priestly influence emphasize the aspect of the appropriation to the sanctuary. Ezra 10.8, the only occurrence of חרם in the book of Ezra–Nehemiah, threatens the confiscation of property belonging to seditious members of the temple community. Corresponding regulations are found in Lev. 27.21, 28-29; Num. 18.14; Ezek. 44.29. The military range of meaning is dominant in the late prophetic and apocalyptic literature. Jer. 25.9 announces the 'banning' of Judah at the hands of the Babylonians authorized by YHWH;[16] Jer. 50.21, 26 and 51.3 conversely predict the 'banning' of the Babylonians by unnamed enemies also obeying the command of YHWH. According to the legends

---

14. It is referred to once more in Josh. 22.20.

15. The change of actors in executing the ban from the Israelites (banning Jericho first, and then Achan) to the people of Ai (banning the Israelites, Josh. 7.12) seems only to be a question of form; in truth God is the real acting subject in the story. G. Michell wants to see in the episodes of the Canaanite Rahab being spared and the Israelite Achan being banned an anti-nationalistic tendency (*Together in the Land: A Reading of the Book of Joshua* [JSOTSup, 134; Sheffield: JSOT Press, 1993], pp. 75-76, 82). Over against his attempt to see the episode of Achan as the key to the understanding of the motif of the banning of nations in the book of Joshua—it was 'the idea of abhorrence and perhaps cultic contamination' which brings Israel to 'social distance from foreigners' (p. 81)—we must observe that this is not the root of the conception of the ban but rather a relatively late form.

16. In the conclusion of W. Thiel (*Die deuteronomistische Redaktion von Jeremia 1-25* [WMANT, 41; Neukirchen–Vluyn; Neukirchener Verlag, 1973], p. 262) even a 'Grundbestand' worked out of Jer. 25.1-13 cannot be 'ein original dtr. Text'. 'Er wird derartig von D-Phraseologie beherrscht, dass er insgesamt als literarisches Produkt von D beurteilt werden muss.'

of Isaiah, the great king of Assyria boasted of having banned countless nations (2 Kgs 19.11[17]). At times it is—oddly—YHWH himself who is waging wars of banning, be it against foreign nations (Isa. 11.15; 34.2, 5) or even against his own people (Isa. 43.28; Mal. 3.24). Here and there one gets the impression of the חרם-terminology being used only as a poetic-archaic stylistic device without the cruel seriousness of the original institution (Mic. 4.13; Zech. 14.11; Dan. 11.44).

Overall the idea of a devotion to annihilation retreats to the background in the post-exilic period. Therefore, while it is not surprising that the root חרם does not occur in the books of Job and Ecclesiastes, it is surprising to find the same to be true for Jonah and Esther and even for the Priestly text[18] and the Psalms, where cult and military do play quite a role. Chronicles, in turn, which reports much and readily about wars (and naturally about the cult), uses the terminology of ban only four times and then mostly in recourse to sources in the Deuteronomistic historical work.[19] The specific conceptions of war in Chronicles are different ones more appropriate to their time.[20]

17. Chr. Hardmeier (*Prophetie im Streit vor dem Untergang Judas* [BZAW, 187; Berlin: de Gruyter, 1990], pp. 132-34) sees 2 Kgs 19.3-36 as secondary narrative reinterpretation of the basic narrative of the Assyrian threat and the liberation of Jerusalem, which he believes in its turn to be datable fairly precisely to the year 588. Accordingly, the addition could not be pre-exilic.

18. Concerning the 'pacifism' of the priestly text, cf. N. Lohfink, 'Die Schichten des Pentateuch und der Krieg', in N. Lohfink (ed.), *Gewalt und Gewaltlosigkeit im Alten Testament* (QD, 96; Freiburg: Herder, 1983), pp. 51-110, specifically 75ff.

19. Concerning 1 Chron. 2.7 cf. Josh. 7; concerning 2 Chron. 32.14 cf. 2 Kgs 19.11 resp. Isa. 37.11-12. Chron. 20.23 seems to refer rather freely to 2 Kgs 3.23, where, of course, the term חרם is not used. The occurrence in 1 Chron. 4.41, which reports in the middle of the genealogy of Judah an episode in the time of King Hezekiah (725–696) in which a חרם is said to have played an important role, is remarkable. Is the Chronicler citing an older source in the passage 4.39-43 which falls strangely out of the context?

20. P. Welten, who has studied the facts thoroughly (*Geschichte und Geschichtsdarstellung in den Chronikbüchern* [WMANT: Neukirchen–Vluyn: Neukirchener Verlag, 42; 1973], pp. 79-172) holds that Chronicles already reflects Greek military principles. A. Ruffing (*Jahwekrieg als Weltmetapher. Studien zu Jahwekriegstexten des chronistischen Sondergutes* [SBB: Stuttgart: Katholisches Bibelwerk, 24; 1992]) arrives in his analysis of a paradigmatic war-narrative at a similar chronological setting but emphasizes much more the theological intent of the texts. They are concerned with the survival of Israel in a troublesome situation in world politics, which not Israel itself (as through war!) but only God is able to

2. *The Praxis of the Ban in the Time of the Israelite Kings*

Nearly all of the occurrences of the root חרם in the Hebrew Bible, then, have been discussed.[21] Just a few places in the books of Samuel and Kings are left. Since they also belong to the Deuteronomistic historical work one might suppose that they also belong to the conception of the ban inserted by the Deuteronomistic authors or redactors as part of their standard intellectual repertory. If this is the case, we are dealing with an ideologoumenon that was born in the exilic period, in the shock of the loss of the land and the fear of losing the special relationship between YHWH and Israel.

Now there is a text whose authenticity and origin in the ninth century BCE cannot be denied even by the most radical critics of the Bible. On a stone inscription found near the end of the last century, King Mesha of Moab boasts of having freed his country and people from the dominion of Israel, and all of this under the command and help of the god Kamosh.[22] He reports with observable pride how he carried out in a most furious way 'ethnic cleansings' in several villages inhabited by Israelites:

> And the people of Gad lived in the land of Atarot from old times. And for himself the king of Israel built (enlarged) Atarot. I assaulted the city and conquered it. And I killed all the people of the town as a sacrifice for Kamosh and for Moab. And I removed the altar of their Dod from there and dragged it before Kamosh in Qaryot (1.10-13).

Here the ban is not mentioned in terminology but in content: the inhabitants are, obviously entirely, exterminated—for the sake of

---

master. Over against this and in contrast to the Deuteronomistic historical work, the problem of Israel's distinct religious existence does not play any role for the Chronicler (so Ruffing, *Jahwekrieg*, p. 359)—and yet the conception of ban in the Deuteronomistic texts is linked precisely with this.

21. The occurrence in Judg. 21.11 is difficult to explain in literary-historical terms. Even if Judg. 17–21 is not an appendix to the (Deuteronomistic) book of Judges (against M. Noth, *Überlieferungsgeschichtliche Studien* [Tübingen: Niemeyer, 1957], p. 54 n. 2), it says nothing about the real age of the traditions used here. Specifically the passage 21.6-15 seems to be an addition inserted by means of *Wiederaufnahme*.

22. In the following I am citing (and translating) in accordance with K. Jaroš, *Hundert Inschriften aus Kanaan und Israel* (Schweiz: Katholisches Bibelwerk, 1982), pp. 41ff.

Kamosh; an altar belonging to YHWH[23] is reassigned to Kamosh; all the rest of the belongings (houses, fields, movable property) probably fell, thanks to Kamosh, to the Moabites. Mesha continues:

> Kamosh said to me: Go and take Nebo (in battle) against Israel... And I conquered it and killed all: seven thousand men and slaves and women and nurses and pregnant women [?]; for I had devoted it to a ban for Kamosh. And I took from there the utensils of Yahweh and dragged them before Kamosh (1.14.16-18).

These lines again describe the extermination of the population—this time with specific mention of the female part of it—with the specific rationale of having first devoted them to the 'ban' (same word as in Hebrew!) and in this way to the deity. And they also describe the reassignment of the utensils to their own deity while the rest of the loot was presumably distributed.

The fact that Mesha speaks about his carrying out the ban and the way he does so allows for several conclusions specifically concerning the previously discussed Deuteronomic-Deuteronomistic occurrences of the term:

1. The silent abandonment of the חרם-terminology in Deut. 20.13-14 and the instruction given there to kill 'only' the men of a conquered city show themselves to be an attempt—in line with the overall quite humane and social Deuteronomic legislation[24]—to humanize the customs of war practiced by Israel's neighbors and certainly by Israel itself.[25]

2. The (first) Deuteronomistic rendering of the taking of the land as a devotion to the ban that resulted in the extermination of the

---

23. The utilized word *dôd* actually means 'darling' (e.g. Song 2.3) but is used in Isa. 5.1 for YHWH. Whether the sequence of letters d-w-d in the newly found inscription of Tell Dan is an epithet for a god or means the name of king David, has become an issue of heated scholarly debate. I fear it will not end favorably for the above-mentioned Young Turks of Copenhagen (who decidedly argue for the former; cf. N.P. Lemche and T.L. Thompson, 'Did Biran Kill David? The Bible in Light of Archaeology', *JSOT* 64 [1994], pp. 3-22).

24. Cf. the noticeably emphatic portrayal of the Deuteronomic Torah by F. Crüsemann, *Die Tora. Theologie und Sozialgeschichte des alttestamentlichen Gesetzes* (Munich: Chr. Kaiser Verlag, 1992), pp. 235ff.

25. Corresponding to this is the prohibition of the cutting of any trees bearing fruit during a siege, Deut. 20.19-20.

whole population seems to be unrealistic only in terms of geography, not in terms of its cruel thoroughness.

3.   Surprisingly, the second Deuteronomistic conception is confirmed as well. According to it, the ban could also cover material goods[26]—at least what related to utensils of the cult; the dedication of every noble metal to the deity (Josh. 6–7) and the burning of all the loot (Deut. 13.17-18) would have reduced human enthusiasm for war since there was no profit to be gained for risking one's life.

The idea of a devotion to the ban is not an invention of the exilic period. The Deuteronomistic conceptions of it are inscribed down to the details in the monument of the Moabite king Mesha. Now, the Deuteronomists probably did not know or appreciate this Moabite icon of victory. Nor was this necessary. The Israelite historical traditions taken up by them spoke repeatedly of the institution of חרם.

Two biblical reports concerning wars in which the ban is executed are to be located chronologically not far from the deeds and the text of King Mesha. They are said to be carried out by Israelite kings against their foreign enemies. The anecdote in 1 Kgs 20.35-43 reports how a member of the prophetic guild condemned a king of northern Israel—in the present context this would have been Ahab. The reason for this was his saving the life of his Damascene adversary in order to make financial agreements with him.

> This is what YHWH says: Because you allowed the man I devoted to the ban to escape,[27] your נפש will be taken for his נפש and your people (of war) for his people (of war) (1 Kgs 20.42).

According to the present prologue, which is highly legendary, *all* Aramean soldiers—totaling 127,000—were killed beforehand (1 Kgs 20.29-30); the term חרם is not used there but may stand in the background. So the whole battle for the Israelites was a war involving the ban and because it took place on Israelite territory[28] 'only' the *men* of Aram

---

26. Of course, Mesha refers expressly to cultic utensils; the words in Josh. 6.19 fit this only conditionally, those in Josh. 7.21-22 not at all.

27. שלח יד 'to send from the hand' is found in various versions with different suffixes; but it does not make a big difference whether the enemy king escaped the hand of YHWH or the hand of the king obliged to ban him.

28. The whole chapter 1 Kings 20 describes the action of the Arameans as a one-sided aggression.

fell under the ban after Israel's victory[29]—thus leaving only one man, of all men the most important and the one primarily responsible for the war.

A close parallel is the story of the breach between Samuel and Saul in 1 Samuel 15. Right from the beginning the war against Amalek is clearly declared as a war involving the ban. Samuel delivers the command to King Saul:

> Go and attack Amalek and subject[30] everything that belongs to it to the ban. Do not spare him. Kill the men, women, children and babies, the cattle, sheep, camels and donkeys (1 Sam. 15.3).

Cruel as this command is, it does not seem exaggerated or incredible when we consider the context of the monument of Mesha on the one hand and the late Deuteronomistic texts presented above on the other. The biblical narrative, then, is not startled in the least about Saul's accepting and completing the command without any opposition. On the contrary, he is rebuked, even 'rejected', for having made an exception with the king of Amalek and the best of their cattle with good reasons, this reproach being exactly analogous to the prophetic narrative in 1 Kgs 20.35ff.

In recent scholarship, 1 Samuel 15 is more and more frequently declared to have no historical value and to be a product of fantasy of very late origin.[31] There may well be late, that is Deuteronomistic, traces of redaction in the narrative, but it seems to originate mainly in the middle of the monarchic period; together with 1 Kgs 20.35-43 and other stories of conflicts between prophets and kings it may have been part of a separate collection of narratives.[32] It is striking how the devotion to the ban plays a role in these narratives time and again.[33]

---

29. We will encounter analogous circumstances in the Davidic traditions. Was it such experiences that led to the regulation in Deut. 20.13-14—even if it is another situation that is described there?

30. The 2nd. masc. pl. suffix appears out of context and is debated in the history of the text, cf. *BHS*.

31. Cf. H. Donner, *Die Verwerfung des Königs Saul* (Sitzungsberichte der Wiss. Gesellschaft an der Johann Wolfgang Goethe-Universität Frankfurt/M., 19.5; Wiesbaden: Franz Steiner, 1983), and F. Foresti, *The Rejection of Saul in the Perspective of the Deuteronomistic School. A Study of 1 Sam 15 and Related Texts* (Rome: Edizioni del Teresianum, 1984).

32. Cf. W. Dietrich, *David, Saul und die Propheten* (BWANT, 122; Stuttgart: Kohlhammer, 2nd edn, 1992), pp. 9ff.

33. Should one consider 1 Chron. 4.41 as belonging here too? This strange notice

The core of the tradition in 1 Samuel 15 seems to be a short account about an expedition of Saul against the Amalekites in the Negev[34]—in my opinion not historically implausible—which was victorious and never led to a clash with the 'prophet' Samuel. This oldest core of the narrative seems to have read as follows:

(4a) And Saul summoned the men and mustered them at Tela'im. (5) And Saul went to the city of Amalek and set an ambush in the ravine. (6*aab) And Saul said to the Kenites, 'Go away, get out from among the Amalekites.' So the Kenite moved away from the Amalekites. (7) Then Saul attacked the Amalekites all the way from Havilah to Shur, to the east of Egypt. (8) He took Agag king of the Amalekites alive [and all his people he totally put to a ban with the sword[35]]. (12) Early in the morning Samuel got up and went to meet Saul, but he was told, 'Saul has gone to Carmel. There he has set up a monument in his own honor and has turned and gone on down to Gilgal.' (13a) And Samuel went to Saul. (31b) And Saul worshipped YHWH. (32) And Samuel said, 'Bring me Agag, king of the Amalekites.' And Agag came to him confidently. And Agag said, 'Surely the bitterness of death is past.' (33) And Samuel said, 'As your sword has made women childless, so will your mother be childless among women.' And Samuel chopped Agag in pieces before YHWH. [(34) Then Samuel went home to Ramah, and Saul went up to his home in Gibeah of Saul.]

The king and the spiritual tribune[36] work hand in hand in the battle against a grim enemy of Israel. They meet at the shrine of YHWH at Gilgal—which constitutes at other times too the geographical and possibly the ideological basis of co-operation between the two.[37] And

is about a group of Judeans having emigrated in the time of the Judean king Hezekiah (that is, towards the end of the eighth century) as it were into Philistine territory, putting to the ban all people who lived there.

34. D. Edelman suggests an attack against an Amalekite territory in the Ephraimite highlands ('Saul's Battle against Amaleq (1 Sam. 15)', *JSOT* 35 [1986], pp. 71-84); but with this assumption one encounters difficulties—maybe not with the topographical name Carmel (this could refer to the mountain range in north Israel) but with Gilgal, which remains precisely to be localized.

35. Verse 8b—maybe together with the preceding ה—*could* have come in here because of the ban-command, v. 3, which is given in the expanded prophetic narrative. But this assumption is not necessary because there have been, as we will see, other wars involving the ban in the period of early monarchy.

36. Here Samuel does not act as prophet, not expressly at any rate.

37. Cf. 1 Sam. 11.14-15 (though Samuel may have been added there later) and 1 Sam. 10.8 and 13.1ff. (here too the co-operation has later been constructed into a confrontation).

'before YHWH' the last part of the Amalekite expedition is executed. Whether this war was declared as war including the ban or not, it was at any rate a war of YHWH.

The reconstruction of the textual basis of an old account about an expedition against the Amalekites by Saul and Samuel is certainly not without risks. Nevertheless, notes on further clashes between Amalekites and Israelites or Judahites respectively in the time of the formation of the state show that the reconstruction does not lead beyond all historical probability. Saul's rival and later successor, David, frequently invaded, when he was still vassal to the Philistines, the (pasture-) 'land of the Geshurites, the Girzites and the Amalekites; and David attacked the land and did not leave alive any men or women; and he took the sheep, oxen, donkeys, camels, and clothing' (1 Sam. 27.8-9). This makes—horrific— sense: with the prey he not only keeps his troops happy but also courts the favor of his countrymen in Judah (1 Sam. 30.26-30), who indeed crown him king shortly thereafter (2 Sam. 2.4). And there is a clearly stated reason for the death of the Amalekite women along with their men: nobody should report any of David's activities to his Philistine feudal lord (1 Sam. 27.11).

In the course of events these raids correspond fairly exactly to the line of action of the victors in ban-wars. But the inner motivation here is different, oriented simply on economical and political goals; accordingly the term חרם is missing. It is also absent in the long list of wars and victories of David in 2 Samuel 8 as well as in the two short stories about Philistine wars in 2 Samuel 5 and in the elaborated Ammonite war narrative in 2 Samuel 10 and 12.26-31. Apparently nobody believed these expeditions to be ban-wars or tried to make them appear as such.

Only in one single seemingly specifically irritating and critical case did David according to the tradition impose the 'ban' upon an enemy. It is strikingly the Amalekites again, who this time in a raid destroyed the residence of David and kidnapped—not slaughtered—wives, sons and daughters of David and his people (1 Sam. 30.3). David pursued them, overtook them and fought them from dusk until evening and devoted them to the ban; and none of them got away, except four hundred young men who rode off on camels and escaped.[38] The previously captured Judean women and children were freed. Some of the material plunder

---

38. Apparently the ban is directed 'only' against the recruitable men; again no word is said about women or children.

taken from the Amalekites David sent to Judah with the words: 'See, a present for you from the plunder of the enemies of YHWH' (1 Sam. 30.26).

The phrasing pricks one's ears, as a little pretentious but rather casual. The Amalekites appear, at least in this case, not only as the enemies of David and his Judahites but also as 'enemies of YHWH', and this caused them to be banned.[39] The ban includes here the extinction of all Amalekite men within reach[40] for the sake of YHWH—just as Saul for the sake of YHWH apparently was supposed to kill the Amalekite warriors, whom he defeated in his expedition, and as Samuel subsequently 'chopped into pieces before YHWH' the Amalekite king Agag—and as Mesha of Moab killed 'the men and slaves', but also 'women, nurses and pregnant women' of Nebo in the name of his god Kamosh. The deity requires the extermination of *its* enemies.

The usually profane appearance of the wars of Saul and David[41]—and if we had records of them probably the wars of Mesha too—and the use of the ban terminology only in certain instances is an indication of important facts. This was apparently an extreme means, an *ultima ratio*, which was not applied in every fight and every war, but only when the existence of the respective group or nation—and with them also their deity—was threatened. The deity and its worshippers were highly provoked and ready to go to the extreme. This the enemies (and also the opposing deity), once they were defeated, were to suffer. In such a case, the blood of the men fallen in battle did not suffice; all men (or even women and children and beasts) had to die. The enemy gods had to pay as well, their penalty being the reassignment of their statues and cultic utensils to the victorious deity. In these circumstances, the usual reasons for war—economic benefits, material profit—were no longer foremost.

39. We may leave it open whether this was the case only once (1 Sam. 30), or yet a second time (1 Sam. 15) or even in general (thus the opinion of Exod. 17.16).

40. The women and children presumably had the good fortune not to be present at this raid.

41. Yet it should be remembered that in antiquity every meaningful action had religious implications. In some way or another deities were involved in every war; cf. M. Weippert, '"Heiliger Krieg" in Israel und Assyrien. Kritische Anmerkungen zu Gerhard von Rads Konzept des "Heiligen Kriegs im alten Israel"', *ZAW* 84 (1972), pp. 460-93. Thus the devotion to the ban—not yet mentioned outside of Palestine—signifies a form of especially intensive involvement of the deity in the war.

It was not a matter of gold, slaves or land, but the existence or non-existence of the people and its god.

These notions and this praxis of the 'devotion to the ban' existed apparently in the middle and even in the early period of the Israelite monarchy. They were probably never central to the spiritual identity and the military actions of Israel (nor of Moab), but were relied upon only in highly critical situations. Records of them were preserved in two lines of Israelite tradition: on the one hand in the historical, which retained among others memories of the first kings; on the other hand in the prophetic—the 'devotion to the ban' with its unreserved (and ruthless!) God-centeredness apparently attracted especially the radical Yahwistic circles.

Both lines, the national-political and the prophetic, meet in the Deuteronomistic historical work. Its first basic form designed its picture of the Israelite conquest of the land under Joshua after the pattern of David's 'banning' of Amalek.[42] Presumably in a later editing, the prophetic strand was inserted; in the example of the 'ban' it was easy to demonstrate the tense relationship between kings and prophets.[43] Finally the 'banning' changed into a means of handling controversy about the right way of fidelity to YHWH *within* Israel.[44]

From Deuteronomism, it seems, the lines continue into the prophetic and apocalyptic sphere as well as into the post-exilic cult congregation. Thus, the tradition of חרם did not expire just after the end of the state of Israel but was rather reawakened once more to an even more intensive if only spiritual life. It could not be realized any more in a political and military way, not in Israel and under the title חרם at any rate. In the light of many examples in history and the present, it is doubtful whether the conduct of war has since become any more humane.[45]

Our observations on the idea and the praxis of the devotion to the ban in Moab and Israel cast a historical glance at a specific narrow area of the early monarchy. Just as the Moabite Mesha reports in his inscription, so the biblical writers relate how David and Saul announced the חרם on their enemy in highly critical situations and subsequently received the

42. Deut. 20.16-17; Josh. 10–11.
43. 1 Sam. 15; 1 Kgs 20.35-43.
44. Deut. 13.13-19.
45. Concerning the theological and ethical implications of the biblical idea of devotion to the ban, cf. W. Dietrich and C. Link, *Die dunklen Seiten Gottes. Willkür und Gewalt* (Neukirchen–Vluyn: Neukirchener Verlag, 1995), pp. 195ff.

victory from their deity. Especially in the case of David the respective details have a rather casual and unpretentious effect—and thus are historically the more credible. This perception gained in a rather peripheral area of the tradition should warn us not to consider the time of the early monarchy in Israel as a mythical past age and the biblical narratives about the first kings as altogether legendary. Certainly, the books of Samuel are not an altogether trustworthy historical source, nor do they claim to be such. But they still contain valuable historical recollection, not only in lists and other erratic material of the tradition, but also in the middle of narratives. It continues to be the task of exegetes and historians to uncover and to ascertain this information. Instead of falling into extreme positions—apologetically or hypercritically—we should try together to gain a picture of the time of the early monarchy in Israel which does justice to the available historical witnesses and is historically plausible. The endeavor is not hopeless and indeed pays off historically as well as theologically.

INDEXES

INDEX OF REFERENCES

OLD TESTAMENT

OTHER ANCIENT AUTHORS

INDEX OF AUTHORS

JOURNAL FOR THE STUDY OF THE OLD TESTAMENT
SUPPLEMENT SERIES